Protagoras and *Logos*

Studies in Rhetoric/Communication
Thomas W. Benson, Series Editor

PROTAGORAS AND *LOGOS*

A Study in Greek Philosophy and Rhetoric
Second Edition

Edward Schiappa

University of South Carolina Press

© 2003 Edward Schiappa

Published in Columbia, South Carolina, by the
University of South Carolina Press

Manufactured in the United States of America

07 06 05 04 03   5 4 3 2 1

Library of Congress Cataloging-in-Publication Data

Schiappa, Edward, 1954–
   Protagoras and logos : a study in Greek philosophy and rhetoric / Edward
Schiappa.— 2nd ed.
      p. cm. — (Studies in rhetoric/communication)
Includes bibliographical references and index.
   ISBN 1-57003-521-0 (pbk. : alk. paper)
   1. Protagoras—Contributions in rhetoric. 2. Rhetoric, Ancient. 3.
Rhetoric—Philosophy. I. Title. II. Series.
B305.P84 S35 2003
183'.1—dc22

                                                          2003016687

For Jacqueline Jean

CONTENTS

Contents

Contents

PREFACE TO THE SECOND EDITION

I begin by expressing my gratitude to the University of South Carolina Press for publishing this revised edition of *Protagoras and* Logos. My sincere thanks to Tom Benson and Barry Blose for their support of this project, and to Wilfred E. Major and John T. Kirby for their helpful suggestions for revisions.

The changes in the book from the first edition can be described as follows. First, I have corrected errors in translation that slipped through the first time and made minor wording changes to claims in the first edition that were unclear or misleading. Second, in my discussion of different research approaches to the Sophists, I have replaced the phrase "rational reconstruction" with "contemporary appropriation"—a phrase somewhat less likely to be misunderstood. Third, I have added an afterword that addresses certain historiographical issues that have been a persistent source of discussion among scholars in rhetorical studies over the past decade.

Although I have not attempted to incorporate all of the scholarship on Protagoras that has appeared since the first edition, I have incorporated into the footnotes of each chapter references to work that has altered or clarified my views on Protagoras and the Sophists. I want to take this opportunity to draw the reader's attention to work that resonates with this project. The same year in which this book originally appeared also saw the publication of Thomas Cole's important book *The Origins of Rhetoric* (Johns Hopkins University Press, 1991). While I do not agree with Cole's attempt to elide the distinction between rhetorical theory and practice, there is much in his book that has encouraged scholars to reconsider the role of the Sophists in early rhetorical theory. I am particularly encouraged by Michael Gagarin's essay "Did the Sophists Aim to Persuade?" (*Rhetorica* 19 [2001]: 275–91) and a follow-up paper, as yet unpublished, titled "What Did the Sophists Teach? The Sophists and the Art of Words." Gagarin takes seriously the idea that "rhetoric" may not be the best word to describe what the Older Sophists taught, and he is building a careful case for a redescription of their educational program. Two books recently have been published devoted to the sophist Gorgias of Leontini: Bruce McComiskey's *Gorgias and the New Sophistic Rhetoric* and Scott Consigny's *Gorgias, Sophist and Artist.* Interest in the Sophists continues, and it is exciting to see the growing sophistication of methodological and theoretical frameworks brought to bear in such scholarship.

For me, the most important part of this book is the reading I provide of the surviving fragments of Protagoras. My sense is that part II and part III of the book generally have proven useful to those interested in the historical reconstruction of Protagorean thought. By far, the most controversial portion of the book has been part I. In particular, my arguments concerning the origins of the Greek word for rhetoric—*rhêtorikê*—and how a revised dating of that term may challenge our understanding both of the Sophists and of early rhetorical theory have provoked considerable discussion. Readers interested in these issues may benefit from my 1999 monograph, *The Beginnings of Rhetorical Theory in Classical Greece.* In many respects that book picks up where this book leaves off. I have attempted to reply to criticisms of the arguments made in this book, both in the opening chapters of *Beginnings* and in the afterword of this edition.

It is said that the worst fate for a book is if it is ignored. Whatever else I might think about the various receptions of this book, I cannot complain that it has been ignored. To my various interlocutors, supportive and otherwise, I owe a tremendous debt of thanks.

Minneapolis, December 2002

PREFACE TO THE FIRST EDITION

A new full-length study of Protagoras and his contribution to early Greek thought is long overdue. Although there is a sizable amount of excellent scholarship concerning Protagoras, much of it tends to be hobbled by one or more problems. Many studies begin with such hostile assumptions about the Sophists that a reasonably productive picture of Protagoras is impossible. Too many studies have relied exclusively on Plato for their understanding of Protagoras, thereby privileging Plato's dramatic interpretations over the Sophist's surviving fragments. Studies that attempt to examine Protagoras' own words, his *ipsissima verba,* have typically focused only on one or another of his surviving fragments and hence have missed the larger picture. Few studies of Protagoras have taken seriously the fact that Greece in the fifth century BCE was in transition from a predominantly oral to a predominantly literate culture. As a result, many translations and interpretations of Protagoras' fragments have missed the influence of changing syntax and word usage.

The purpose of this book is to defend a reconstruction of Protagoras' contributions to ancient Greek philosophy and rhetoric that is more complete than is currently available. In order to accomplish that purpose it is necessary to construct a picture of Protagoras' world view based on all of his significant fragments, using the assumption that Protagoras and his fellow Older Sophists were serious and important thinkers. It is my hope that what follows will encourage resistance to the Platonic tradition of treating the Sophists of the fifth century BCE as rarely—if ever—capable of philosophically important ideas or of a morally acceptable rhetoric, and will stimulate future full-length studies of the Older Sophists. It is through such efforts that these interesting figures of the Greek enlightenment can be more fully appreciated for the depth and breadth of their contributions to the history of philosophy and rhetoric.

ACKNOWLEDGMENTS

The following study began as my doctoral dissertation at Northwestern University. I wish to thank Leland M. Griffin for chairing my committee and for providing needed encouragement. Thanks also to Michael J. Hyde, Charles Kauffman, and David Zarefsky for serving on my committee and providing challenging and beneficial feedback.

The first section of chapter 3, "Did Plato Coin *Rhêtorikê?*," originally appeared, in a slightly different form, in the *American Journal of Philology* 111 (1990): 460–73. I am grateful for permission to include it here; and for George A. Kennedy's valuable editorial suggestions. Chapter 3 benefited from advice from Robin Smith, Michael Cahn, Tony M. Lentz, and John T. Kirby.

An earlier version of chapter 4 appeared as "Neo-Sophistic Rhetorical Criticism or the Historical Reconstruction of Sophistic Doctrines?" in *Philosophy and Rhetoric* 23 (1990): 192–217. My thanks to the Pennsylvania State University Press for permission to reproduce it here, and to Henry W. Johnstone, Jr., Christopher L. Johnstone, and Beth S. Bennett for their comments on earlier drafts.

John T. Kirby read the manuscript in its penultimate form and made a number of useful suggestions. A special thanks is owed to Richard Henninge for his generous help with some of the German sources cited. Though we part ways on many issues, I also am grateful to John Poulakos; his spirited criticisms have greatly enriched my thinking. Thanks also to Theodore F. Brunner, director of *Thesaurus Linguae Graecae,* for his assistance with several *TLG* searches.

I am deeply indebted to Carroll C. Arnold, the previous editor of this series, for his thoughtful comments and careful editing. His support and advice have done much to ease my trepidations concerning publication.

It cannot be assumed that any of the above mentioned individuals agree with my conclusions. The remaining faults of the book are entirely my responsibility.

TRANSLATIONS AND ABBREVIATIONS

Unless otherwise noted, English translations of Greek authors are from the following sources: for Plato, Edith Hamilton and Huntington Cairns, *The Collected Dialogues of Plato* (Princeton University Press, 1961); for Aristotle, Jonathan Barnes, *The Complete Works of Aristotle*, 2 vols. (Princeton University Press, 1984); for other ancient authors, see the appropriate volume in the Loeb Library collection. For Greek texts, unless otherwise noted, I have used the editions available in the Oxford Classical Texts series.

The standard collection of surviving fragments concerning the Older sophists is that of Hermann Diels and Walther Kranz, traditionally abbreviated DK. Fragments are divided into sections A and B, the first of which consists of statements by later writers concerning the life, writings, and doctrines of the person in question. The second records fragments that Diels and Kranz believe are actual quotations from the person's writings. Hence, Protagoras' "human-measure" fragment is cited as DK 80 B1. English translations of fragments of or about the Older Sophists (DK 79 through DK 90) are from *The Older Sophists,* edited by Rosamond Kent Sprague (Columbia: University of South Carolina Press, 1972).

BOOKS

Classen, *Sophistik*   Carl Joachim Classen, ed., *Sophistik,* Wege der Forschung 187 (Darmstadt: Wissenschaftliche Buchgesellschaft, 1976).

DK	Hermann Diels and Walther Kranz, *Die Fragmente der Vorsokratiker,* 3 vols., 6th ed. (Berlin: Weidmann, 1951–52).
DL	Diogenes Laertius, *Lives of Eminent Philosophers,* 2 vols., trans. R. D. Hicks (Cambridge, MA: Harvard U. Press, 1925).
Dupréel, *Sophistes*	Eugène Dupréel, *Les Sophistes: Protagoras, Gorgias, Hippias, Prodicus* (Neuchâtel: Éditions du Griffon, 1948).
Gomperz, *SR*	Heinrich Gomperz, *Sophistik und Rhetorik* (1912; Aalen: Scientia Verlag, 1985).
Guthrie, *HGP*	W. K. C. Guthrie, *History of Greek Philosophy,* 6 vols. (Cambridge: Cambridge U. Press, 1962–81).
Kahn, *Verb*	Charles H. Kahn, *The Verb "Be" in Ancient Greek* (Dordrecht: D. Riedel, 1973).
Kennedy, *APG*	George A. Kennedy, *The Art of Persuasion in Greece* (Princeton: Princeton U. Press, 1963).
Kerferd, *Legacy*	G. B. Kerferd, ed., *The Sophists and Their Legacy* (Wiesbaden: Franz Steiner, 1981).
Kerferd, *SM*	G. B. Kerferd, *The Sophistic Movement* (Cambridge: Cambridge U. Press, 1981).
KRS	G. S. Kirk, J. E. Raven, and Malcolm Schofield, *The Presocratic Philosophers: A Critical History with a Selection of Texts,* 2nd ed. (Cambridge: Cambridge U. Press, 1983).
LSJ	Henry George Liddell and Robert Scott, *A Greek-English Lexicon,* 9th ed., rev. and augmented by Henry Stuart Jones (Oxford: Clarendon Press, 1940).
Untersteiner, *Sophists*	Mario Untersteiner, *The Sophists,* trans. Kathleen Freeman (Oxford: Basil Blackwell, 1954).

JOURNALS

AJP	*American Journal of Philology*
CJ	*Classical Journal*
CM	*Communication Monographs*
CP	*Classical Philology*
CQ	*Classical Quarterly*
CR	*Classical Review*
CSSJ	*Central States Speech Journal*
GRBS	*Greek, Roman, and Byzantine Studies*
HPQ	*History of Philosophy Quarterly*
HSCP	*Harvard Studies in Classical Philology*
JHP	*Journal of the History of Philosophy*
JHS	*Journal of Hellenic Studies*
JP	*Journal of Philology*
JVI	*Journal of Value Inquiry*
PR	*Philosophy and Rhetoric*
QJS	*Quarterly Journal of Speech*
RE	*Paulys Real-Encyclopädie der classischen Altertumswissenschaft*
RSQ	*Rhetoric Society Quarterly*
SSCJ	*Southern Speech Communication Journal*
TAPA	*Transactions of the American Philological Association*
WJSC	*Western Journal of Speech Communication*
YCS	*Yale Classical Studies*

PART I

PROLEGOMENON TO
THE STUDY OF EARLY
GREEK RHETORICAL THEORY

1

WHY A STUDY OF PROTAGORAS?

An important part of comprehending the place of Protagoras, the first and most influential of the Older Sophists, is understanding how the profession he helped to spawn was perceived in ancient Greek thought and in subsequent histories of thought. So many of the issues concerning the Sophists are shrouded in controversy that it is difficult even to begin to describe who the Sophists were, let alone to discuss the content and significance of their work. My purpose in what follows is to summarize how the meaning of the word "sophist" has undergone successive redefinition by ancient and contemporary philosophers. Such a summary is appropriate since the term currently suffers from distinctly pejorative connotations, despite the fact that it originally was considered honorific. Understanding why such a transformation has taken place sheds light on how to interpret the role of the Sophists in their own time and explains the disparate treatment the Sophists have often received at the hands of historians and philosophers.

DEFINING "SOPHIST"

The word "sophist" has been defined in important ways by ancient and modern writers. These definitions have altered the interpretive frameworks within which Sophists have been studied and understood. To comprehend scholarship concerning the Sophists in general, and Pro-

3

tagoras in particular, one must be able to place that scholarship in its proper context and interpretive tradition.[1]

The most familiar definition of "sophist" is pejorative: "one who makes use of fallacious arguments; a specious reasoner." This sense of "sophist" is clearly the sense that enjoys the most popular use, as almost any pocket dictionary will show. This negative sense of "sophist" is what guided the initial construction of such pejorative terms as "sophisms," or "sophistical" arguments. The oldest and broadest definition of the word is "one who is distinguished for learning; a wise or learned man."[2] This definition has roots in the Greek term *sophia*, meaning wisdom or skill. Accordingly, as George Grote and G. B. Kerferd have pointed out, a wide variety of people in ancient Greece were called Sophists, including poets, musicians, rhapsodes, diviners, and persons now called philosophers.[3] Even Socrates and Plato were called Sophists (Aristophanes, *Clouds;* Isocrates, *Against the Sophists*). Protagoras, in the Platonic dialogue of the same name, claims that Sophists have a long-standing tradition, and he names as his predecessors the poets and prophets of the past, including Homer, Hesiod, Simonides, Orpheus, and Musaeus (316d). Protagoras went on to claim that current teachers of music and physical training also practice the "sophist's art" (316e). It is clear then that the broadest notion of "sophist" would include almost anyone who demonstrates and imparts wisdom (*sophia*).

Beginning in the mid-fifth century BCE, the word "sophist" began to take on narrower and more technical meanings. The definition listed first in the *Oxford English Dictionary* describes a Sophist as "one specially engaged in the pursuit or communication of knowledge; esp. one who undertook to give instruction in intellectual and ethical matters in return for payment." So conceived, the Sophists were the first professional teachers in Western history. Missing from this definition is any reference to the practice and teaching of rhetoric, which, for Heinrich Gomperz, was the distinguishing characteristic of the Sophists.[4] Gomperz exaggerated a point that was otherwise well taken. Virtually every person considered a Sophist by posterity was concerned with instruction in *logos*. According to most accounts, the teaching of the skills of public argument was the key to the Sophists' financial success,[5] and a good part of the reason for their condemnation by Plato.

Where did the modern negative definition of "sophist" originate? Karl Popper claimed that Plato "by his attacks on the 'Sophists' *created* the bad associations connected with the word."[6] Grote claimed that Plato "stole the name out of general circulation" and connected with it "discreditable attributes."[7] W. K. C. Guthrie opposed that view, claiming that the term already possessed negative connotations in pre-Platonic writings such as Aristophanes' *Clouds*.[8] Eric A. Havelock has offered the most plausible explanation: prior to Plato, the term "sophist" could be given either a respectful or a contemptuous meaning, not unlike the word "intellectual" today. The playwrights of the "Old Comedy" of Plato's youth played upon, and perhaps fostered, an anti-intellectual prejudice in the populace which helped to diminish the respectability of the title *Sophistês*.[9]

The fact that the term *sophistês* was used disparagingly prior to Plato's writings does not, however, decrease the significance of his role in reconceptualizing the word. Plato's dialogue *Sophist* is the first recorded attempt to provide a systematic definition in answer to the question "What is a Sophist?" Plato's interlocutors agree that a Sophist is 1) a paid hunter after the young and wealthy, 2) a kind of merchant of knowledge of the soul, 3) a retailer of these same wares (perhaps implying that the knowledge is sold in small quantities), 4) a seller of his own productions of knowledge, 5) an athlete in contests of words—specifically disputation (*eristikê*), and, though the speakers are dubious, 6) a purger of souls, who removes opinions that obstruct learning through *elenchus* (231d–e).[10]

The conclusion of Plato's analysis is that a Sophist does not offer true knowledge, but merely an opinion (*doxa*) of things (*Sophist* 233c). The dialogue concludes with the following summary: "The art of contradiction making, descended from an insincere kind of conceited mimicry, of the semblance-making breed, derived from image making, distinguished as a portion, not divine but human, of production, that presents a shadow play of words—such are the blood and lineage which can, with perfect truth, be assigned to the authentic Sophist" (268c–d).

To this rather reprehensible character Plato contrasts the philosopher, the "lover of wisdom" (*Phaedrus* 278d). It is important to recognize, however, that the term "philosopher" was not common prior to Plato. As Havelock pointed out, "The noun *philo-sophia* appears in Plato's *Charmides* and *philo-sophos* in his *Apology*.... It is likely that these words first became professionalized in Plato's Academy. It is reasonably certain that Athenians would regard Presocratic intellectuals such as Anaxagoras or Diogenes as 'sophists,' or as 'meteorologists,' never as 'physicists' or 'philosophers'."[11]

The significance of such a contrast is not inconsequential. Plato was attempting to enact what Chaim Perelman and L. Olbrechts-Tyteca describe as "dissociation."[12] Dissociation is a rhetorical strategy whereby an advocate attempts to break up a previously unified idea into two concepts: one which will be positively valued by the target audience and one which will be negatively valued. A definition functions as an "instrument" of the dissociation of a concept, "especially whenever it claims to furnish the real, true meaning of the concept as opposed to its customary or apparent usage."[13] In this instance Plato was attempting to dissociate the general and traditional meaning of *sophistês* as a wise person or teacher into two concepts, one of which (the Sophist as possessor of counterfeit knowledge) would be negatively valued, the other (the philosopher as the seeker of true wisdom) would be positively valued.

As Charles L. Stevenson has noted, many of Plato's dialogues can be described as promulgating *persuasive definitions*: "The purport of the definition is to alter the descriptive meaning of the term, usually by giving it greater precision within the boundaries of its customary vagueness; but the definition does not make any substantial change in the term's emotive meaning."[14] One of the rhetorical objectives of the dialogues was to dissociate the usual or "commonsense" usage of a term such as "knowledge," "justice," or "sophist" from what Plato believed should be the correct usage. Thus, by giving the terms "sophist" and "philosopher" more precise technical meanings and portraying his characters as more or less attractive—depending on the objective of the dialogue—Plato provided a favorable emotive and technical meaning for "philosophers" and a negative emotive and technical meaning for "sophists." To be sure, at times even Socrates was presented as obnoxious, as in the *Protagoras*, while the title character was treated with respect. But there can be no question, even in the *Protagoras*, about what Plato's final verdict was. It is important to keep in mind that Plato apparently planned to write a companion dialogue to his *Sophist* and *Statesman* to define the "philosopher" (*Statesman* 257a, *Sophist* 217a).[15] Despite the absence of such a dialogue, there is no doubt of how, in Plato's overall system, the Sophist and the philosopher compare.

Perelman and Olbrechts-Tyteca have suggested that rhetors rarely offer dissociations in isolation. Rather, "the philosopher will establish a *system* that will lead essentially to the relating of the various philosophical pairs with each other."[16] The authors illustrate their claim with examples of sets of "philosophical pairs" drawn from various philosophers' works. From Plato's *Phaedrus* they extracted the following pairs: appearance/reality, opinion/knowledge, sensible knowledge/rational knowledge, body/soul, becoming/immutability, plurality/unity, and human/divine (*Phaedrus* 247e, 248b). In each pair the second term is preferred by Plato over the former, and with each pair one can find in the pages of such dialogues as *Gorgias, Sophist,* and *Thaeatetus* the second term associated with philosophy and the first term linked to sophistry.

The effect of Plato's giving "sophist" a more precise and technical meaning, combined with his powerful prose style, was nothing short of overwhelming.[17] For over two thousand years our understanding of who the Sophists were has been dominated by Plato's writings.

Aristotle's treatment of the Sophists paralleled Plato's. As C. J. Classen has argued, Aristotle grasped the Sophists' ideas and practices by means of his own conceptual scheme.[18] As a result, his description of the Sophists' thoughts is almost always in contrast to his own superior system. In modern terminology, one can say that Aristotle differentiated his system from the Sophists' supposed system epistemologically, ontologically, and ethically. In *On Sophistical Refutations* Aristotle described what "appear to be refutations but are really fallacies" (164a), and claimed that "the art of the Sophist is the semblance of wisdom without the reality, and the Sophist is one who makes money from an apparent but unreal wisdom" (165a). In his *Metaphysics* he said that "dialectic is merely critical where philosophy *claims to know,* and Sophistic is what appears to be philosophy but is not" (1004b). In his discussion of the different meanings of "being" in the *Metaphysics* Aristotle stated that Plato was correct (in the *Sophist*) to claim that Sophists dealt with "that which is not" or "nonbeing" since the Sophists' arguments dealt with "accidental being" (1026a–b). Finally, Aristotle in several places claimed that what defined a Sophist was his deficient moral purpose, rather than his practice of the art of rhetoric or dialectic.[19] According to W. M. A. Grimaldi, Aristotle considered a Sophist as one who "misuses" the art of dialectic in order "to deceive."[20]

So powerful was the combined indictment by Plato and Aristotle that their judgments concerning the Sophists remained the standard view in most modern histories of ancient Greece. Plato's and Aristotle's respective rhetorical definitions became accepted as accurate *descriptions* of the Sophists. According to Grote, the Sophists came to be understood as

> ostentatious imposters, flattering and duping the rich youth for their own personal gain, undermining the morality of Athens public and private, and encouraging their pupils to the unscrupulous prosecution of ambition and cupidity. They are even affirmed to have succeeded in corrupting the general morality, so that Athens had become miserably degenerated and vicious in the latter years of the Peloponnesian war, as compared with what she was in the time of Miltiades and Aristeides. Socrates, on the contrary,

7

is usually described as a holy man combating and exposing these false prophets—standing up as the champion of morality against their insidious artifices.[21]

The next significant redefinition of "sophist" did not take place until the nineteenth century. Kerferd identified the key to this stage of scholarship as the publication of G. W. F. Hegel's *Lectures on the History of Philosophy* in the 1830s.[22] Hegel described the history of thought as a movement through the triadic scheme he called dialectic: through thesis, antithesis, and synthesis. According to Kerferd's interpretation, Hegel saw the Presocratics (from Thales to Anaxagoras) representing the first step through their search for an objective philosophical account of the world. Socrates and the Sophists represented the antithesis by their supposed support of the principle of subjectivity. Hegel found the synthesis of both positions in the works of Plato and Aristotle.

Two aspects of Hegel's thoughts on the Sophists deserve comment. First, Hegel's description of the Sophists as subjectivist philosophers grouped with Socrates was a step toward restoring the Sophists to the "philosophical" limelight. Subsequent accounts of ancient Greek philosophy began to include sections devoted to treatments of "sophistic philosophy." Eduard Zeller's and Wilhelm Windelband's histories of Greek thought, considered influential classics of the nineteenth century, both contain chapters devoted to the Sophists.

Second, though Hegel may have returned the Sophists to philosophical significance, it was in a decidedly negative manner. According to Kerferd, "To many in the nineteenth century it seemed that subjectivism from its very nature was anti-philosophical."[23] Truth and reality were considered objective, not subjective, and accordingly the Sophists were not only not considered philosophers, but they were the enemies of philosophy.[24] Thus, Zeller considered Sophists such as Protagoras and Gorgias radical skeptics, and Windelband claimed that the "majority of the Sophists did not take truth seriously from the beginning."[25] The Sophists fared little better in Hegel's discussion of their role in Greek political thought. In contrast with "objective morality," through which laws are laid down by "great men" and the oracles are consulted on all great ventures, the Sophists "first introduced subjective reflection, and the new doctrine that each man should act according to his own conviction." This subjectivity "plunged the Greek world into ruin."[26] In sum, Hegel's redefinition of the Sophists held that they were a necessary and important step in Greek philosophy, but that they were rightfully opposed and

8

defeated by Plato and that they were somehow instrumental to the downfall of Greece. Windelband claimed that "however seriously and scientifically the theories of skepticism were held, even by Protagoras, they nevertheless led to the demoralization of science, and resulted finally in a frivolous diversion in daily life."[27]

The next redefinition of the Sophists is rooted in George Grote's famous chapter 67 of his *History of Greece*. Grote has been described as a reformer and utilitarian very much concerned with challenging the "dead hand of tradition."[28] Believing the Sophists misconceived as well as "misesteemed," Grote rejected the traditional assessment and offered a case for considering the Sophists a positive force in Greek culture and philosophy. For my purposes his most important arguments were as follows.

First, Grote pointed out that even Plato's attacks on the Sophists were not as vicious as those by modern historians: "I know few characters in history who have been so hardly dealt with as these so-called Sophists."[29] Plato's dialogues did not justify such harsh claims. Plato's characterizations of Protagoras, Hippias, Gorgias, and other Sophists may have been unflattering, but Plato did not present them as morally corrupt.[30] Grote cited examples from the commentaries of his time to demonstrate what he felt was unfair bias against the Sophists by interpreters of the Platonic dialogues:

> We continually read from the pen of the expositor such remarks as these—"Mark how Plato puts down the shallow and worthless Sophist"— the obvious reflection, that it is Plato himself who plays both games on the chessboard, being altogether overlooked. And again—"This or that argument, placed in the mouth of Socrates, is not to be regarded as the real opinion of Plato: he only takes it up and enforces it at this moment, in order to puzzle and humiliate an ostentatious pretender"—a remark which converts Plato into an insincere disputant and a Sophist in the modern sense, at the very moment when the commentator is extolling his pure and lofty morality as an antidote against the alleged corruption of Gorgias and Protagoras.[31]

Second, Grote noted that the main charge against the Sophists was that they accepted pay for their services. Professors on salary, Grote commented, should not be throwing stones.[32] There is no evidence that the fees the Sophists charged were exorbitant. In fact, Plato indicated that Protagoras gave the option to his pupils of either paying the fee he requested or going to a temple to state under oath what the pupil felt was the worth of his instruction (*Protagoras* 328b).[33]

9

Third, Grote defended the Sophists as teachers of public argument. Any citizen could end up in court with the need to defend himself, hence the Sophists' teaching of *logos* was essential and helpful.[34] As Aristotle put it, "It is absurd to hold that a man ought to be ashamed of being unable to defend himself with his limbs, but not of being unable to defend himself with speech and reason, when the use of rational speech is more distinctive of a human being than the use of his limbs" (*Rhetoric* 1355b).

Fourth, Grote claimed that recent German historians had created a "fiend" whom they called *Die Sophistik*, or "Sophistic." He argued that the Sophists shared few if any common doctrines, principles, or methods; they had nothing in common but their profession as paid teachers. In fact, there is evidence in the Platonic dialogues indicating that the Sophists often disagreed with each other on a wide variety of topics. Hence, censure of the entire body of Sophists was inappropriate, inaccurate, and "unbecoming."[35]

Finally, Grote defended the Sophists against the charge that they were responsible for the decline of Athens during the fifth century (specifically, 480–415 BCE). Grote argued that there is simply no evidence of a decline in Athenian character during the period in question.[36] And if there was such a decline, he believed the Sophists were not singly responsible. The ethical lessons embodied in Xenophon's version of Prodicus' "Choice of Heracles" suggest that at least some of the Sophists were interested in teaching conservative and traditional morals.[37] Furthermore, Grote argued, it was unfair for historians to single out the Sophists, since the Platonic dialogues attacked almost everyone—poets, statesmen, musicians, and rhetors alike.[38] Indeed, in the *Republic* (492) the Sophists are portrayed not only as sharing Plato's interest in improving Athenian education but also as relatively powerless in light of the overall problems of society. Only "the multitude" believed that young men were corrupted by the Sophists.

In sum, the term "sophist" has been defined four ways. Or, put another way, the Sophists of the fifth century have been contextualized four times. What I have said to this point should not imply that each definition succeeded in completely replacing its predecessors. Henry Sidgwick's summary in 1872 of the prevailing opinion regarding the Sophists suggests that, decades after Hegel's and Grote's writings, the Platonic definition was still dominant:

> The old view of the Sophists was that they were a set of charlatans who appeared in Greece in the fifth century, and earned an ample livelihood

10

by imposing on public credulity: professing to teach virtue, they really taught the art of fallacious discourse, and meanwhile propagated immoral practical doctrines. That gravitating to Athens as the *Prytaneion* of Greece, they were there met and overthrown by Socrates, who exposed the hollowness of their rhetoric, turned their quibbles inside out, and triumphantly defended sound ethical principles against their plausible pernicious sophistries. That they thus, after a brief success, fell into well-merited contempt, so that their name became a byword for succeeding generations.[39]

In modern writings one still finds elements of the Platonic tradition. In Robert S. Brumbaugh's chapter on the Sophists, subtitled "How to Succeed in Athens," he follows the dichotomy initiated by Plato: "The Sophists, who were engaged in training young men to live successfully, suggested that rhetoric—the art of persuasive discourse—*not philosophy*, should be studied."[40] In supporting his claim that "on balance, the Sophists did not offer a major constructive advance in Western philosophy," Brumbaugh argues that the Sophists' "use of rhetoric, with which they persuaded their hearers that science and philosophy are impractical, was an alternative to philosophy, not a contribution to it."[41] More recently, Bruce A. Kimball writes that the Sophists "attended more to devising persuasive techniques than to finding true arguments, and this amoralism exacerbated the disintegration of the ethical tradition and led to their condemnation."[42]

Strong elements of the Hegelian tradition persist as well. Kerferd has suggested that Guthrie's treatment is in this tradition, since the Sophists' "empiricism" and "skepticism" are contrasted with the idealism of Plato on one hand and the physical theories of the Presocratics on the other.[43] It is tempting also to place Mario Untersteiner's treatment of the Sophists in the Hegelian tradition, since he describes the Sophists as anti-idealistic realists and phenomenalists.[44] In Guthrie's case, his sympathies lie with the idealist tradition, and he specifically stops short of endorsing Grote's position.[45] Untersteiner may be guilty of employing inappropriate twentieth-century notions to explicate a sophistic "philosophy," but he attempted to treat each of the Sophists as an individual thinker in his own right, and did not find it necessary to demonstrate preference for certain ancient philosophical traditions over the doctrines of the Sophists.[46]

Despite the lingering of the Platonic and Hegelian traditions, most contemporary students of the Sophists accept Grote's general position, at least insofar as his position implies a rejection of a Platonic condemnation of the Sophists and an avoidance of what Kerferd believes the Hegelian framework encourages: a "premature schematisation of the his-

11

tory of thought."[47] Grote's interpretation suggests that the Sophists were a positive force in fifth-century Greece, and that the Platonic and Hegelian interpretive frameworks missed their significance by assuming more doctrinal commonality than the Sophists actually shared. It may be the case, therefore, that Grote's most valuable contribution was and is procedural. To understand the Sophists, Grote argued, one must study them on their own terms: as *individuals* situated in a culture dominated by an oral tradition. Following Grote, I question the notion that "Sophists" were somehow bound together by "doctrine" and that they thought more or less alike. Anticipating an argument developed in a later chapter, I suggest that the Sophists ought to be examined as individuals, and that we ought to be as sensitive to their differences as we have been to their similarities. It follows that the concept "sophist" should be treated loosely and not doctrinally.

An additional definitional stipulation I shall follow in this book is that the term "sophist" will refer specifically to those first professional educators who, more often than not, are associated with the *technê* (art or skill) of prose speech. The purpose of this definition is to provide conceptual clarity, not to make any particular philological or philosophical point. Based on my definition, the most relevant figures of fifth-century Greece include Protagoras, Gorgias, Prodicus, Hippias, Antiphon, Critias, and Thrasymachus. The preceding list is that used by John Poulakos in his work on the Sophists, and it may be thought of as the "traditional" list.[48] Lists of Sophists differ from source to source. Grote did not include Critias but did include Polus, Euthydemus, and Dionysodorus in his list; Kerferd included Callicles and Socrates, and the authors of the *Dissoi Logoi,* the *Anonymus Iamblichi,* and the *Hippocratic Corpus.* Guthrie included Antisthenes, Alcidamas, and Lycophron among his Sophists.[49] All of these individuals are properly called Sophists, but for clarity and simplicity I choose to focus on the traditional group.

PROTAGORAS' SIGNIFICANCE

There are at least four reasons that justify singling out Protagoras from among the traditional group and focusing on his role in early Greek philosophy and rhetoric. First, the Sophists deserve study as individual thinkers and not simply as a movement. Second, solid evidence suggests that Protagoras' doctrines had very significant practical and philosophical consequences. Third, Protagoras' thinking has been neglected by students of rhetorical theory. Fourth, the Sophists in general, and Protagoras in particular, had significant roles in the Greek transition from a mythic-poetic to a more humanistic-rationalistic culture.

One need only compare the amount of literature on the Older Sophists with the literature on the presocratic "philosophers" to realize how little attention the Sophists have received. For some of the presocratic philosophers there are literally no extant fragments, yet the available literature on those thinkers is enormous compared to that on the Sophists. The number of full-length studies of the Sophists that have been published in the past fifty years is surprisingly small.[50] Kerferd has argued that before further debate proceeds on the characteristics of the "sophistic movement" as a whole, a much more detailed approach to the individual Sophists is necessary; otherwise, interpretations of the Sophists as a group will continue to be inhibited by the Platonic and Hegelian traditions.[51] Such studies, he suggests, may well lead to the conclusion that the Sophists were not as far apart in doctrines and intentions from the Presocratics and Plato as is typically assumed: "What is now wanted is a series of detailed studies of the actual evidence relating to individual Sophists, which will take this evidence seriously and will not be inhibited at its very starting point by the conviction that any attribution of significant doctrines to a particular Sophist is unlikely to be correct because 'the Sophists were not the kind of people to entertain serious doctrines'."[52]

If Kerferd's counsel is followed, one of the first items of business ought to be the comprehensive study of Protagoras. There is evidence that he was the first of the professional Sophists (DL 9.52; Philostratus, DK 80 A2; Plato, *Greater Hippias* 282d; *Protagoras* 349a), and there is a consensus that he was the most famous and influential.[53] Protagoras' fame and influence can be amply demonstrated. Protagoras was friend and adviser to the Greek leader Pericles. J. S. Morrison has claimed that Protagoras achieved such a position because of his ability to provide a theoretical justification for the practice of Periclean democracy.[54] The claim is plausible, for it was reported by Heraclides Ponticus that Pericles appointed Protagoras to draft the legal code for the important new colony of Thurii (DL 9.50), a mission I shall address in a later chapter.

Further evidence of Protagoras' importance can be provided by noting his contributions to the politics and philosophy of his time. His human-measure tenet was at the heart of a sophistic move to democratize *aretê* and knowledge, and hence the public life of Athens.[55] It has been argued that Protagoras' teachings influenced the political content of

13

Euripides' *Supplices* and Sophocles' *Antigone,* and another scholar maintains that Aeschylus' *Prometheus Bound* was a mythological account of the Sophists—in particular Protagoras—bringing knowledge to the *polis.*[56]

Protagoras also left his mark on fifth- and fourth-century Greek philosophy. It is appropriate to classify Protagoras' interests as philosophical as long as it is kept in mind that the term is used in a modern sense. His human-measure statement was examined by Plato in the *Theaetetus,* a dialogue concerned with the definition of knowledge. The dialogue titled *Protagoras* dealt with the teachability of *aretê* (excellence or virtue), making the dialogue an early effort in what we now call educational philosophy. These and other references in the dialogues testify to Protagoras' philosophical importance to Plato.[57] Classen has argued that Aristotle likewise treated Protagoras as a serious thinker.[58] Other than Aristotle's attack on Protagoras' supposed claim to "make the weaker argument stronger" (*Rhetoric* 1402a22), his treatments of Protagoras in the *Rhetoric* (1407b5), *Poetics* (1456b15), *Nicomachean Ethics* (1164a22), and *Sophistical Refutations* (173b17) are generally positive. Aristotle's most serious disagreement with Protagoras occurs in the *Metaphysics* (1007b18, 1009a6–1011b22, 1047a6, 1062b13–1063b33). There Aristotle devotes several chapters to taking Protagoras' doctrines to task for violating the law of noncontradiction. It is clear that Aristotle considered Protagoras a serious thinker, one whose doctrines were sufficiently influential long after his death to require refutation. Interestingly enough, one way Aristotle shows respect for Protagoras is by refraining from calling him a Sophist.[59]

Other writers of antiquity also considered Protagoras a philosopher to be reckoned with. Isocrates compared Gorgias and Protagoras with Zeno and Melissus (*Helen* 2–3), and a variety of other ancient writers took the trouble to support or refute statements pertaining to Protagoras' doctrines (DK 80A, various).

There is also a fairly recent philological rationale to support the claim that Protagoras thought and spoke as did the other philosophers of his time. Charles H. Kahn's seminal work on the Greek verb "to be" will be discussed later. For the moment it is sufficient to note that there were certain technical constructions of the verb "to be" that occurred very rarely in pre-Platonic writings. According to Kahn, at least one of the technical uses—the negative form of *einai*—was employed exclusively by "philosophers."[60] Protagoras' human-measure statement employs such a negative form of *einai.* Kahn also credits Protagoras with what may be the earliest surviving technical use of the verb "to be" as a purely existential predicate.[61] If Kahn is correct, then Protagoras must be ranked as a first-rate philosophical thinker of the Greek enlightenment.

A final bit of evidence concerning Protagoras' influence is relayed by Kerferd:

> In the years 1851–54 some eleven statues in a half-circle of wall facing the end of the so-called Sphinx alley leading to the Serapeum at Memphis in Egypt were uncovered.... On the eastern half of the semi-circle we have Plato, Heraclitus, Thales, and Protagoras identified by the inscription of their names on the statues.... The date is uncertain, except that the statues certainly belong to the Ptolemaic period. What is remarkable is that Protagoras should be included in a series of philosophers facing a set of poets on the opposite side, a clear testimony, it would seem, to the importance with which he was invested in the Hellenistic period.[62]

While there seems to be wide support for crediting Protagoras with important philosophical contributions, there is considerable disagreement over just how his contributions should be characterized. Protagoras has been called the first *positivist,* the first *humanist,* the forerunner of *pragmatism,* a *skeptic,* an *existentialist,* a *phenomenalist,* an *empiricist,* an early *utilitarian,* a *subjective relativist,* and an *objective relativist.*[63] To reconcile all of these disparate views may be impossible, but an attempt at conceptual ground-clearing is in order.

Those who have interested themselves in reconstructing the early history of rhetorical theory have given Protagoras strikingly little attention. Since Bromley Smith's 1918 essay in *The Quarterly Journal of Speech* nothing directly concerning Protagoras has appeared in major journals of communication studies. By contrast, communication scholars have "rehabilitated" and explored implications of the ideas of Gorgias of Leontini, a contemporary of Protagoras.[64] Given the importance of the teaching and practice of persuasive speech to the Sophists, and given the eventual centrality of rhetoric in the Greek educational process, the relative lack of attention to Protagoras' contributions to rhetorical theory is as surprising as it is necessary to correct. Accordingly, in the pages to follow I hope to "rehabilitate" Protagoras as an important transitional figure in the evolution of Greek rhetorical theory.

There is another reason why a new study of Protagoras is appropriate. Over the past sixty years the essentially preliterate of oral character of ancient Greek culture has been firmly established. The emerging literacy in classical Greece facilitated the sort of abstract thinking necessary for philosophical analysis. Eric A. Havelock has argued that one of Plato's

15

primary objectives, particularly in the *Republic,* was to advocate abandonment of the mythic-poetic tradition—its forms of discourse, patterns of explanation, and modes of reasoning. Drawing on evidence from Plato and others, Havelock argued that the Sophists were Plato's allies in his educational campaign against the poets and that they shared the presocratic philosophers' role in reshaping Greek language and thought.[65] As provocative as Havelock's analysis is, I can identify few studies of the Sophists that have made significant use of it.

Additional reasons for a study of Protagoras as an individual will emerge as various fragments are explicated in later pages of this book. For the moment the reasons can be summarized as follows. Understanding the so-called sophistic movement requires careful study of the individual Sophists. Protagoras is an obvious case in point since he was the first and most important of the professional Sophists, both in terms of cultural influence and in terms of philosophical importance. Efforts toward recovering Protagoras' doctrines have been virtually nonexistent in the field of communication studies, and efforts elsewhere have resulted in a multitude of conflicting interpretations. In particular, little effort has been made to recover Protagoras' implicit rhetorical theory, and recent findings on the development of Greek language and thought during the sophistic era have yet to be exploited. This book is an attempt to correct these deficiencies.

NOTES

1. For summaries of interpretive traditions in scholarship concerning the Sophists see: C. J. Classen, "Einleitung," in *Sophistik,* 1–18; Kerferd, *Legacy,* 1–6; Guthrie, *HGP III,* 3–13; Kerferd, *SM,* 4–14. See also John Poulakos, *Sophistical Rhetoric in Classical Greece* (Columbia: U. of South Carolina Press, 1995).

2. "Sophist," *The Compact Edition of the Oxford English Dictionary* (Oxford: Oxford U. Press, 1971).

3. George Grote, *A History of Greece* (London: John Murray, 1851), 8:479–81; G. B. Kerferd, "The First Greek Sophists," *CR* 64 (1950): 8–10. See also R. J. Mortley, "Plato and the Sophistic Heritage of Protagoras," *Eranos* 67 (1969): 24–32.

4. Gomperz, *SR;* cf. Guthrie, *HGP III,* 176.

5. Ibid.; Kerferd, *SM,* 25–28; T. A. Sinclair, *A History of Greek Political Thought* (London: Routledge and Kegan Paul, 1951), 44–45.

6. Karl R. Popper, *The Open Society and Its Enemies* (London: Routledge and Kegan Paul, 1966), 1:263 n52; emphasis added.

7. Grote, *History,* 484.

8. Guthrie, *HGP III,* 12–13, 33–34.

9. Eric A. Havelock, *The Liberal Temper in Greek Politics* (New Haven: Yale U. Press, 1957), 158–59.

10. Paraphrased from H. N. Fowler's translation of *Sophist* in the Loeb collection.

Cf. Havelock, *Liberal,* 159; Kerferd, *SM,* 4–5. Guthrie's *HGP III,* somewhat surprisingly, does not discuss the passage.

11. Eric A. Havelock, "The Linguistic Task of the Presocratics," *Language and Thought in Early Greek Philosophy,* ed. Kevin Robb (La Salle, IL: Hegeler Institute, 1983), 57.

12. Chaim Perelman and L. Olbrechts-Tyteca, *The New Rhetoric: A Treatise on Argumentation* (Notre Dame: U. of Notre Dame Press, 1969), 411–59.

13. Ibid., 444.

14. Charles L. Stevenson, *Ethics and Language* (New Haven: Yale U. Press, 1944), 210; see also his discussion of Plato, 224–26.

15. Guthrie, *HGP V,* 123.

16. Perelman and Olbrechts-Tyteca, *New Rhetoric,* 421.

17. Giovanni Reale, *A History of Ancient Philosophy: From the Origins to Socrates* (Albany: State U. of New York Press, 1987), 150. For an example of a contemporary Platonic effort to define sophists and philosophers, see Clarence W. McCord, "On Sophists and Philosophers," *SSCJ* 29 (1963): 146–49.

18. C. J. Classen, "Aristotle's Picture of the Sophists," in Kerferd, *Legacy,* 7–24.

19. Ibid., 17; Aristotle, *Rhetoric* 1355b15–21 and *Metaphysics* 1004b22–25 are the best examples.

20. W. M. A. Grimaldi, *Aristotle's Rhetoric: A Commentary* (New York: Fordham U. Press, 1980), 1:33.

21. Grote, *History,* 485.

22. Kerferd, *SM,* 6–8; *Legacy,* 2–3.

23. Kerferd, *Legacy,* 2.

24. Kerferd, *SM,* 8.

25. Wilhelm Windelband, *History of Ancient Philosophy* (New York: Scribner's, 1924), 120; Eduard Zeller, *A History of Greek Philosophy* (London: Longmans, Green, 1881), 2:445–69.

26. G. W. F. Hegel, *Lectures on the Philosophy of History* (London: G. Bell and Sons, 1914), 263. For the argument that Hegel's efforts to "rehabilitate" and "normalize" the Sophists destroyed the vitality of their rhetoric, see John Poulakos, "Hegel's Reception of the Sophists," *WJSC* 54 (1990): 218–28.

27. Windelband, *History,* 119.

28. Kerferd, *SM,* 8; Guthrie, *HGP III,* 11. Grote's portrayal of the Sophists was critiqued in a series of articles by E. M. Cope, "The Sophists," *Journal of Classical and Sacred Philology* 1 (1854): 145–88; "On the Sophistical Rhetoric," 2 (1855): 129–69; 3 (1856): 34–80, 252–88.

29. Grote, *History,* 495.

30. Ibid., 518–23.

31. Ibid., 495.

32. Ibid., 497–98.

33. For the argument that Plato did not uniformly condemn the Sophists' practice of charging fees, see Michael Gagarin, "Protagoras and Plato" (Ph.D. diss., Yale University, 1968), 181–87; "The Purpose of Plato's *Protagoras,*" *TAPA* 100 (1969): 138–39. The evidence concerning the conflicting attitudes toward payment for teaching is collected and discussed by David L. Blank, "Socratics versus Sophists on Payment for Teaching," *Classical Antiquity* 4 (1985): 1–49 (on Protagoras see 26–29).

34. Grote, *History,* 464, 499.

35. Ibid., 509–10. Cf. Gomperz, *SR,* 39.

36. Grote, *History,* 511–15.

37. Ibid., 515–18.

38. Ibid., 541–50.

39. Henry Sidgwick, "The Sophists," *JP* 4 (1872): 289. The summary quoted did

17

not represent Henry's position. Sidgwick praised Grote's vindication as an important historical discovery.

40. Robert S. Brumbaugh, *The Philosophers of Greece* (New York: Crowell, 1964), 112; emphasis added.

41. Ibid., 115.

42. Bruce A. Kimball, *Orators and Philosophers: A History of the Ideal Liberal Education* (New York: Teachers College Press, 1986), 17. Robert J. Brake documented the persistence of the Platonic tradition in "Pedants, Professors, and the Law of the Excluded Middle: On Sophists and Sophistry," *CSSJ* 20 (1969): 122–29. For another recent (predominantly pejorative) discussion of the Sophists, see Tony M. Lentz, *Orality and Literacy in Hellenic Greece* (Carbondale: Southern Illinois U. Press, 1989), ch. 7. Such portrayals are usually a result of relying almost exclusively on Plato's dialogues for information about the Sophists.

43. Kerferd, *SM,* 11.

44. Untersteiner, *Sophists.*

45. Guthrie, *HGP III,* 11–13.

46. Cf. R. F. Holland, "On Making Sense of a Philosophical Fragment," *CQ* 6 (1956): 215–20.

47. Kerferd, *SM,* 13. For a useful discussion of the interpretive frameworks of contemporary scholarship about the Sophists, see Susan C. Jarratt, "The First Sophists and the Uses of History," *Rhetoric Review* 6 (1987): 67–77. See also Steven Mailloux's introduction to *Rhetoric, Sophistry, Pragmatism* (Cambridge: Cambridge U. Press, 1995), 1–31.

48. John Poulakos, "Towards a Sophistic Definition of Rhetoric," *PR* 16 (1983): 47 n1.

49. Grote, *History,* 486; Kerferd, *SM,* 42–58; Guthrie, *HGP III,* 261–319.

50. On the Sophists as a group: Eugène Dupréel's *Les Sophistes* was published in 1948 and is devoted to the four earliest Sophists: Protagoras, Gorgias, Hippias, and Prodicus. Mario Untersteiner's 1949 *I sofisti* was translated into English as *The Sophists* in 1954 by Kathleen Freeman (a 2nd revised Italian edition was published in 1967). W. K. C. Guthrie's *The Sophists* was orginally published in 1969 as roughly half of volume 3 of his classic *History of Greek Philosophy*. G. B. Kerferd's *The Sophistic Movement* is a concise presentation of thirty years of his study of the Sophists. Two useful article collections are C. J. Classen's compilation of previously published essays concerning the Sophists in his 1976 *Sophistik,* and Barbara Cassin's *Positions de la Sophistique* (Paris: Vrin, 1986). Previous book-length studies of Protagoras include: Antonio Capizzi, *Protagora* (Firenze: G. C. Sansoni, 1955); Italo Lana, *Protagora* (Torino: Università di Torino Pubblicazione, 1950); and Stelio Zeppi, *Protagora e la filosofia del suo tempo* (Firenze: La Nuova Italia, 1961).

51. Kerferd, *Legacy,* 3.

52. Kerferd, *SM,* 14.

53. See, e.g., Guthrie, *HGP III,* 263; Kerferd, *SM,* 42; Windelband, *History,* 114.

54. J. S. Morrison, "The Place of Protagoras in Athenian Public Life," *CQ* 35 (1941): 10.

55. Kerferd, *SM,* 85, 145; Untersteiner, *Sophists,* 87; Werner Jaeger, *Paideia: The Ideals of Greek Culture* (New York: Oxford U. Press, 1945), 1:286ff.; Milton C. Nahm, *Selections from Early Greek Philosophy* (Englewood Cliffs, NJ: Prentice-Hall, 1964), 212; Philip Wheelwright, *The Presocratics* (New York: Odyssey Press, 1966), 236.

56. For Euripides and Sophocles, see Morrison, "Place of Protagoras," 13–16; for Aeschylus, see J. A. Davison, "The Date of the *Prometheia,*" *TAPA* 80 (1949): 66–93.

57. Sinclair, *History,* 53. For the argument that Plato's *Republic* is aimed at Protagoras' defense of democracy, see Stanley Moore, "Democracy and Commodity Exchange: Protagoras versus Plato," *HPQ* 5 (1988): 357–68.

58. Classen, "Aristotle's Picture."

59. Ibid., 23.

60. Kahn, *Verb*, 366–70.
61. Ibid., 302.
62. Kerferd, *SM*, 44. See also J. Ph. Lauer and Ch. Picard, *Les statues ptolémaïques du Sarapieion de Memphis* (Paris: Presses Universitaires de France, 1955), 120–27; K. Schefold, "Die Dichter und Weisen in Serapieion," *Museum Helveticum* 14 (1957): 33–38.
63. **Positivist:** Otto Neurath, quoted in Jaap Mansfeld, "Protagoras on Epistemological Obstacles and Persons," Kerferd, *Legacy*, 49; see also Windelband, *History*, 116. **Humanist:** F. C. S. Schiller, *Plato or Protagoras?* (Oxford: Basil Blackwell, 1908), 7–8; Harold Bennett, *The Sophists: Rhetoric, Democracy, and Plato's Idea of Sophistry* (Novata, CA: Chandler and Sharp, 1987), 36; George C. Simmons, "The Humanism of the Sophists with Emphasis on Protagoras of Abdera," *Educational Theory* 19 (1969): 29–39. **Pragmatist:** Dupréel, *Sophistes*, 55; James Haden, "Did Plato Refute Protagoras?" *HPQ* 1 (1984): 229–32; Robert F. Davidson, *Philosophies Men Live By* (New York: Holt, Rinehart, 1952), 11; P. S. Burrell, "Man the Measure of All Things: Socrates versus Protagoras," *Philosophy* 7 (1932): 27–41, 168–84. **Skeptic:** Windelband, *History*, 116; Zeller, *History*, 446. **Existentialist:** Milton K. Reimer, "The Subjectivism of the Sophists: A Problem of Identity," *Journal of Thought* 13 (1978): 50–54. **Phenomenalist:** Untersteiner, *Sophists*, 48. **Empiricist:** Theodor Gomperz, *Greek Thinkers* (London: John Murray, 1901), 1:455; Windelband, *History*, 118. **Utilitarian:** S. Moser and G. L. Kustas, "A Comment on the 'Relativism' of Protagoras," *Phoenix* 20 (1966): 111–15. **Subjective relativist:** Guthrie, *HGP III*, 186; A. E. Taylor, *Plato: The Man and His Work* (London: Methuen, 1949), 325–33; Gregory Vlastos, *Plato's "Protagoras"* (Indianapolis: Bobbs-Merrill, 1956), xii–xvi; Newton P. Stallknecht, "Protagoras and the Critics" [concerning aesthetics], *Journal of Philosophy* 35 (1938): 39–45. **Objective relativist:** Gomperz, *SR;* Francis M. Cornford, *Plato's Theory of Knowledge* (London: Routledge and Kegan Paul, 1935), 32–36; David K. Glidden, "Protagorean Relativism and *Physis*," *Phronesis* 20 (1975): 209–27; G. B. Kerferd, "Plato's Account of the Relativism of Protagoras," *Durham University Journal* 42 (1949): 20–26; Adolfo J. Levi, "Studies on Protagoras: The Man-Measure Principle: Its Meaning and Applications," *Philosophy* 40 (1940): 158.
64. Richard A. Engnell, "Implications for Communication of the Rhetorical Epistemology of Gorgias of Leontini," *WJSC* 37 (1973): 175–84; Richard Leo Enos, "The Epistemology of Gorgias' Rhetoric: A Re-examination," *SSCJ* 42 (1976): 35–51; Bruce E. Gronbeck, "Gorgias on Rhetoric and Poetic: A Rehabilitation," *SSCJ* 38 (1972): 27–38.
65. Havelock, *Preface to Plato* (Cambridge, MA: Harvard U. Press, 1963), 8, 280, 285–86, 305–6; see also "Task."

19

2

INTERPRETING ANCIENT FRAGMENTS

Plucked out of context and dropped into the twentieth century, the few extant lines by Protagoras appear trivial if not nonsensical. Not only are there pitifully few statements attributed to Protagoras, but much of what is available has been filtered through sources not altogether friendly to Protagoras' project.[1] T. A. Sinclair, deploring the scanty remains of Protagoras' writings, noted that "when the evidence is so meagre, interpretation is hazardous and subjective, and it is not surprising that even in antiquity conflicting opinions were held and conflicting traditions current."[2]

The problem I want to address is how to give Protagoras' fragments their "best-accessible reading"—a phrase I borrow from Thomas S. Kuhn's description of the method of historical interpretation with which he tries to provide the most plausible and coherent reading to otherwise implausible and incoherent texts.[3] The operating assumption is that what may seem implausible to a modern reader may make perfect sense if understood in the text's historical context. Hence, the question is: In reconstructing Protagoras' contributions to early Greek philosophy and rhetoric, how does one construct the most reasonable and interesting account of his words and the narratives about him?[4]

20

PROBLEMS FACING THE MODERN INTERPRETER

The issue of competing methods of interpretation of ancient Greek texts has received renewed attention. Havelock has suggested that the training of classicists emphasizes distrust for the "use of theory" and "a priori" approaches to interpretive problems.[5] Such distrust notwithstanding, Havelock insists that previous readings of most ancient and classical texts have in fact been influenced by unstated assumptions about the language and literary habits of Greek culture.[6] Much of Havelock's work can be read as an effort to identify and correct these unstated assumptions and provide an alternative way of reading Greek texts. Similarly, Charles H. Kahn noted that all interpretation is informed by presuppositions. He concludes: "If we do not deliberately construct or select our own interpretive framework, we become unconscious and hence uncritical prisoners of whatever hermeneutical assumptions happen to be 'in the air.'"[7] Following Havelock, Kahn, and others, I think it is important to identify the presuppositions guiding the reading of Protagoras I defend in this book.

In addition to the traditional prescriptions of sound reasoning and appropriate use of evidence, I posit the following hermeneutic practices for recapturing Protagoras' contributions: 1) Protagoras' fragments make the most sense when viewed as intelligent responses to issues and concerns of his own time. 2) Modern philosophical concepts should be bracketed as much as possible when one initially interprets Protagoras' fragments and doctrines in order to avoid improper and premature schematization of the history of ideas. 3) The ancient sources of information about Protagoras' doctrines must be treated with the same cautiousness as modern commentaries. 4) The influence of the Greek transition from a mythic-poetic to a more literate, humanistic-rationalistic culture must be considered in interpreting texts of the sixth, fifth, and fourth centuries BCE. 5) Four hermeneutic principles useful for translating and interpreting Protagoras' fragments are *ipsissima verba* primacy, triangulation, linguistic density, and resonance.

Discourse is not produced in a vacuum. It is accepted that Plato's writings on rhetoric, for example, were written in response to various sophistic writings and teachings. Aristotle, in turn, wrote in response to Plato as well as to the Sophists. It is hard to imagine that Protagoras was speaking and writing in a manner other than in response to influential writers and thinkers of his time.

21

As simple as this point is, its significance for interpreting fragments should not be underestimated. An example can help to illustrate the point: Gorgias' tract *On Not-Being* seems patently absurd on first reading. The traditional interpretation has Gorgias arguing that nothing exists, that if anything did exist it is inapprehensible to humans, and that even if it were apprehensible it would be incommensurable and inexpressible.[8] Some scholars cite Gorgias' argument as proof that he was unphilosophical and a nonserious thinker.[9] Others, such as Guthrie, see the text as a creative and amusing parody of Parmenides' poem "On Nature or That Which Is" which proves Gorgias' disdain for idle philosophical speculation.[10] Yet another interpretation, by Kerferd, suggests that Gorgias' treatise was a serious and seminal work on the philosophical problem of meaning and reference.[11] Each interpretation varies according to how Gorgias' writing is juxtaposed to that of other thinkers. Brumbaugh and Dodds view Gorgias' text in a vacuum. Guthrie and Kerferd make far more sense out of Gorgias' arguments by framing them as responses to particular writers and issues of his time. Similar effort must be made to frame Protagoras' statements.

Unfortunately, previous efforts to interpret Protagoras' extant statements often have imposed latter-day contexts on Protagoras, and so rendered him patriarch of various Western traditions. Protagoras has been called the father of debate, the father of grammar, the first educational philosopher, the first political philosopher, the first positivist, the first humanist, and the forerunner of pragmatism. As mentioned in the last chapter, he also has been called a skeptic, a phenomenalist, an empiricist, a utilitarian, and a relativist. The use of some of these labels implies that certain intellectual boundaries existed in Protagoras' time when, in fact, they did not. The very concept of a specially trained thinker called a "philosopher" originated with Plato.[12] Hence, the idea that Protagoras regarded himself as a "philosopher" (let alone a specialist!) is impossible. As Havelock argues, the use of such labels "subtly distorts the story of early Greek thought by presenting it as an intellectual game dealing with problems already given and present to the mind, rather than as a groping after a new language in which the existence of such problems will slowly emerge, as language emancipates itself from the oral-poetic tradition."[13]

The overreliance on modern concepts and categories manifests what modern sociologists call an unexamined "natural attitude" toward ancient Greek thought that misses Protagoras' (and others') contributions. The basis of the natural attitude is the taken-for-granted presumption that the things of the world are an unproblematic "given." The world is defined by its externality, its being "out there" to be "discovered."[14] It is tempting to think that there were such *things* as "grammar," "positivism," or "educational philosophy" waiting for Protagoras to discover them. However, as Michel Foucault pointed out, certain descriptions of history ("Protagoras invented grammar" would be an example) tend to understate the subjective process of formulating discourse that makes something like "the study of grammar" possible.[15]

A more defensible position is to recognize that such labels are largely modern constructions and, as such, ought to be bracketed whenever possible as one initially attempts to recover the ancients' ideas. Often there is a grain of useful information revealed in the employment of modern labels to describe Protagoras, but not much more than a grain. Protagoras may remind us of modern-day positivists when he professes agnosticism in the absence of surer evidence of the gods, but that is where the similarities end.

Second, to use such labels misses an important fact of Greek life. Greek discourse was not neatly divided into categories such as political or philosophical, and there was primarily one audience for public discourse. As Alasdair MacIntyre has noted:

> We ought to recognize that the categories *political, dramatic, philosophical* were much more intimately related in the Athenian world than in our own. Politics and philosophy were shaped by dramatic form, the preoccupations of drama were philosophical and political, philosophy had to make its claims in the arena of the political and the dramatic. At Athens the audience for each was potentially largely and actually to some degree one and the same; and the audience itself was a collective actor.[16]

It is impossible, of course, to forget completely all of our modern ways of thinking when interpreting ancient fragments. New phenomena are understood largely in terms of already experienced and understood phenomena. Nevertheless, avoidance of what Kerferd has called the "premature schematization of the history of thought" is possible if care is taken in using categories and labels that carry considerable historical baggage. Further, any analytical breakdown of Protagoras' doctrines into such parts as political philosophy, epistemology, and the like must be recognized as a contemporary act of reconstruction. Protagoras created his doctrines as parts of a complete and whole way of understanding his world.[17] His work deserves to be approached and understood on his terms—even if later a dissection is made in order to serve modern interests.

Much of what is known about Protagoras is based on two of Plato's dialogues, the *Theaetetus* and the *Protagoras*. The reliability of Plato as a witness to Protagoras' doctrines is a hotly disputed issue. Joseph P. Maguire has argued that Plato deliberately distorted Protagoras' doctrines in both dialogues in order to refute them more easily.[18] F. C. S. Schiller has argued that Plato simply did not understand Protagoras' theory of knowledge, but reproduced it as best he could.[19] Theodor Gomperz suggested that the *Protagoras* faithfully portrayed Protagoras, but that the portrait in the *Theaetetus* was a sham.[20] Guthrie and Michael Gagarin, on the other hand, argue that the criticism of Plato has been excessive, and that—at least in the *Protagoras*—Plato's treatment of the Sophist is actually flattering.[21]

Aristotle and his student Theophrastus also have been challenged as historians of their "philosophical" predecessors.[22] Richard L. Enos has argued that Aristotle distorted the history of the sophistic tradition and the history of rhetoric in general.[23] The complaint against Aristotle has been that his interest in advancing his own philosophical doctrines often led him to reformulate the ideas of his predecessors in order that they might be better explained, refuted, or assimilated by his own system.

The issue is not whether to consult the records of Plato or Aristotle, for it would be impossible to attempt a reconstruction of almost any presocratic thinker without reference to Plato and Aristotle. Rather, a more constructive prejudice would be to accept the methodological requirement that claims regarding *specific* passages require specific evidence to support or to question reliability. Any broader assumption about the reliability of Plato and Aristotle as sources cannot help but adopt a basically pro or con bias toward the Sophists. As Guthrie noted, it is important to resist the tempting assumption that negative references to the Sophists must be wrong, and positive ones right.[24]

LITERACY AND GREEK PHILOSOPHY

Eric A. Havelock inaugurated an ambitious project of reading early Greek philosophical literature in light of the fact that Greece underwent a transition from a predominantly oral to a predominantly literate culture in the sixth, fifth, and fourth centuries BCE. Since Havelock's views have influenced my reading of the texts of and about Protagoras, a discussion is in order of his orality-literacy thesis and of certain necessary attenuations.

Two related discoveries in the first half of the twentieth century concerning the Greek language provided the starting point for Havelock's later theorizing. The first was the hypothesis that Greek culture was wholly oral until approximately 750 BCE. Though controversial for decades, Rhys Carpenter's thesis that the Greek written alphabet developed as late as the last quarter of the eighth century is now widely (though not universally) accepted.[25] A complementary development was Milman Parry's case that the *Iliad* and *Odyssey* were originally oral compositions, handed down by memory from generation to generation.[26] The epic poems of "Homer" were not written down until sometime around 700 BCE. These two developments support the theory that literacy developed in classical Greece at about the same time as presocratic philosophy emerged.

Is it merely an accident of history that philosophy flourished at the same time literacy became a pervasive part of Greek culture? Havelock and writers such as Jack Goody insist that it was not.[27] In fact, they claim literacy and philosophy grew up side by side in classical Greece so that the latter cannot be understood fully without reference to the former. From the time of the presocratic philosophers and the Sophists up through the time of Plato, Greek culture was in a slow but steady transition from a predominantly nonliterate to a predominantly literate culture. During this transition the uses of (and attitudes toward) written documents changed radically. What I will refer to as book-oriented literacy was a relatively late development. As writers such as Rosalind Thomas, Brian Street, and Ruth Finnegan point out, "oral" and "literate" are difficult to define because the *uses* to which literacy is put differ from society to society. As Thomas notes: "Different degrees of literacy are demanded and encouraged by the running of a farm, active and energetic participation in the proposing of decrees, and reading philosophical or poetic texts."[28] In this study "literacy" refers primarily to the consistent habit of reading and writing books. Since books were fairly rare in Athens until after Protagoras' career, book-oriented literacy was restricted to a fairly small number of intellectuals—even if a more basic sense of literacy was widespread.

Rudolf Pfeiffer has suggested that, from the standpoint of classical scholarship, literacy can be described as developing in four stages or periods. The first period was wholly oral. The second began with the introduction of the alphabet and involved the preservation of important oral compositions (such as Homer). During this stage there is no evidence for book production on a large scale for a general reading public. The third period began in the fifth century and marks the beginning of book-oriented literacy. During this period books became available for purchase, but they were still sufficiently rare and novel to evoke curiousity and amusement (see Aristophanes, *Frogs 52*, 1109–18). The fourth and final stage, reached well after the age of the Older Sophists, is characterized by the widespread distribution of books plus a change in attitude such that a library would no longer seem odd or novel.[29]

Havelock has argued that much of our understanding of the philosophical writings of the sixth and fifth centuries is badly tainted because it has not considered the impact of such a cultural transition on the content and the style of those writings. To begin with, widespread, book-oriented literacy potentially facilitates new ways of thinking and understanding the world. Language in oral Greek society evolved to serve the needs of memory, since it was through repetition and memorization that one generation passed on to the next what it had learned. For example, the vocabulary of an oral dialect is usually limited to a few thousand words, while modern English has a recorded vocabulary of one and a half million words.[30] The need to remember also affects syntax and composition, making verse, song, and story the best vehicles to store the records of Greek oral culture.

Based on Havelock's writings and his own research on oral and literate cultural characteristics, Walter S. J. Ong has identified nine points of difference between oral and literate cultures. Of these, five are particularly relevant for this study. Accounts of the cognitive differences between oral and literate cultures, such as the following by Ong and Havelock, have been severely criticized by various anthropologists, classicists, and sociologists. Even the ability to identify clearly "oral" and "literate" cultures has been challenged. It will be useful, however, to understand Havelock's and Ong's position in a fairly undiluted form before discussing certain required attenuations.

1) An oral culture's thought and expression are additive rather than subordinate. In English, phrases are often joined with connectives that point to the different logical statuses of the phrases. The connective may imply, for example, a temporal or causal ordering of the phrases (if, then, thus, when, while). In Greek oral culture the primary connective was "and"—the term most capable of keeping a story flowing. One of the tasks faced by the philosophers of classical Greece was the development of a technical vocabulary that would encourage analytic manipulations of ideas and phrases.

2) An oral culture's thought and expression are aggregate rather than

26

analytical/partitioning: "The elements of orally based thought and expression tend to be not so much simple integers as clusters of integers, such as parallel terms or phrases or clauses, antithetical terms or phrases or clauses, epithets.... Oral expression thus carries a load of epithets and other formulary baggage which high literacy rejects as cumbersome."[31] The need for clustering ideas plays an important role in the composition of the writings of the Sophists and Presocratics, and it provides yet another reason an oral culture resists logical analysis: "Once a formulary expression has crystallized, it had best be kept intact. Without a writing system, breaking up thought—that is, analysis—is a high-risk procedure."[32]

The two points discussed so far represent what can be described as the additive or amplificatory cognitive function of oral poetry. Of course, written prose can amplify notions as well, but for the moment the most important cognitive functions of written prose can be described, according to Havelock's and Ong's analysis, as abstractive and analytical.[33] While the amplificatory function was ideal for transmitting the already known, it was not always as useful for the purposes of advancing the insights of persons devoted to inquiry as were analytical thinking and prose communication.

3) The thought and expression of an oral culture are close to the human life world. A literate culture has greater power to objectify people, objects, and events in ways that divorce them from a context of human action, while in Greek oral culture this was far more difficult.[34] Hence, the preliterate Greeks thought of justice not as an abstract principle but as a word that described specific human experiences: acting-unjustly, receiving-justice, etc.[35]

4) Thought and expression in an oral culture are empathetic and participatory rather than objectively distanced. An oral culture's history, myths, traditions, values, and beliefs—in other words, all cultural knowledge considered worth remembering—are preserved in rhythmic verse. In ancient Greece the task of memorizing the wisdom of Homer and Hesiod fell on all members of society, not just the specialists (poets, rhapsodes, and actors). Hence the performance of epic poetry made psychological demands on both speaker and audience.[36] Havelock hypothesized that the psychomotor demands of recollecting and performing epic poems created a hypnotic, almost trancelike state in both minstrel and hearer during performances.[37] In addition to being the source of a culture's collective wisdom, poetic performances were also a pleasurable form of recreation.[38] One can participate in such a performance

only by yielding to the rhapsode's "spell": "Psychologically it is an act of personal commitment, of total engagement and of emotional identification."[39] Hence, according to Havelock, the poetic experience and the cognitive habits of Greek oral culture were at odds with what would now be called critical thinking. Additionally, Havelock has argued that distinctions and dichotomies such as thinking and feeling, subject and object, knower and known, did not occur in the strictly oral culture of Homeric Greece. Literacy facilitated changes in Greek syntax irrespective of the implications for memorization. Such changes, in turn, advanced changes in patterns of explanation. Havelock suggested that the transition from expressing "me identifying with Achilles" to expressing "me thinking about Achilles" was facilitated by the technology and psychology of the written word.[40]

5) Thought in an oral culture is situational rather than abstract. Reporting on field research by Luria and others, Ong has described some of the ways in which oral cultures understand the world differently from literate cultures. The most potent intellectual power literacy serves is that of analysis and abstraction. Ong summarizes: "An oral culture simply does not deal in such items as geometrical figures, abstract categorization, formally logical reasoning processes, definitions, or even comprehensive description, or articulated self-analysis, all of which derive not simply from thought itself but from text-formed thought."[41] So, for example, *aretê* (excellence or virtue) was originally thought of not as an abstract moral concept (as it is found in Plato) but as a concrete skill or ability—the *aretê* of a fast runner or of a brave and cunning warrior.[42]

The supposed differences between an oral and literate culture can be summarized as follows: An oral culture's thought and expression are additive rather than subordinate, aggregate rather than analytic, close to the human life world, empathetic and participatory rather than objectively distanced, and situational rather than abstract.

There are two major objections to the preceding description of the differences between oral and literate cultures. First, posited as crosscultural generalizations, they are highly questionable. Recent studies suggest that predominantly oral groups are capable of the abstract cognitive abilities and self-conscious verbal skills that Ong, Goody, and others suggest are only evident in literate cultures.[43] Furthermore, what counts as properly "analytical" or "objective" discourse may be more a result of the researcher's ethnocentric biases than a legitimate account of the qualitative differences between the reasoning of oral and literate people.[44] Accordingly, critics such as Ruth Finnegan and Brian Street conclude that most of the literature concerning the cognitive and verbal differences between oral and literate cultures has overgeneralized from the available data.[45] The "great divide" between oral and literate cultures, they conclude, has been exaggerated.

The second objection is that the causal qualities attributed to literacy are excessively "autonomous." That is, it is assumed that literacy *by itself* causes certain cultural changes. Luria's study, for example, compared schooled with unschooled subjects and hence did not isolate literacy as the only, or even the most important, potential variable at work. In contrast to the autonomous model, Street offers an ideological model that focuses on the specific uses of literacy in a particular society. As Finnegan puts it, "The mere technical existence of writing cannot affect social change. What counts is its *use*, who uses it, who controls it, what it is used for, how it fits into the power structure, how widely it is distributed—it is these social and political factors that shape the consequences."[46] Viewed within the framework of the ideological model, literacy is seen as an enabling or facilitating factor, rather than as a sufficient cause for certain cognitive or social changes.[47]

An example of a description based on an autonomous model can illustrate the force of the two objections discussed above. Tony M. Lentz's *Orality and Literacy in Hellenic Greece* equates orality with "concrete observation" and literacy with "abstract thought." He concludes: "Thus abstract thought and logical argument from the written world merge with common knowledge and concrete evidence from the oral world in the pursuit of an ever-growing wisdom. The strength of this relationship between the two modes of thought forms the foundation of Western culture, and leads, ultimately, to contemporary scientific methods."[48] By implying that literacy is always and only associated with abstract thought, and orality always and only with concrete observation, Lentz's description is an overgeneralization. Furthermore, almost all cultures are characterized by a mix of orality and literacy. Since it is not always the case that such a mix ultimately leads to contemporary scientific methods, Lentz's description implies a fallacious causal relationship.

Another benefit of literacy, Lentz declares, is that it "fosters the abstract ideals that make democracy possible." Democracy can survive only when citizens are able "to compromise" and "to think abstractly, to allow that there are different perspectives on the world."[49] However, Ruth Finnegan's study of the nonliterate Limba people of Sierra Leone demonstrated that multilingualism facilitates the very type of perspective-taking abilities that Lentz says are required for democracy.[50] Furthermore, since various forms of fascism have flourished in highly literate societies, it follows that literacy cannot, by itself, "cause" democracy. In short, literacy is neither a necessary nor a sufficient condition for democracy.

Advocates of the ideological model do not claim that literacy had nothing to do with the rise of philosophy in classical Greece. The point is that the relationship is not as direct and causal as Goody, Havelock, and Ong sometimes suggest. Even critics of orality-literacy theories concede that the sort of ivory tower scholasticism and speculative thought we now associate with philosophy depends, in part, on written modes of communication and records.[51] But early Greek "philosophizing" was also influenced, in important ways, by oral traditions and by the prevailing political and social conditions. Furthermore, Greek culture in the sixth, fifth, and fourth centuries BCE was never strictly oral or strictly literate. Greek society was characterized by a mix of oral and literate practices, even if the emphasis on literate practices became more pronounced as time went by.[52]

By employing the ideological model for studying the uses to which Greek society put literacy, I hope to avoid the pitfalls of the autonomous model while still stressing the philosophical importance of growing literate habits during the fifth century. While I often follow Havelock's lead on such matters, I wish to attenuate his claims that imply a direct causal relationship between literacy and certain forms of analytical thought. The clash Havelock perceived between orality and literacy in classical Greece is best viewed as a larger ideological struggle between competing ways of life. The first I will refer to as the Greek "mythic-poetic tradition." Implicit in this phrase is a constellation of certain social practices, including specific forms of discourse (primarily oral poetry), patterns of explanation (typically theistic), and political orientations (elitist). The second I will refer to as the "humanistic-rationalistic" movement associated with certain Greek intellectuals. A variety of social practices underwent substantial changes during the fifth century. Oral and written prose challenged poetry, anthropocentric or "scientific" explanations challenged theistic traditions, and radical democracy challenged more elitist forms of government. Protagoras' place in this struggle will often be the focal point of this study.

My terminology is similar to the traditional habit of dividing Greek thought into *mythos* versus *logos*. The problem with the *mythos/logos* dichotomy is that, in some scholars' writings, it implies that there was a sudden rupture or discontinuity between the mythic-poetic and humanistic-rationalistic traditions. Homer's oral poetry is thought of as typical of the mythic-poetic tradition and Aristotle's analytical written prose is assumed to be representative of the rationalism of *logos*. As a result, the transitional nature of fifth-century theory and practice is missed. A good example of the transitional character of sophistic discourse is Protagoras' "Great Speech" as related in Plato's dialogue (*Protagoras* 320c–328d). Protagoras combined what he called a myth (*mythos*) and a rational account (*logos*) in a way that was characteristic of the Older Sophists. Accordingly, a persistent theme of this study is that Protagoras and his fellow Sophists were transitional theorists and practitioners of discourse. They hold a distinct place in the history of Greek consciousness that should not be reduced to a narrow sense of *mythos* or *logos*.[53]

The Sophists engaged in giving lectures and writing texts, thereby providing prose as a competitor to poetry as a vehicle of wisdom and entertainment. These Greek intellectuals shared a didactic purpose, yet were constrained by the practical need to maintain an entertained audience for their works. They treated language itself as an object of analysis for the first time in Greek history. In short, they were trying to develop and to practice abstract and analytical thinking through a mixture of oral and literate practices. In that sense, what the Presocratics, the Sophists, and Plato had in common "was of greater importance than what separated them."[54]

Though the Presocratics, the Sophists, and Plato all opposed certain mythic-poetic traditions and beliefs of sixth- and fifth-century Greece, they nonetheless were thinking and speaking in a primarily oral culture. Accordingly both the style and the content of their writings were constrained by the influences of an oral age. With respect to style, it should be noted that books were read aloud before audiences, requiring that the language be so "managed as to provide maximum appeal to the ear and evoke maximum response from the ear."[55] Thus Parmenides and Empedocles wrote their famous texts as poems, and the writings of Zeno, Melissus, Anaxagoras, and especially Heraclitus are best described as a series of aphorisms—self-contained sayings "designed for memorization and often containing elements of rhythm to further this end."[56] The famous fragments of Protagoras also were composed in the manner of aphorisms—an important fact to consider in their translation and interpretation.

There is an important sense in which the content of pre-Aristotelian philosophical thought was also constrained by the oral tradition. For example: the vocabulary inherited by the Presocratics was relatively non-

31

abstract and nonconceptual. My point here is empirical, not theoretical. Even if Street and Finnegan's examples prove that nonliterate societies *can* think abstractly and analytically, such societies do not always do so. In the case of ancient Greece, the evidence is clear that new words were invented, particular syntactical practices were revised, old metaphors were stretched, and the dominant patterns of reasoning underwent substantial change after the introduction of literacy.[57] All of the Presocratics criticized the language currently in use, which "they sometimes identify as that spoken by Homer and Hesiod, and at other times by men generally."[58] Such critical efforts were continued in the writings of Plato, which can be viewed as systematic efforts to correct and purify use of language. One of the rhetorical objectives of the dialogues was to dissociate the usual or commonsense meaning of terms such as "knowledge" or "justice" from what Plato believed to be the true meanings.

In short, between the times of Thales and Aristotle philosophical terminology underwent a difficult birth and maturation. The result for modern philologists is that great care must be taken in understanding the subtle changes even common words like *logos* and *einai* (to be) underwent from generation to generation, or even from writer to writer. Accordingly, while some of Havelock's most provocative claims require attenuation, his writings on orality, literacy, and early Greek philosophy are indispensable for understanding Protagoras' contribution to fifth-century philosophy and rhetoric.

FOUR HERMENEUTIC PRINCIPLES

Foremost, the place to recover Protagoras' doctrines is in his own words. As scanty as Protagoras' *ipsissima verba* are, they exceed those available for many thoroughly studied Presocratics and provide an adequate basis for at least a partial reconstruction of his doctrines. The method I shall employ in this study is to grant primacy to Protagoras' actual words and to consider Plato's treatments as derivative and in some cases distortive.

As straightforward as the preceding principle may appear, Catherine Osborne's recent *Rethinking Early Greek Philosophy* provides an important objection to it that deserves discussion. Osborne suggests that there are no such things as authentic fragments representing *ipsissima verba* of the Presocratics. Instead, what we are left with "are often paraphrases quoted from memory, and may be adapted to the context in which they

32

are used; they may be given in reported speech, the terms are sometimes glossed or changed to a more familiar wording. In all these cases we read the text in the form in which it is presented by the ancient interpreter, and his presentation is governed by what he thought the text ought to say."[59] As a remedy Osborne suggests that we abandon the search for the "original context" or "a single conclusive reading" and concentrate on exploring "the range of meaning brought out by the creative use of the text."[60] Specifically, we should abandon the exegesis of "context-free" fragments and study the "embedded text" as found in various ancient commentators. In the case of Protagoras, Osborne's approach calls for the study of what "Protagoras" meant to Plato, Aristotle, and later commentators. The search for Protagoras' original words and what they may have meant to his fifth-century peers should be given up for lost.

As pointed out in a review by Jonathan Barnes, Osborne's objection contains true and false arguments. Even though the ancients did not have quotation marks, they nonetheless "had and used unambiguous devices for marking off quotations."[61] In the case of Protagoras there are clear instances of where later writers purport to quote his famous sayings. Accordingly, it is unnecessarily pessimistic to claim that it is impossible to identify any authentic Protagorean fragments. It is true to note that the contexts in which discussions of Protagoras appear are vital for understanding what Protagoras was saying: "If you snip a fragment out of context, then you will overlook the fact that the quoting author—from bias or indolence—may have changed or twisted the text to suit his own ends."[62] While I differ with Osborne on the possibility of identifying authentic *ipsissima verba,* I agree that the context of Protagoras' surviving words are a source of information about the fragments that cannot be ignored.

Once the genuine fragments are identified, the best guides for translating Protagoras' words are fellow fifth-century writers. For example, *kreittôn* and *hêttôn* had a moral sense in the mid-fourth century BCE, and they are often translated in Plato's writings as "better" and "worse," respectively. Extant sixth- and fifth-century usages have no such moral force. The words were used generally to describe "stronger" or "weaker" physical forces. Accordingly, when *kreittôn* and *hêttôn* appear in Protagoras' fragments, they should be translated as "stronger" and "weaker" rather than "better" and "worse."

Sometimes, however, the fifth-century meaning of a word is not evident, and in such cases I employ a procedure best described as *triangula-*

tion. Just as one might try to locate the source of a radio transmitter by calculating the distance from two known points of reception, so might one attempt to understand Protagoras' words by comparing his usage with that of better-known writings. The known points are the usages of the pre-Protagorean sources of Homer and Heraclitus on one side and the post-Protagorean writings of Plato and Aristotle on the other. Greek philosophical language underwent considerable change during the sixth, fifth, and fourth centuries BCE, and the evidence is solid that Protagoras contributed to the development of various concepts. Accordingly, it is reasonable to hypothesize that Protagoras' usage shows some advancement over his predecessors while not reaching the sort of sophistication found in Plato and Aristotle. Havelock, for example, suggests that Protagoras' use (and possible invention) of the word *dikaiosunê* (justice as a personal excellence) represents a conceptual advancement over the Homeric sense of *dikê* (justice as paying one's debts), yet falls short of the Platonic notion of justice as a purely abstract principle.[63]

Two other useful analytical tools for interpreting Protagoras' fragments are suggested by Kahn in the course of his study of the fragments of Heraclitus. Kahn describes two hermeneutic aids: linguistic "density" and "resonance."[64] Linguistic density refers to the fact that the meaning of a particular phrase may be magnified by a writer's deliberate choice of words with multiple meanings. Density is apparent particularly when word choice is aided by ambiguous syntax, which occurs often in the construction of aphorisms. In the case of Protagoras' extant fragments, linguistic density is useful for explaining the varied readings by later commentators. Furthermore, since Protagoras became known for his interest in correct language (*orthos logos*), it seems reasonable to assume that words with a wide range of meanings were chosen deliberately.

Linguistic resonance refers to the fact that the meaning of a particular fragment may be better understood when viewed in relation to other fragments with similar words or phrases by the same author. The significance of one fragment may not be fully appreciated unless one notes how it "resonates" with others. As I show in Part 2, Protagoras' fragments fit together and resonate with each other in ways unnoticed in previous studies.

Martin Heidegger pointed out that a "presuppositionless apprehending" of a text is impossible, since all interpretation is influenced by one's previous understanding.[65] Any act of interpretation is limited by the historicity of the interpreter, but some historical accounts are more defensible than others.[66] That is, some interpretations better withstand the tests of time and argument than others. By identifying the presuppositions of previous interpretations of the fragments of Protagoras (and other Sophists), certain distortions and anachronisms can be avoided, and by identifying my own hermeneutic presuppositions the usefulness of my study can be better assessed. What follows is not the last word on Protagoras. It is, I hope, a helpful contribution to an ongoing dialogue on the Sophists—one that promises to continue as long as the study of philosophy and rhetoric persists.

NOTES

1. Theodor Gomperz, *Greek Thinkers* (London: John Murray, 1901), 1:440.
2. T. A. Sinclair, *A History of Greek Political Thought* (London: Routledge and Kegan Paul, 1951), 44.
3. Thomas S. Kuhn, see preface, *The Essential Tension* (Chicago: U. of Chicago Press, 1977), esp. xii. The analogy to the history of science is appropriate, claims Richard Rorty, since in both cases the historian should strive to understand the past on its own terms—even if those terms are incompatible with modern theories and beliefs. ("The Historiography of Philosophy: Four Genres," *Philosophy in History: Essays on the Historiography of Philosophy,* ed. Richard Rorty, J. B. Schneewind, and Quentin Skinner [Cambridge: Cambridge U. Press, 1984], 49).
4. Stephen Makin, "How Can We Find Out What Ancient Philosophers Said?" *Phronesis* 33 (1988): 121. There are many ways to read or interpret ancient texts. In chapter 4 I discuss in more detail the difference between historical reconstructions and other, more contemporary, ways of reading the Sophists. A short but useful discussion of interpretation can also be found in Richard Robinson, *Plato's Earlier Dialectic* (Oxford: Clarendon Press, 1953), 1–6.
5. Eric A. Havelock, *The Literate Revolution in Greece and Its Cultural Consequences* (Princeton: Princeton U. Press, 1982), 220.
6. Ibid., 220–60.
7. Charles H. Kahn, *The Art and Thought of Heraclitus* (Cambridge: Cambridge U. Press, 1979), 88.
8. Jonathan Barnes, *The Presocratic Philosophers* (London: Routledge and Kegan Paul, 1982), 173.
9. See, e.g., Robert S. Brumbaugh, *The Philosophers of Greece* (New York: Crowell, 1964), 116–17; E. R. Dodds, *Plato: Gorgias* (Oxford: Clarendon Press, 1959), 6–10.
10. Guthrie, *HGP III,* 194.
11. Kerferd, *SM,* 99. See also chapter 8 of Edward Schiappa, *The Beginnings of Rhetorical Theory in Classical Greece* (New Haven: Yale U. Press, 1999).
12. Eric A. Havelock, "The Linguistic Task of the Presocratics," *Language and Thought in Early Greek Philosophy,* ed. Kevin Robb (La Salle, IL: Hegeler Institute, 1983), 57.
13. Ibid.
14. Alfred Schutz and Thomas Luckmann, *The Structures of the Life-World* (Evanston: Northwestern U. Press, 1973). Edmund Husserl introduced the term "natural attitude" (Robert C. Solomon, *From Rationalism to Existentialism* [New York: Harper, 1972], 157–66).
15. Michel Foucault, *The Archaeology of Knowledge* (New York: Pantheon, 1972). Saul Levin, "The Origin of Grammar in Sophistry," *General Linguistics* 23 (1983): 41–47,

does a good job of identifying some of the subjective elements of formulating a discipline while still placing Protagoras in the historical development of grammar (even if his verdict on the Sophists is unduly harsh).

16. Alasdair MacIntyre, *After Virtue: A Study in Moral Theory* (Notre Dame: Notre Dame U. Press, 1981), 129.

17. Untersteiner, *Sophists*, 19–91.

18. Joseph P. Maguire, "Protagoras—or Plato?" *Phronesis* 18 (1973): 115–38; "Protagoras . . . or Plato? II. The *Protagoras*," *Phronesis* 22 (1977): 103–22.

19. F. C. S. Schiller, *Plato or Protagoras?* (Oxford: Basil Blackwell, 1908).

20. Gomperz, *Greek Thinkers*, 1:458.

21. Guthrie, *HGP III*, 9–11, 37, 39 n2, 265–66; Michael Gagarin, "The Purpose of Plato's *Protagoras*," *TAPA* 100 (1969): 133–64; see also Gregory Vlastos, *Plato's "Protagoras"* (Indianapolis: Bobbs-Merrill, 1956), viii.

22. Harold Cherniss, *Aristotle's Criticism of Presocratic Philosophy* (New York: Octagon Books, 1935); J. B. McDiarmid, "Theophrastus on the Presocratic Causes," *HSCP* 61 (1953): 85–156; W. K. C. Guthrie, "Aristotle as Historian," *JHS* 77 (1957): 35–41; Havelock, "Task."

23. Richard Leo Enos, "Aristotle's Disserve to the History of Rhetoric" (Paper presented at the Speech Communication Association Convention, Washington, DC Nov. 1983).

24. Guthrie, *HGP III*, 34.

25. Rhys Carpenter, "The Antiquity of the Greek Alphabet," *American Journal of Archaeology* 37 (1933): 8–29; "The Greek Alphabet Again," *American Journal of Archaeology* 42 (1938): 58–69. According to Kevin Robb, "The issue of the late arrival of the Phoenician script into Hellas is no longer a live one" (introduction, *Language and Thought in Early Greek Philosophy*, 3). The issue has been resurrected: see Martin Bernal's discussion of the latest literature in his *Black Athena: The Afroasiatic Roots of Classical Civilization* (New Brunswick: Rutgers U. Press, 1987), 427–33; Joseph Naveh, *Early History of the Alphabet* (Jerusalem: Magnes Press, 1982). Even if the Greek alphabet was introduced earlier than Carpenter suggested, there was clearly a widespread change in the social uses of literacy in the mid-eighth century (see William V. Harris, *Ancient Literacy* [Cambridge, MA: Harvard U. Press, 1989], viii). As long as oral traditions were predominant until the fifth century, the precise date of the invention of the Greek alphabet is a secondary matter for the purposes of this study.

26. Milman Parry, "Studies in the Epic Technique of Oral Verse-Making" (in 2 parts), *HSCP* 41 (1930): 73–147; 43 (1932): 1–50. Harris suggests that, even by mid-fourth century, the literacy rate for Attica was not likely to have been "much above 10–15%" (*Ancient Literacy*, 328).

27. Jack Goody and Ian Watt, "The Consequences of Literacy," *Literacy in Traditional Societies*, ed. Jack Goody (Cambridge: Cambridge U. Press, 1968), 27–68.

28. Rosalind Thomas, *Oral Tradition and Written Record in Classical Athens* (Cambridge: Cambridge U. Press, 1989), 18–19. See also Harris, *Ancient Literacy*, 25–42, 66–93 (Harris includes a helpful chronology of the use of written texts in Athens on 92–93). Robert Pattison, *On Literacy: The Politics of the Word from Homer to the Age of Rock* (New York: Oxford U. Press, 1982) presents a rather different perspective on the uses of literacy in Greece.

29. Rudolf Pfeiffer, *History of Classical Scholarship from the Beginnings to the End of the Hellenistic Age* (Oxford: Clarendon Press, 1968), ch. 2, esp. 25–27. On the scarcity of books and the changing attitudes toward books in the fifth century, see Thomas, *Oral Tradition*; Leonard Woodbury, "Aristophanes' *Frogs* and Athenian Literacy: *Ran.* 52–53, 1114," *TAPA* 106 (1976): 349–57; E. G. Turner, *Athenian Books in the Fifth and Fourth Centuries B.C.* (London: H. K. Lewis, 1977); Harris, *Ancient Literacy*, 84–88. Alfred Burns suggests that literacy was more widespread than the above authors believe: "Athe-

36

nian Literacy in the Fifth Century B.C.," *Journal of the History of Ideas* 42 (1981): 371–87. The evidence concerning the extent of literacy is ably summarized in Harris, *Ancient Literacy*, 93–115.

30. Walter S. J. Ong, *Orality and Literacy: The Technologizing of the Word* (London: Methuen, 1982), 8.

31. Ibid., 38.

32. Ibid., 39. The potentially adverse effects of literacy on memory was noted even in ancient times (see Harris, *Ancient Literacy*, 30–33).

33. Carroll C. Arnold contributed the notion of oral poetry's additive/amplificatory and written prose's abstractive/analytical functions.

34. Bruno Snell, *The Discovery of the Mind* (Oxford: Basil Blackwell, 1953).

35. Eric A. Havelock, *The Greek Concept of Justice* (Cambridge, MA: Harvard U. Press, 1978).

36. Ong, *Orality and Literacy*, 45–46.

37. Eric A. Havelock, *Preface to Plato* (Cambridge, MA: Harvard U. Press, 1963), 145–64. Havelock's hypothesized trancelike state only occurred during performances and not all the time, as some have implied (see, e.g., Friedrich Solmsen's review of *Preface to Plato* in *AJP* 87 [1966]: 99–105).

38. Havelock, *Preface to Plato*, 152.

39. Ibid., 160.

40. Ibid., 209.

41. Ong, *Orality and Literacy*, 55.

42. LSJ, s.v. *aretê;* see also MacIntyre, *After Virtue*, 115; H. D. F. Kitto, *The Greeks* (Harmondsworth: Penguin, 1957), 171–72.

43. Ruth Finnegan, *Orality and Literacy: Studies in the Technology of Communication* (Oxford: Basil Blackwell, 1988), ch. 3.

44. Brian V. Street, *Literacy in Theory and Practice* (Cambridge: Cambridge U. Press, 1984), ch. 1. It is clearly an Enlightenment bias to assume that the later rationalistic forms of discourse and patterns of explanation were *better* than what preceded them. A good deal of postmodern thought is now in the process of critiquing just this bias. A preference for Enlightenment or postmodern thought should not, however, prevent us from noting the historical role of fifth-century Sophists in promoting new forms of discourse and patterns of explanation that were later codified by Plato and Aristotle.

45. Finnegan, *Orality and Literacy*, 151: "Certainly if we take cognitive processes in a *general* sense, the existence of rich classificatory systems, symbolism, traditions of judicial reasoning, highly developed languages and complex literature among the many non-literate peoples (all amply demonstrated in anthropological research), makes one dubious about the dependence of abstraction on literacy, while the more specific claims about particular logical skills and verbal manipulation are at best too controversial and elusive for any definitive conclusion to be asserted." Finnegan is not ready to reject a possible connection between literacy and certain cognitive skills. On the same page she continued: "It is *possible* that there is indeed some necessary connection between literacy and the ability to conceptualize abstractly and argue rationally. My own prejudices suggest that there is."

46. Ibid., 41–42.

47. Ibid., 159: "Literacy (or indeed orality) can be more fruitfully looked at not as an effective cause, but as an enabling factor: something which *can* facilitate particular forms of cognitive development, etc., but does not of itself bring them about."

48. Tony M. Lentz, *Orality and Literacy in Hellenic Greece* (Carbondale: Southern Illinois U. Press, 1989), 178.

49. Ibid., 179.

50. Finnegan, *Orality and Literacy*, ch. 3. On the relationship between literacy and democracy see Harris, *Ancient Literacy*, 62–63, 79–80, 332–35.

51. Finnegan, *Orality and Literacy*, 56. As Harris put it, "At the very least, the desire of the early Ionian philosophers to perpetuate and diffuse their opinions by writing them down inevitably created a sort of rudimentary dialectic, since all ambitious thinkers were increasingly compelled to confront the ideas of their best-regarded predecessors." Thus, he concludes, "The accumulation of texts was a necessary though not sufficient condition for many of the literary and intellectual achievements of the classical world" (*Ancient Literacy*, 63, 336). For a recent and balanced study of the cognitive contributions of literacy, see Leonard F. M. Scinto, *Written Language and Psychological Development* (Orlando, FL: Academic Press, 1986).

52. Thomas, *Oral Tradition*.

53. Susan C. Jarratt suggests a *mythos-nomos-logos* framework to emphasize the transitional role of the Older Sophists: "The Role of the Sophists in Histories of Consciousness," *PR* 23 (1990): 85–95.

54. Havelock, *Preface*, 290.

55. Havelock, "Task," 8.

56. Ibid., 11.

57. The following studies are just a few of the many that document the evolution of patterns of explanation and forms of discourse in the fifth and fourth centuries: Havelock, *Literate, Justice;* Snell, *Discovery of Mind;* Lentz, *Orality and Literacy*, ch. 8; Friedrich Solmsen, *Intellectual Experiments of the Greek Enlightenment* (Princeton: Princeton U. Press, 1975).

58. Havelock, "Task," 15.

59. Catherine Osborne, *Rethinking Early Greek Philosophy* (London: Duckworth, 1987), 7.

60. Ibid., 8, 10.

61. Jonathan Barnes, "The Presocratics in Context," *Phronesis* 33 (1988): 330. See also the review of Osborne's book by A. P. D. Mourelatos in *Ancient Philosophy* 9 (1989): 111–17.

62. Barnes, "Presocratics," 331.

63. Havelock, *Justice*, 305. I freely admit that triangulation provides no more or less than an educated guess. It is certainly possible that Protagoras was ahead of his time, or even behind it! What I find persuasive is that, in the process of writing Part 2 of this study, triangulation made more sense of Protagras' fragments than Homeric or Platonic readings.

64. Kahn, *Heraclitus*, 89–92.

65. Martin Heidegger, *Being and Time* (New York: Harper, 1962), 191–92.

66. Charles P. Segal, "Literature and Interpretation: Conventions, History, and Universals," *Classical and Modern Literature* 5 (1984/5): 80–83; Edward Schiappa, "History and Neo-Sophistic Criticism: A Reply to Poulakos," *PR* 23 (1990): 307–15.

3

THE "INVENTION" OF RHETORIC

One of the objectives of this book is to identify Protagoras' contributions to fifth-century rhetorical theory and practice. Before those contributions can be recovered, a certain amount of ground-clearing is necessary. Most scholarship concerning sophistic rhetoric is informed by what has become the "standard account" of the early history of rhetorical theory and practice.[1] The basic assumptions of the standard account are as follows: The overthrow of tyranny in Sicily around 466 BCE and the resulting establishment of a democracy created a sudden demand for the teaching of the art of rhetoric for citizens' use in the law courts and in the assembly. Two Sicilians, Corax and Tisias, responded to this demand by "inventing" rhetorical theory through the introduction of the first written *Art of Rhetoric*. The primary theoretical contributions of Corax and Tisias were the identification of the parts of forensic speeches and the theory of the "argument from probability." By the end of the fifth century BCE written technical handbooks (known as *technai*) were commonly available for people wishing to learn the art of rhetoric. About the same time a competing approach to the teaching of rhetoric appeared in the teachings of the Older Sophists: Students learned rhetoric through imitating exemplary speeches. The Sophists earned substantial amounts of money as itinerant orators and teachers of rhetoric. However, because their teaching was theoretically modest, philosophically relativistic, and emphasized political success above all else, the Sophists motivated Plato and Aristotle to develop more philosophical treatments of rhetoric as an

39

art. Accordingly, three traditions of rhetorical theory are identifiable in the fifth and fourth centuries: technical, sophistic, and philosophical.

Despite the popularity of this account, I believe that it is fundamentally flawed on almost every point. The argument developed in this chapter is that rhetoric as a discipline was not recognized or defined as such prior to the time of Plato. Prior to that time, sophistic theorizing centered on *logos* and was as "philosophical" (truth-seeking) as it was "rhetorical" (success-seeking). Accordingly, accounts of sophistic theorizing about rhetoric that are based on the Platonic definition of sophist discussed in chapter 1 are anachronistic.

The word "rhetoric" in English can refer to a specific instance of discourse, to an art, or even to a philosophy. The Greek *rhêtorikê* (ῥητο-ρική), from which the English "rhetoric" is derived, is somewhat different. The root *rhêtôr* meant "public speaker" or "politician." The words *rhêtor-eia* (oratory) and *rhêtor-ikê* (rhetoric) were innovations with specific, technical meanings: oratory as the product of a *rhêtôr,* and rhetoric as the art or skill of the *rhêtôr.* The appearance of the term *rhêtorikê* thus signaled the emergence of a discipline distinct from other verbal activities or arts. The standard account of the history of rhetoric assumes that the notion of *rhêtorikê*—rhetoric as an art—orginated in the fifth century. Instead, as argued below, the Greek *rhêtorikê* and *rhêtoreia* are of *fourth*-century BCE, rather than fifth-century, origin. The relatively late coinage of "rhetoric" must be taken into consideration in examining sophistic teaching and doctrine if a reductionistic approach to the Sophists' activities is to be avoided. Sophistic teaching is better understood if scholars focus on the Sophists' role in privileging *logos* over the mythic-poetic tradition rather than by imposing fourth-century conceptions of *rhêtorikê* on fifth-century practices and doctrines.

DID PLATO COIN *RHÊTORIKÊ?*

The proposition advanced here is that the word *rhêtorikê* may have been coined by Plato in the process of composing the *Gorgias* around 385 BCE. I believe that the evidence for such a proposition is surprisingly clear, though the inferences one might draw from such a historical claim are far from obvious. I offer two arguments in support of the proposition that Plato coined *rhêtorikê.* The first is that the surviving instances of the word demonstrate that its use in Plato's *Gorgias* is novel. The second is that Plato's penchant for coining terms ending in *-ikê,* which I document

40

below, makes it highly probably that *rhêtorikê,* like most other terms denoting specific verbal arts, was originally coined by Plato.

Evidence for the first argument is straightforward: *Rhêtorikê* does not appear in fifth- and early fourth-century texts where it would be expected to appear if the term were in common, or even in specialized, usage. Though *rhêtêr* is found in the *Iliad* (9.443), the earliest surviving use of *rhêtôr* is in the Brea Decree, ca. 445 BCE.[2] In the late fifth century, and through much of the fourth, *rhêtôr* was a technical term designating politicians who put forth motions in the courts or the assembly.[3] Accordingly, by the time of Plato's *Gorgias, rhêtôr* was recognized as delimiting a very specific group of people—politicians who spoke often in the courts or the assembly.[4] It is usually taken for granted that a term specifying the art or skill of being a *rhêtôr* was in use prior to Plato, but the evidence simply does not support such a conclusion.

Rhêtorikê does not appear in any of the fifth-century sources where it would be expected to be found if it was a term in use. A search for all forms of *rhêtorik-* in the texts of the *Thesaurus Linguae Graecae* indicates that the earliest documented use of the term is from the fourth century.[5] Prior to the fourth century *logos* and *legein* were used to describe what later would be called rhetoric. Both terms are far broader in their meanings than the term *rhêtorikê,* hence the appearance of *rhêtorikê* signals a new level of specificity and conceptual clarity concerning different verbal arts. Prior to the appearance of the term *rhêtorikê,* both Sophist and philosopher claimed the province of *logos.*

Fifth-century drama provides compelling evidence for a later date for the coining of the word *rhêtorikê.* Euripides, who is generally assumed to have been familiar with sophistic doctrines regarding rhetoric, used *legein* to describe speeches or speakers, *peithô* for persuasion, and *logos* for argument or speech.[6] Aristophanes' well-known diatribe against sophistic training in the *Clouds* never once used the word "rhetoric." *Legein* is used repeatedly for "oratory," *logos* for "argument" or "speech," and "sophist"—not *rhêtôr*—for a trained speaker.[7] *Clouds* was originally presented in 423 BCE, at which time the Older Sophists were well known and their educational practices well established. Had the word *rhêtorikê* been used by the Sophists or had it even been associated with them, Aristophanes certainly would have targeted it as one of the objects of his attack. Given Aristophanes' penchant for poking fun at new or technical terms, the fact that *rhêtorikê* does not appear even once in this play is strong evidence that the term had not yet been invented.[8]

41

There is no record of Protagoras having used the word *rhêtorikê*, even in the Platonic dialogue named after him. Protagoras' fragments make it clear that his focus was on *logos*. There is no evidence that Gorgias ever used the word *rhêtorikê* other than the Platonic dialogue named after him (which is discussed below). In the two tracts by Gorgias most likely to discuss *rhêtorikê*, *On Not-Being* and *Encomium to Helen*, it is the power of *logos* that is described and praised; *rhêtorikê* is never mentioned. Likewise, there are no surviving *ipsissima verba* from other fifth-century Sophists such as Antiphon, Prodicus, or Hippias that indicate the word *rhêtorikê* was in use in their time.[9] Neither *rhêtorikê* or *rhêtoreia* appear in the work of Herodotus, who was quite familiar with sophistic teachings.[10] A passage in the treatise *Dissoi Logoi*, ca. 400 BCE, is noteworthy in this regard.[11] Section 8 specifically addresses the characteristics of a person who wishes to give sound advice to the city: "The man acquainted with the skills (*technê*) involved in argument (*logon*) will also know how to speak correctly (*orthos legein*) on every topic."[12] To speak well, a person must know the laws and the "truth of things" of which he would speak. If there was a late fifth-century sophistic passage in which one would expect to find the word *rhêtorikê*, this surely is one.

In short, as surprising as it may seem, neither *rhêtorikê* nor *rhêtoreia* appears where one would expect it to if, in fact, either word was in popular or even in specialized use in the fifth century. Accordingly, it is difficult to justify any conclusion other than that *rhêtorikê* originated in the early fourth century.

Rhêtorikê not only does not appear in the literature of the fifth century, its use in the fourth century is surprisingly rare. Once again *rhêtorikê* does not appear where one would expect if it were a term in either common or specialized usage. Beyond the works of Plato and Aristotle the two best-known sources for fourth-century theorizing about rhetoric are Anaximenes' *Rhetoric to Alexander* and the texts of Isocrates. *Rhêtorikê* appears in neither. The *Rhetoric to Alexander* is considered the oldest extant full-length sophistic treatment of rhetorical theory other than the works of Isocrates. References in chapter 8 date the text no earlier than 341 BCE and possibly much later—hence the work appeared more than a generation after the *Gorgias*.[13] Neither *rhêtorikê* or *rhêtoreia* is ever used in the work except in the title—which was almost certainly added later when the work was recast as addressed from Aristotle to Alexander. *Logos* is the term used to describe the capacity the work offers to improve. If *rhêtorikê* was a term denoting an established specialty, as implied by Plato and Aristotle, it is remark-able that the *Rhetoric to Alexander* never once used the word.

The first documented use of the word *rhêtoreia,* or "oratory," is in Isocrates' *Against the Sophists* (21). This programmatic work appears to date from the beginning of Isocrates' school, approximately 392 BCE. Unfortunately, the surviving lines of *Against the Sophists* end after only a few pages, so it is impossible to know how consistently Isocrates used the term, but the term appears only twice in other works of Isocrates (*To Philip* 26; *Panathenaicus* 2). *Rhêtorikous* appears in *Nicocles* (8), pub-lished in 374, and in *Antidosis* (256), *ca.* 354/3 BCE. In 346 *rhêtor-euesthai* appeared in the address *To Philip* (25). The scarcity of all these terms testifies to their novelty, particularly in light of Isocrates' preferred use of *logos* and *legein* to describe what he was teaching. Throughout his extant writings Isocrates describes the education he provided as *logôn paideia.* What translators have rendered as speech, discourse, and ora-tory (except for the cases cited above) are from the Greek *logos* and *legein.*

In *Antidosis*—the famous defense of his life's work—Isocrates de-scribed his training as *philosophia* and called it training for the mind as physical training is for the body (181). Philosophy teaches all forms of *logos,* according to Isocrates, and hence makes students stronger in their thinking (183–85). When Isocrates praised the art of discourse as that which makes humans superior to other animals, it is the art of *logos* that was praised (253–57). There certainly is no doubt that Isocrates taught oratory as it is now understood. However, the dominance of the term *logos* in his writings, the rarity of *rhêtoreia,* and the absence of *rhêtorikê* suggest that Isocrates did not professionalize the word *rhêtorikê.* His art, like that of the fifth-century Sophists, was that of *logos.*

Though the term "rhetoric" is quite common in post-Aristotelian lit-erature, its use during most of the fourth century is quite sparse. Though references to the *rhêtôr* became increasingly common in that century, the specific notion of an art of being a *rhêtôr—rhêtorikê*—appears to be limited to Plato and Aristotle throughout much of the fourth century.

So far the evidence suggesting that Plato first coined *rhêtorikê* has been indirect; namely, it seems clear that there are no extant uses of *rhêtorikê* that can be confidently dated prior to the *Gorgias.*[14] The man-ner in which Plato used the term *rhêtorikê* throughout his dialogues also points to its novelty in the *Gorgias.* Despite Plato's well-known reputa-tion for controversy with the Sophists and rhetoric, *rhêtorikê* appeared rarely in his works. *Rhêtoreia* appeared only once (*Statesman* 304a1).

Instances of the various forms of *rhêtorikê* are curiously distributed. In the middle and late dialogues *Euthydemus, Theaetetus, Cratylus,* and *Statesman, rhêtorikê* appeared a combined total of only five times.[15] The word is noticeably absent in *Protagoras, Hippias Major* and *Minor,* and *Sophist.* Even in the *Phaedrus* the word appeared only a bit more than a dozen times. The earliest documented use of the word is in the *Gorgias*—which is also the most extensive usage found in Plato. The *Gorgias* used the word nearly ninety times. Thus the earliest documented use of the word *rhêtorikê* is also the first time it is defined and examined theoretically.[16]

The ready use Plato makes of *rhêtorikê* gives the reader the impression that the word is a "conceptual constant," a "given." Is it plausible that Plato, of all people, invented the word and in a sense the concept *rhêtorikê*? Further, *why* would Plato invent a term for a skill he obviously mistrusted?

Though it cannot be proved conclusively that Plato first coined the word *rhêtorikê,* there is inductive evidence supporting such a possibility. Plato's creative use of language is well established, as is his need to invent a proper "philosophical" vocabulary.[17] In particular, it is significant that Plato was a prolific coiner of words ending with *-ikê,* denoting "art of." The use of such terms was an essential part of Plato's philosophical analysis of the relationship between *technê* and *epistêmê*—art or skill and knowledge. In the dialogues *Gorgias, Euthydemus,* and *Sophist,* for example, Plato coined literally dozens of terms ending in *-ikê.*[18] Plato made conceptual breakthroughs with such linguistic innovations, by which he linked knowledge and skill with an assortment of activities and professions.

Not only was Plato a prolific inventor of *-ikê* terms in general, he invented an important series of *-ikê* terms for verbal arts in particular. The Greek words for eristic (*eristikê*), dialectic (*dialektikê*), and antilogic (*antilogikê*) all originated in Plato's writings, hence it would be remarkable if *rhêtorikê* were *not* coined by Plato.[19]

Morphologically, once *rhê-* was made into *rhêtôr,* as it was in the mid-fifth century, it was a simple step to extend the word to *rhêtoreia* and *rhêtorikê.* Renato Barilli's premise that *rhêtorikê* was originally coined by adding "toric" (*torikê*) to the root *rhê* (to say) is unsupported by the available philological evidence I have already cited.[20] Hence his conclusion that *rhêtorikê* originally meant "the art of discourse" requires amendment. By the time *rhêtorikê* was coined, *rhêtôr* had an established, specific meaning: a politician who put forth motions in court or the assembly. Accordingly, *rhêtor-ikê* meant "art of the rhêtôr."

For decades most scholars have accepted the premise that *rhêtorikê* is derived from *rhêtôr*. From this premise it has been concluded that *rhêtorikê* was used in the fifth century to describe sophistic teachings. Yet no *ipsissima verba* of the Sophists are cited for authority. Rather, scholars such as Stanley Wilcox claim that passages in Plato's *Gorgias* "confirm the derivation." The possibility that Plato himself coined the derivation has not been considered seriously.

There were good reasons for Plato to coin the term *rhêtorikê*. The *Gorgias* was written about the same time as the *Menexenus,* a piece in which Plato also attacked *rhêtorikê*—despite providing what came to be regarded by Athenians as a good example of a funeral oration.[21] The combined target of the *Gorgias* and *Menexenus* was nothing less than the most important public-speaking practices in Athens: defense in the law courts, speaking in the assembly, and the important political act of eulogizing the war dead.[22] If Plato could identify the "product" of his rival Isocrates' training as something unnecessary or undesirable, so much the better for the reputation of Plato's school. Gorgias, it should be remembered, was the teacher of Isocrates, hence a dialogue on public discourse titled *Gorgias* that included thinly veiled references to Isocrates would easily have been recognized in the fourth century as an attack on the training afforded by Isocrates.[23] It is significant, I think, that the portion of the dialogue devoted to "What is rhetoric?" begins with an exchange between the *students* of Gorgias and Socrates (Polus and Chaerephon), perhaps symbolically paralleling the conflict between Isocrates and Plato. The portions of the dialogue concerned explicitly with the nature of *rhêtorikê* involve Gorgias; afterward his character fades from the dialogue. If, as I have conjectured, *rhêtoreia* was a novel term associated with the training offered by Isocrates, then Gorgias' explicit declaration at 449a5 that he teaches the art of oratory (*rhêtorikê*) would have been a clear signal to fourth-century readers that the target of the passage was Isocrates.

A more "philosophical" rationale is possible as well. There is no question but that one valuable feature of value in sophistic training in the skill of *logos* was its use in politics. Fifth- and fourth-century Athens was an exceptionally litigious society; careers and fortunes were won and lost in the law courts.[24] Plato's treatment of justice in the *Gorgias* was designed, in part, to prove that sophistic training was unnecessary; the worst that could happen was that one would lose unjustly, in which case one was still better off than one's unjust accuser (468e–481b). Similarly, Plato has Socrates conclude that orators in the assembly end up having less power than anyone else, not more, again making an art of public speaking unnecessary (466b–e). Hence, Plato may have coined *rhêtorikê* to designate and limit the the sophistic art of *logos* to affairs in the law courts and the assembly—affairs which, in Plato's view, could only lead to mischief.

For both pragmatic and philosophical reasons Plato wanted to establish a distinction between his own "philosophical" art of *logos* and that of his rivals. In order to contrast clearly the training of philosophy to that of his sophistic competitors, Plato needed a conceptual target that would not be confused with the training offered by his own school. The *Phaedo* contains a passage in which Socrates attributes misology (*misologia*), the dislike of all *logoi*, to an improper knowledge of *logôn technê*, the art of *logos*. Socrates blames misology on those who practice antilogic, the *antilogikoi*, by whom Plato meant Protagoreans and Sophists in general. Their training only led to smugness and a casual attitude toward truth, Plato suggested. Only some *logoi* are true, and it is the task of the student of philosophy to learn to tell the difference between good and bad *logoi* (*Phaedo* 89d1–91c5).

The *Gorgias*' historical context is crucial to its proper interpretation. The *Gorgias* documents Plato's growing disillusionment with public life, and its writing was, in Guthrie's words, a result of an "emotional crisis" experienced by Plato after Socrates' death.[25] The *Gorgias* was not written as a philosophical treatise on rhetoric but as a broader attack on the life of fourth-century politicians. The issue is made explicit by Socrates: "Our argument now concerns ... the way one ought to live: whether it is the life to which you summon me, doing such manly things as speaking in public, practicing rhetoric, engaging in politics as you do now; or whether it is this life of mine in philosophy" (500c1–8).[26] As I have said, the term *rhêtôr* in the fourth century designated a specific class of individuals who spoke often in court or the assembly.[27] Plato opposed education aimed at producing such orators because he did not trust the training to produce proper statesmen. Hence, whether he originated the term or not, *rhêtorikê* was a useful label for Plato to use to distinguish Isocrates' (and others') training from his own.

Rhêtorikê is used sparingly in the *Phaedrus* compared to the *Gorgias*. It is noteworthy that in the *Phaedrus*, where the possibility of philosophical rhetoric is outlined, Plato contrasts his conception of rhetoric with that of those teaching the "art of speech"—*logôn technê* (266d–274c).

Guthrie has described aptly Plato's intention to differentiate between good and bad arts of *logoi:* "The rhetorical art was also known as 'the art of the *logoi*,' and the wide meaning of this word (from talking or speech-making to argument, reason, thought) made possible very different conceptions of the art of which it was the subject. Plato's aim was to get it out of the hands of superficial persuaders and special pleaders, and show that, properly applied and based on knowledge of the truth, it was coextensive with philosophy."[28]

There is a tendency to treat rhetoric as a given in Plato's *Gorgias.* That is, it is usually assumed that there was a discrete set of activities or a body of teachings that were consensually regarded as *rhêtorikê* and toward which Plato directed his critical abilities. A more likely situation was that Plato thought the Sophists' art of *logos* was in danger of being ubiquitous and hence in need of definitional constraint. Just as in the *Sophist* Plato broke the preliterate concept of Sophist as "wise one" into two concepts, in the *Gorgias* he sought to contrast the ideal art of *logos* with the art of *rhêtorikê.*

Textual support for this view can be found in the *Gorgias.* Socrates asks Gorgias, "Of what objects does *rhêtorikê* provide knowledge?" (*peri ti tôn ontôn estin epistêmê*). Gorgias answers *peri logous,* which many translators oversimplistically render as "about words" (449d9–e1). The dialogue then addresses the question, "With what sorts of *logoi* is rhetoric concerned?" Gorgias makes the unlikely concession that not all kinds of *logoi* fall under *rhêtorikê,* only some. Though Socrates and Gorgias agree the art concerns *legein* and *peithô,* Socrates obtains Gorgias' admission that many if not all arts involve speaking and persuasion, including medicine, physical training, mathematics, astronomy, and business. Finally, Gorgias is limited to defending *rhêtorikê* as training for persuasion in public gatherings. The remainder of Plato's treatment of rhetoric in the *Gorgias* and in the *Phaedrus* need not be examined here. The point is to note the process that Plato went through to enable discussion to focus on the utility of *rhêtorikê* as an art of *logos* for the law courts and the assembly. The art of discourse professed by Isocrates, the fourth-century successor of the sophistic tradition, was nothing less than training the mind to think; for Plato in the *Gorgias* rhetoric was reduced to (unnecessary) training for political persuasion.

The evidence for an early fourth-century origin of *rhêtorikê* can be summarized as follows. The word does not appear in fifth-century literature where one would expect to find it if, in fact, it was a term in use. The occurrence of *rhêtorikê* in Plato's *Gorgias* is the earliest recorded usage. While the term appears extensively in a Platonic work well known for its polemic intent, its relatively rare use in other Platonic dialogues gives the impression that *rhêtorikê* is not a common word. The absence of *rhêtorikê* in any other theoretical literature from 400 to 350 BCE further suggests that it was an early fourth-century derivation.

A skeptical interlocutor could object that evidence found in the *Gorgias* itself points to an earlier origin. At 448d9 Socrates introduces rhetoric into the dialogue with the phrase *tên kaloumenên rhêtorikên,* typically translated as "what is called rhetoric." Later Plato presents Gorgias as unequivocally claiming to teach *rhêtorikê* (449a5). These passages have given commentators the impression that *rhêtorikê* was a term in common use.[29] However, an alternative interpretation is justifiable.

There are good reasons *not* to treat *Gorgias* as historically precise. Plato's objective was not to describe accurately Gorgias' views on the persuasive use of language—a fact illustrated by the substantial differences between the defense of *logos* found in the speeches of Gorgias and his floundering performance in Plato's dialogue.[30] In addition, Socrates makes the uncharacteristic claim that he alone practices the true political art—*politikê technê*—and hence is Athens' only true statesman (521d6–8). R. E. Allen describes the dialogue as so "riddled with anachronism that no dramatic date can be assigned to it." In light of "intentional and repeated conflicts of dates," Allen believes that "tense distinctions lose their relevance" in the dialogue.[31] What matters is the *agôn* between the life of the philosopher and the life of the orator. If Plato was willing to put unhistorical sayings in the mouth of Socrates for the sake of argument, there is no reason why he should not do the same with Gorgias.

In any case, the evidence adduced so far plainly points to the conclusion that the term was novel when the *Gorgias* was written. As I noted earlier, it cannot be proved conclusively that Plato first coined *rhêtorikê*. However, even if the term was coined by someone else, it was still new enough to require the phrase *tên kaloumenên rhêtorikên* ("what is called rhetoric") to introduce it. If *rhêtorikê* was not coined by Plato, he may have believed it to be an important and useful term to define (and hence limit) from the perspective of his philosophy. As the seminal analytical treatment of *rhêtorikê,* the *Gorgias* stands in marked contrast to the descriptions of the art of *logos* as found in Gorgias and Isocrates.

It is my contention that some, perhaps much, previous scholarship has misunderstood fifth-century theory because the term "rhetoric" has been used uncritically to interpret the texts and fragments of and about the period. Intellectual enterprises change, in part, through the evolution of a specialized vocabulary, hence historical accounts of the development of what is now called rhetorical theory that fail to consider the move from *logos* to *rhêtorikê* are likely to be misleading.[32] At the very least it can be said that any treatment of the Older Sophists, or even of the fourth-century rivals of Plato, that takes the notion of rhetoric as a given or as a conceptual constant is likely to be in need of revision. *Logos* and *legein* cannot be reduced to *rhêtorikê*. The terms cannot simply be substituted without distorting our understanding of what was happening in fifth-and fourth-century Greece. Examples of the sort of misreadings possible if the proper origins of *rhêtorikê* are not considered are offered below.[33]

THE "INVENTION" MYTHS RECONSIDERED

A further consequence of the relatively late appearance of the word "rhetoric" is that the traditional accounts of the "invention" of rhetoric must be qualified. The two most popular accounts are the Corax/Tisias story and Aristotle's mention of Empedocles as the inventor of rhetoric. Examination of each account sheds light on both the development of the art of *logos* and the possible intentions of the accounts' originator, Aristotle.

The primary authority for the story that Corax and Tisias invented rhetoric as an art is Aristotle. Though Plato referred to Tisias in the *Phaedrus* (272e–274a), he did not claim that Tisias invented *rhêtorikê*. In fact he referred to Tisias' innovation regarding probability as part of a *technê logôn* (273d7). Aristotle stated in the now-lost *Synagôgê* that Corax and Tisias were the first rhetorical theorists (Cicero, *Brutus* 46), and in *Sophistical Refutations* he mentioned Tisias as coming after un-named "first founders" of rhetoric (183b32). Cicero (*de Inventione* 2.6) and Quintilian (*Institutio Oratoria* 3.1.8) also identified Corax and Tisias as originators of the art, but they probably did so on the authority of Aristotle.

A. W. Verrall's essay "Korax and Tisias" accepted the testimony of Aristotle, as did R. C. Jebb, who proclaimed, "The founder of Rhetoric as an Art was Korax of Syracuse."[34] Rhys Roberts accepted the originating role accorded Corax and Tisias in "the development of the art of rhetoric by means of written treatises," as did J. H. Freese in his introduction to Aristotle's *Rhetoric*.[35]

Bromley Smith continued the tradition by claiming that "Rhetoric was born" in Sicily.[36] Corax was "the founder" of rhetoric, "who made the discovery, who wrote the first treatise on the art of the orator (*rhêtorikê technê*)" and who first "defined Rhetoric."[37] D. A. G. Hinks's account of "Tisias and Corax and the Invention of Rhetoric" accepted Aristotle's report, and his interpretation has become a standard reference work on Corax and Tisias.[38] A. E. Douglas, despite noting that Aristotle's history was "highly tendentious," nevertheless accepted the Corax and Tisias legend without question.[39] More recent scholarship tends to regard the story of Corax and Tisias as doubtful only with regard to details. The writings of Guthrie, Kennedy, Wilhelm Kroll, Donald C. Bryant, and James J. Murphy are all standard reference works or textbooks that accept the essential validity of the Corax and Tisias legend.[40]

Despite this strong tradition of granting credibility to the Corax and Tisias story, there are two respects in which the legend is clearly wrong. First, whatever Corax and Tisias taught was not taught under the rubric of *rhêtorikê*. Most accounts agree on an early fifth-century date for Corax's teaching, about 466 BCE.[41] Had Corax or Tisias used the word *rhêtorikê* as early as 466, it should have surfaced in one of their fragments, or at least the word would have been appropriated by someone familiar with their work prior to 387. We may conclude that the surviving references to Corax and Tisias (other than Plato's and Aristotle's) fairly represent customary usage when they identify *logos* and *legein* as the objects of Corax's and Tisias' concern.

It is also likely that traditional accounts of Corax and Tisias' doctrines are also in error. Once again there has been a tendency to take Plato and Aristotle at their word. Two characteristics of Corax and Tisias' *technê* are taken for granted: that it dealt with probability (*to eikos*) and that it represented training for the law courts. Both characteristics have basis in historical fact, yet both have been distorted by Plato and Aristotle.

Even if it is assumed that *eikos* represents a word used by Corax and Tisias, the question remains: What did the term mean? In Plato the term's meaning is twofold: in the *Theaetetus* it is contrasted with geometric proof (162e–163a), giving *eikos* a logical sense, while in the *Phaedrus*, *eikos* is described as *plêthei dokoun*—that which "most people think"—a psychological sense (273b1–2). In Aristotle's writings *eikos* is given a technical, logical sense in contrast to the certainty that is possible with infallible signs or syllogisms (*Rhetoric* esp. 1357a34; *Prior Analytics* 70a4).[42] But there is no reason to believe *eikos* was understood by Corax and Tisias in the limited sense given it by Plato and Aristotle. There is no evidence that they were constructing an epistemological or logical theory of the sort sought by Plato and Aristotle. In fifth-century usage as found in Herodotus (7.103), Thucydides (1.121, 4.17, 6.18), Aeschylus (*Agamemnon* 575) and Sophocles (*Philoctetes* 230) *eikos* meant "likely," "fitting," "meet," "right," or "reasonable." As Havelock has pointed out, a shift in syntax from using a word as an adjective or adverb to the use of a neuter singular construction (i.e., the use of a generic article in the neuter singular paired with a neuter adjective or adverb) may indicate the emergence of a technical sense of the word which signals its professionalization.[43] There is no evidence that Corax and Tisias used the neuter singular construction (*to eikos*) as found in Plato and Aristotle.

It is unlikely, then, that Corax and Tisias espoused a theory that a "probable" *logos* was preferable to stricter, absolute, or more careful logic, as suggested by Smith and Hinks.[44] Equally unlikely is Guthrie's description of the invention of rhetoric as the "introduction of the appeal to probability *instead of* fact."[45] It is more likely that Corax and Tisias attempted simply to teach would-be orators how to plead reasonable and hence believable cases. In such an effort the new rationalistic spirit of *logos* was clearly more useful than anything that could be found in epic poetry.

The second traditionally accepted feature of Corax and Tisias' *technê* is that it resulted in a training manual for the law courts. The question is: *In what way* did the early writings address what would later be called "forensic rhetoric"? Modern commentators, apparently influenced by the sort of treatment forensic rhetoric received in Aristotle's *Rhetoric,* have assumed that previous works were essentially the same in character and function. That is, it has been assumed that "manuals" functioned as "how to" books that coached would-be litigants. Clark charged that the manuals represented rhetoric at its worst: "The whole aim of rhetoric was to win cases, to win the verdict by hook or by crook, and if truth was trampled on in the process, so much the worse for truth."[46] Not all judgments of early rhetorical handbooks have been as harsh as Clark's, but all generally take it for granted that the speaking needs of a would-be litigant were obvious and a given, and that Corax and Tisias stepped in to fill such needs.

A fact often overlooked by historians of rhetoric is that the law courts were mostly fifth-century innovations. Homicide courts may have had an older history, but the popular law courts in which so many fortunes were won and lost flourished at roughly the same time as the Older

Sophists.[47] Thus, instead of a strict causal relationship between the rise of the courts and the rise of *technai,* it is possible that the relationship was that of mutually dependent and interactive development. That is, it is possible that what is commonly referred to as the early sophistic rules for speaking before the law courts were just that—regulations governing the counter talk *(antilegein)* of the law courts. Such a possibility was anticipated by Havelock, who suggested that Plato's *Protagoras* and fifth-century writings imply that the Sophists first promulgated norms for the conduct of political discourse.[48] This idea sounds strange to the modern ear, since the categories of teaching and court procedures belong to different fields. But no such categories held firm in the fifth century. Given that Protagoras was selected by Pericles to write the laws of Thurii in 444 BCE, it is entirely possible that Sophists were involved in the process of writing manuals for speaking procedures in the law courts. For example, the basic structuring of the parts of a speech attributed to Corax and Tisias would have been useful for the audience and for the speaker as analytical and organizational guides.[49]

The preceding analysis shows in at least preliminary fashion how different a picture one receives once Corax and Tisias are examined apart from the Platonic and Aristotelian traditions. Not only is it misleading to call them the inventors of *rhêtorikê,* but our understanding of what they accomplished is skewed by accepting the standard account.

The objection may be raised that there is no apparent reason why Aristotle would mislead his readers. However, as noted in chapter 2, Aristotle consistently sought to contrast his philosophical system with that of his predecessors even if the contrast required distortion of his predecessors' doctrines.[50] Accordingly, it should not surprise us if Aristotle reduced the origin of rhetoric to the study of probability, thereby accommodating the history of rhetoric to his own system of logic and giving his own treatment precedence. Just as Aristotle fictionalized some of his history of presocratic philosophy in order to offer his own as the final solution, his designation of Corax and Tisias as originators of a probabilistic rhetoric could be similarly motivated by a desire to offer his *Rhetoric* as the final product of an art in evolution. The fact that the Corax and Tisias story appeared in the *Synagôgê,* or "Collection," of previous rhetorical theories makes such inferences about Aristotle's motives still more plausible.

Aristotle named the presocratic Empedocles (494–434 BCE) as the inventor of rhetoric in the lost dialogue *Sophist* (Sextus Empiricus,

Against the Logicians I.6; Quintilian 3.1.6; DL 8.57). Modern assessments of Aristotle's claims have varied considerably. D. O'Brien's book makes a point of defending Aristotle as a reliable historian, but it never mentions Aristotle's claim concerning Empedocles and rhetoric.[51] At the other extreme is Helle Lambridis's emphatic rejection of Aristotle's statement: Rhetoric "is the art of covering ignorance with seemingly rational arguments; in a word, it is an art of deceit." The rhetorician "believes in nothing and has no theory of his own to expound." Since Lambridis describes Empedocles as a "dedicated philosopher who tried to arrive at truth," he rejects the possibility that Empedocles was the originator of rhetoric.[52]

Two other studies of Empedocles provide more moderate judgments. Guthrie did not render a verdict on Aristotle's statement one way or another, but he noted that Gorgias was reportedly a student of Empedocles (DK 82 A3, A10), and he suggested that "he taught [rhetoric] by example rather than precept, for both his career and some of his poetry support the ancient verdict that he was an outstanding orator."[53] M. R. Wright also withheld an explicit verdict but noted that Empedocles apparently spoke persuasively and successfully on behalf of democracy in Acragas. No prose fragments by Empedocles are extant, hence it is impossible to assess what his "invention" was.[54]

As is the case with Corax and Tisias, whatever Empedocles taught or invented was surely not called rhetoric at the time. So, in what sense would Aristotle find it plausible to call Empedocles the inventor of rhetoric? The question can never be settled with certainty, but an explanation is possible. According to Guthrie, Aristotle's dialogues were probably expansions or explanations of the Platonic works of the same name, which "aimed at bringing them into line with more recent thought."[55] If Aristotle was trying to update Plato's definitional treatment in the *Sophist,* he may have attempted to identify the predecessors of well-known fifth-century Sophists such as Protagoras and Gorgias. Since by Aristotle's time rhetoric had become a defined discipline, Aristotle may have tried to give it a more honorable birth by indentifying the inventor as Gorgias' teacher, Empedocles, for whom Aristotle had high regard.[56] Empedocles was an innovator in poetic composition and had a reputation as a successful persuasive speaker; this combination would make him a believable candidate for the inventor of a poetic-logical style of discourse further advanced by Gorgias and others. Such an explanation is inconsistent with Aristotle's motives for portraying Corax and Tisias as rhetoric's inventors, but it is difficult to imagine an alternative explanation that would better reconcile both of Aristotle's accounts.

SOPHISTIC TEACHING RECONSIDERED

Logos, of course, was a far more comprehensive term than the fourth-century term "rhetoric." The term *logos* was so comprehensive, in fact, that knowing the Older Sophists taught an art of *logos* rather than rhetoric might not appear helpful. However, to treat *logos* as identifying a restricted and clearly defined art is to give the term an anachronistic interpretation. As Havelock has put it, to do this "subtly distorts the story of early Greek thought by presenting it as an intellectual game dealing with problems already given and present to the mind, rather than as a groping after a new language in which the existence of such problems will slowly emerge, as language emancipates itself from the oral-poetic tradition."[57]

Difficulties that arise when unqualified claims are made about the Sophists teaching rhetoric can easily be illustrated. Once it is said that the Sophists were teachers of rhetoric, there is a tendency to conclude that *all* aspects of sophistic activity had to do with rhetoric. Among sources that illustrate this unfortunate reductionism is Douglas J. Stewart's introduction to the fragments of Prodicus. He asserts that rhetoric was the "chief preoccupation of all the Sophists." He then endorses the "prevailing opinion" that the "real interests" of all the Sophists were rhetorical, and hence "their reported views and writings on special questions in science, history, or politics are normally taken as mere methodological devices and stances bound up with their prime goal of teaching their pupils cultural and political adroitness."[58] C. J. Classen similarly explains sophistic fragments concerning language: "The linguistic studies of the Sophists were carried out not for *philosophical* reasons, not to examine the means by which a statement can be made, but for *rhetorical* purposes: to persuade people successfully, even at the expense of truth; and it was more or less *accidental* when some of these investigations produced philosophically important results."[59] Kennedy once asserted that in the tracts of Sophists such as Gorgias, "The subject matter was apparently of only incidental importance—a fact which awakened the opposition of Socrates. The technique was the thing: the Sophist is purely rhetorician."[60]

54

Such interpretations of the Sophists are misleading because they assume that the status and function of rhetoric was as obvious and given in the fifth century as some might believe it is today. Not only is the conceptual creativity and intellectual breadth of the Sophists thereby missed or underestimated, but whatever picture of the Sophists is left is prejudiced by pejorative preconceptions concerning the value of rhetoric. Bruce A. Kimball's *Orators and Philosophers: A History of the Idea of Liberal Education* exemplifies this tendency: "The Sophists thus attended more to devising persuasive techniques than to finding true arguments, and this amoralism exacerbated the disintegration of the ethical tradition and led to their condemnation."[61] Even when rhetoric is highly regarded by a scholar, there is still a tendency to treat the Sophists simplistically once rhetoric is introduced into the picture. So, for example, Kennedy claims that "Sophistry was in large part a product of rhetoric, which was by far the older and in the end the more vital [art]."[62] Heinrich Gomperz's often-cited work went so far as to claim a near total identity of *Sophistic und Rhetorik,* yet he cited either fourth-century sources or fifth-century fragments concerning *logos,* not *rhêtorikê.*[63] Wilhelm Kroll similarly suggested that the teaching of rhetoric ran through the entire sophistic movement "like a red thread."[64]

Even G. B. Kerferd's otherwise thorough and positive portrayal of the Sophists has been affected by modern prejudices concerning rhetoric. In the surviving fragments of the Older Sophists, Kerferd claims "we have already the elements of a theory of rhetoric which can stand comparison with modern accounts of the technique of advertising." The rhetorical theory the Sophists "inaugurated," according to Kerferd, is best understood as covering "the whole art of public relations and the presentation of images."[65] Though Kerferd's overall treatment of the Sophists is one of the best available, our understanding of sophistic contributions to the historical development of rhetorical theory is not advanced by such comparisons.

Once it is accepted that the Sophists' theorizing concerned *logos* rather than *rhêtorikê* per se, a different picture of their teachings emerges. The Sophists were representatives of an intellectualist movement that favored abstract thinking over what Havelock has called the poetic mind. The Sophists were continuing and expanding a "movement" started by the presocratic philosophers, teaching and speaking in a culture still dominated by preliterate practices and modes of thinking.[66]

The *logos* of the Sophists challenged the traditions of poetic discourse both in substance and in style. Substantively, the Sophists introduced new topics which later would become disciplines.[67] Thinking differently about such topics forced changes of style. For example, when Protagoras attempted to set aside the issue of the existence of the gods, he was both challenging the traditional status granted to *mythos* and preparing the way for what now would be called an anthropological approach to theology. This called for *arguing* rather than merely *telling*. The substantive challenges to traditional ways of thinking brought a new humanism of *logos*.

The Sophists also contributed to significant stylistic changes from tradition. Specifically, the Sophists helped to usher in the ascendancy of prose over poetry as the preferred medium of education. In a predominantly oral culture, "the rhapsodist was also the teacher."[68] The rise of the Sophists was part of the end of poetry's hegemony over knowledge. Calling the switch from poetry to prose "stylistic" does not imply that the content of discourse stayed the same while only the form changed. Considerable evidence indicates that the Older Sophists, through their concern for *logos*, were defending a new humanism that competed with mythic-poetic tradition. It is noteworthy that one of the few times Plato counted the Sophists as his allies was in the *Republic*, where he launched his most thorough attack on the poets (600c6 ff.).[69] In the *Protagoras*, Socrates and Protagoras engage in an analysis of a passage by the poet Simonides (338e–348a). Commentators have viewed Socrates' outrageous (mis)interpretation of the passage as evidence of Plato's distrust of poetry and poetic interpretation.[70] But the section also provides clues about Protagoras as well: "It seems likely that he saw the importance of literary criticism rather in developing the critical faculty and the exact use of language than in promoting the understanding and appreciation of poetry as an end in itself."[71] In his analysis Protagoras points out a contradiction in Simonides' poem, and claims that it is important to be able to evaluate poetry and give a *logos* when questioned (339a). Even allowing for some degree of distortion by Plato, Protagoras made a crucial analytical leap: from repetition of poetry to the critical analysis of poetry. His analysis was metapoetic in the sense that poetry became an *object* of study rather than simply the medium through which the world was understood.

Aristotle also provides evidence of Protagoras' critical approach to poetry. In *Sophistical Refutations* Aristotle reports that Protagoras was concerned with the proper gender of words (173b17, also *Rhetoric* 1407b), and in *Poetics* he claims Protagoras criticized the opening of

Homer's *Iliad* for using the mode of command rather than request (1465b15). Ammonius quotes Protagoras as critically analyzing another passage in the *Iliad* (DK 80 A30). The *Gnomologium Vaticanum* records the following anecdote: "When a maker of verses cursed Protagoras because he would not approve of his poems, his answer was, 'My good sir, I am better off enduring your abuse than enduring your poems'" (DK 80 A25). In short, there is evidence that Protagoras broke from the poetic tradition by making poetry a subject of critical analysis. The cultural break was not total, obviously, for Protagoras and other Sophists were heavily influenced by various mythic-poetic compositional habits. Even in Aristotle's writings the influence of training in Homer remains clear. But the step from generally railing against the poets (as in Heraclitus) to critically analyzing and evaluating their work (as in Protagoras) was a significant one.

Though Protagoras seems to have been the first Sophist to privilege *logos* over the mythic-poetic tradition, virtually all the Sophists can be so characterized. Gorgias' tract "On Not-Being" places him squarely in a rationalistic tradition (in response to Parmenides) and contrasts him with the mythic-poetic tradition.[72] His "Encomium of Helen" praises the power of *logos,* of which poetry was deemed a subset: *logos* "with meter" (DK 82 B11, line 9). Gorgias may have critically analyzed Homer in a manner similar to Protagoras (DK 82 B27), and he held certain "scientific" theories (DK 82 B5, B31).[73] Philostratus claimed that Gorgias founded extemporaneous oratory. Though Gorgias' famous style demonstrated obvious affinities with the heavily rhythmic sentence patterns of the mythic-poetic tradition, there is little doubt that his teaching and practice represented a humanist-rationalist turn from the tradition of *mythos.*

Prodicus was well known for his interest in the correct use of language, alternatively referred to as *orthos logos, orthotês onomatôn,* and *orthoepeia.*[74] Hippias' well-known talent for memorization should not have been considered remarkable in an age when the whole of Homer and Hesiod was known by many. A possible explanation is that his techniques of memorization were directed toward unpoeticized discourse, and in this sense represented a significant achievement. The argument also has been made that Hippias was the first "systematic doxographer," or collector of the opinions of earlier writers.[75] In any case, the rise of prose writing permitted for the first time the treatment of poems and myths as objects of knowledge to be stored, manipulated, and rearranged for the purpose of analysis.

Sophistic discourse can be understood better if the Sophists are identified as transitional figures who, while privileging *logos,* were nonetheless still heavily influenced by mythic-poetic traditions. As Robert J. Connors' analysis of fifth- and fourth-century oratory has demonstrated, the speeches of the Sophists were still controlled by the listening needs of preliterate audiences. For example, the "grand style" of Gorgias seemed strange and affected to those reading his speeches after around 350 BCE when literacy was widespread, but in the primarily oral culture of the fifth century his speeches were impressive and powerful, in part because of the power of poetic syntax and style to re-create the rhapsode's "spell."[76] In the surviving fragments of the Sophists, especially those of Gorgias and Protagoras, the marks of an mythic-poetic culture are clear. It is not surprising that Aristotle comments in the *Rhetoric* that prose began with a poetic style like that of Gorgias (1404a 24). Nor should it be surprising that Hippias and Gorgias wore the purple robes of the rhapsode; in a sense the Sophists were *prose* rhapsodes whose discourse constituted both education and entertainment (DK 82 A9). Fifth-century Sophists, like other presocratic philosophers, were "poised between literacy and non-literacy."[77] They were constrained by the demands of the ear and of poetic syntax and style, but not so constrained that they could not develop and advance oral prose and hence introduce the art of *logos.* Some of the most recent scholarship concerning sophistic theorizing about rhetoric and *logos* is the subject of the next chapter.

NOTES

1. A recent study reported that George A. Kennedy's *Classical Rhetoric and Its Christian and Secular Tradition from Ancient to Modern Times* (Chapel Hill: U. of North Carolina Press, 1980) is the most commonly used secondary source in graduate courses on early classical rhetorical theory (Theresa Enos, "The Course in Classical Rhetoric: Definition, Development, Direction," *RSQ* 19 [1989]: 45–48). This and his earlier work, *APG,* have become the standard reference works on early Greek rhetoric from which other reference works differ only marginally. As Michael Gagarin recently commented, Kennedy is "the most important contemporary scholar of Greek rhetoric writing in English" ("The Nature of Proofs in Antiphon," *CP* 85 [1990]: 23 n3). Accordingly, my description of the "standard account" focuses primarily on Kennedy's version. A more thorough description and critique of the standard account can be found in Part One of Edward Schiappa, *The Beginnings of Rhetorical Theory in Classical Greece* (New Haven: Yale U. Press, 1999).

2. Stanley Wilcox, "The Scope of Early Rhetorical Instruction," *HSCP* 46 (1942): 127; Josef Martin, *Antike Rhetorik: Technik und Methode* (München: Beck, 1974), 2. For

rhêtôr in the Brea Decree see I.G. i.³ 46:25 = Marcus N. Tod, *Greek Historical Inscriptions*, new ed. (Chicago: Ares, 1985), 88–90; Russell Meiggs and David Lewis, *A Selection of Greek Historical Inscriptions to the End of the Fifth Century BCE* (Oxford: Clarendon Press, 1969), 128–33.

3. Mogens Herman Hansen, "Initiative and Decision: The Separation of Powers in Fourth-Century Athens," *GRBS* 22 (1981): 368–70; Josiah Ober, *Mass and Elite in Democratic Athens: Rhetoric, Ideology, and the Power of the People* (Princeton: Princeton U. Press, 1989), 104–27; R. K. Sinclair, *Democracy and Participation in Athens* (Cambridge: Cambridge U. Press, 1988): 136–37; S. Perlman, "The Politicians in the Athenian Democracy of the Fourth Century B.C.," *Atheneum* 41 (1963): 327–55. See also Mogens Herman Hansen, "The Athenian 'Politicians,' 403–322 B.C.," *GRBS* 24 (1983): 33–55; and "*Rhêtores* and *Stratêgoi* in Fourth-Century Athens," *GRBS* 24 (1983): 151–80.

4. Werner Pilz, *Der Rhetor im attischen Staat* (Weida: Thomas and Hubert, 1934). On the dating of the *Gorgias* see E. R. Dodds, *Plato: Gorgias* (Oxford: Clarendon Press, 1959), 18–30; Guthrie, *HGP IV*, 284–85; and Gerard R. Ledger, *Re-counting Plato: A Computer Analysis of Plato's Style* (Oxford: Clarendon Press, 1989).

5. A computer search through all corrected and uncorrected TLG texts was conducted by TLG Director Theodore F. Brunner on May 5, 1989. The results support the hypothesis that *rhêtorikê* was coined in the early fourth century (see Appendix B of this book). Over fifty years ago Werner Pilz noted in passing that "ῥητορική findet sich nicht vor Plato" (*Der Rhetor* 15 n1). Similarly, Wilhelm Kroll noted: "Das Wort ῥητορική begegnet zuerst bei Platon" ("Rhetorik," *RE* supp. 7 [1940]: 1039). The same point is made by Josef Martin, *Antike Rhetorik*, 2; LSJ, s.v. "ῥητορεία"; J. W. H. Atkins, "Rhetoric, Greek," *The Oxford Classical Dictionary* (Oxford: Clarendon Press, 1949), 766; H. Hommel (and Konrat Ziegler), "Rhetorik," *Der Kleine Pauly* (München: A. Druckenmüller, 1972), 4:1396.

6. See, e.g., *Medea* (for *logos* see 252, 546, 776, 801, 819, 965; for *peithô* see 802, 941, 944, 964, 984; for *legein* see 316, 475, 522, 580, 585), and *Hecuba* (for *logos* see 130, 250, 271, 294, 334, 840, 1190, 1239; for *peithô* see 133, 294, 340, 816, 819, 1205; for *legein* see 257, 293, 1189). On Euripides and the Sophists see Paul Decharme, *Euripides and the Spirit of His Dramas* (New York: Macmillan, 1906), 34–42; T. B. L. Webster, *The Tragedies of Euripides* (London: Methuen, 1967), 22–23; R. G. A. Buxton, *Persuasion in Greek Tragedy: A Study of Peithô* (Cambridge: Cambridge U. Press, 1982); Ann Norris Michelini, *Euripides and the Tragic Tradition* (Madison: U. of Wisconsin Press, 1987), 142–44.

7. For *legein* see lines 239, 260, 430, 486–87, 1106, 1211, 1314, 1334, 1398, 1422; *logos* appears throughout, but see esp. the debate between the two *logoi,* 882–1104. For the date of *Clouds* see K. J. Dover, *Aristophanes: Clouds* (Oxford: Clarendon Press, 1968), and Alan H. Sommerstein, *Aristophanes: Clouds* (Warminster: Aris and Phillips, 1982). For the absence of *rhêtorikê* in Aristophanes see also Henry Dunbar, *A Complete Concordance to the Comedies and Fragments of Aristophanes* (Oxford: Clarendon Press, 1883).

8. J. D. Denniston, "Technical Terms in Aristophanes," *CQ* 21 (1927): 113–21. See also Charles W. Peppler, "The Termination *-kos*, as Used by Aristophanes for Comic Effect," *AJP* 31 (1910): 428–32.

9. Later writers often describe the teachings of the Older Sophists as being concerned with *rhêtorikê*, but no fragment regarded as authentically fifth-century contains the word. References to fifth-century sophistic manuals of *rhêtorikê* are centuries removed and most likely refer to collections of speeches or "commonplaces." Notably, Aristotle's reference to earlier manuals entitles them *technas tôn logôn* (*Rhetoric* 1354a12).

10. Kennedy, *APG*, 44–47.

11. On the dating of the *Dissoi Logoi* I follow T. M. Robinson, *Contrasting Arguments: An Edition of the Dissoi Logoi* (Salem, NH: Ayer, 1979), 34–41. The traditional dating has been challenged by Thomas M. Conley, "Dating the So-called *Dissoi Logoi*: A

Cautionary Note," *Ancient Philosophy* 5 (1985): 59–65.

12. Trans. Robinson, *Contrasting,* 139.

13. Kennedy, *APG,* 114–24; H. Rackham, introduction, *Rhetorica ad Alexandrum* (Cambridge, MA: Harvard U. Press, 1937), 258–62.

14. A possible exception is the pamphlet by Alcidamas titled *On the Sophists* or *On the Writers of Written Discourses,* dated by LaRue Van Hook as "published" between 390 and 380 BCE. I believe that Hook's estimate is off by several decades. See Appendix B of this book and LaRue Van Hook, "Alcidamas versus Isocrates," *Classical Weekly* 12 (1919): 89–94.

15. See Leonard Brandwood, *A Word Index to Plato* (Leeds: J. S. Maney and Sons, 1976), 809. Masculine forms that do not connote "art of" were not counted as an instance of "rhetoric." On the different periods of Plato's dialogues, see Francis M. Cornford, "The Athenian Philosophical Schools," *Cambridge Ancient History* (1927), 6:310–32; and Ledger, *Re-counting Plato.*

16. The fifth-century text that is most theoretical in its treatment of persuasive *logos* is Gorgias' *Encomium to Helen*; see Charles P. Segal, "Gorgias and the Psychology of the Logos," *HSCP* 66 (1962): 99–155. In a sense Gorgias' *Helen* is misleading as a guide to sophistic thinking; there is no other surviving fifth-century text about discourse of comparable theoretical depth. I do not think this is because the works were lost. Rather, I think the interest in theoretical treatments of persuasive discourse coincided with the growing literacy of the late fifth and early fourth century. As Kathy Eden notes, "We have no substantial evidence for the theoretical discussions of either rhetorical or interpretive strategies before the fourth century"; see her "Hermeneutics and the Ancient Rhetorical Tradition," *Rhetorica* 5 (1988): 59–86.

17. See Eric A. Havelock, *Preface to Plato* (Cambridge, MA: Harvard U. Press, 1963).

18. I limit myself to the following thirty examples of terms with an *-ikê* ending (denoting a *technê*) which, according to LSJ, first appear in Plato's writings. **Gorgias:** *rhêtorikê* s.v. *"rhêtoreia"*; *arithmêtikê* s.v. *"arithmeô"*; *logistikê* s.v. *"logisteia"*; *gymnastikê* s.v. *"gymnasidion"*; *stochastikê* s.v. *"stochazomai"*; *opsopoiêtikê* s.v. *"opsopoieion"*; *kommôtikê* s.v. *"kommoô"*; *sophistikê* s.v. *"sophisteia"*; *nomothetikê* s.v. *"nomotheteô"*; *kolakeutikê* s.v. *"kolakeia."* **Euthydemus:** *eristikê* s.v. *"eristês"*; *aulopoiikê* s.v. *"auloboas"*; *basilikê* s.v. *"basileus"*; *thêreutikê* s.v. *"thêrepôdos"*; *kitharistikê* s.v. *"kithara"*; *lyropoiêtikê* s.v. *"lyropoiêtikos"*; *logographikê* or *logopoiikê* s.v. *"logopoieô"*; *skytikê* s.v. *"skytikos"*; *tektonikê* s.v. *"tektoneô"*; *chrêmatistikê* s.v. *"chrematagôgos."* **Sophist:** *mimêtikê* s.v. *"mimauleô"*; *poiêtikê* s.v. *"poiêseiô"*; *ktêtikê* s.v. *"ktêteos"*; *aspalieutikê* s.v. *"aspalieuomai"*; *halieutikê* s.v. *"halieuma"*; *plêktikê* s.v. *"plêkteon"*; *lêstikê* s.v. *"lêsteia"*; *andrapodistikê* s.v. *"andrapodessi"*; *polemikê* s.v. *"polemêios"*; *dikanikê* s.v. *"dikanikos."* According to Pierre Chantraine, of the more than 350 different *-ikos* words in Plato, more than 250 are not found in earlier texts (*Études sur le vocabulaire grec* [Paris: Klincksieck, 1956], 97–171).

19. *LSJ,* s.v. *"antilogeô," "dialekteon,"* and *"eristês."* Additionally, a search through the entire (corrected and uncorrected) TLG data bank for *antilogik-, eristik-,* and *dialektik-* has confirmed that Plato's use of the *-ikê* forms was original. On the Platonic origins of the word "dialectic" see Richard Robinson, *Plato's Earlier Dialectic* (Oxford: Clarendon Press, 1953), 90–92. On eristic, antilogic, and dialectic in Plato's writings see Kerferd, *SM,* 59–67; Robinson, *Plato's Earlier Dialectic,* 84–92; and Alexander Nehamas, "Eristic, Antilogic, Sophistic, Dialectic: Plato's Demarcation of Philosophy from Sophistry," *HPQ* 7 (1990): 3–16.

20. Renato Barilli, *Rhetoric* (Minneapolis: U. of Minnesota Press, 1989), vii-xi.

21. Guthrie, *HGP IV,* 312–23; Dodds, *Plato: Gorgias,* 23–25.

22. See Richard Garner, *Law and Society in Classical Athens* (New York: St. Martin's Press, 1987), esp. ch. 2; Nicole Loraux, *The Invention of Athens: The Funeral Oration in the Classical City* (Cambridge, MA: Harvard U. Press, 1986), esp. 264–70, 311–27.

23. As R. L. Howland observed, "The attack on rhetoric [in the *Gorgias*] is intended to refer to Isocrates as the most influential contemporary teacher of it"; see his "Attack on Isocrates in the *Phaedrus*," *CQ* 31 (1937): 151–59; cf. Guthrie, *HGP IV*, 308–11.

24. Garner, *Law and Society*.

25. Guthrie, *HGP IV*, 299.

26. Trans. R. E. Allen, *The Dialogues of Plato* (New Haven: Yale U. Press, 1984), 1:289. See *Gorgias* 472c6-d1, 487e7–488a4, 492d3–5, and Plato's *Seventh Letter*. E. R. Dodds' classic study of the *Gorgias* documents the fact that even the earliest commentators noted that the purpose of the dialogue is to address the moral basis of politics. According to Dodds, by 492d3 "the ostensible question of rhetoric has vanished into the background" (*Plato: Gorgias*, 299).

27. See the essays by Hansen, cited above in note 3; Sinclair, *Democracy*, Ober, *Mass and Elite*, Perlman, "Politicians."

28. Guthrie, *HGP III*, 177; cf. Plato, *Phaedrus* 261b6–7, 278b-d. Even in Aristotle rhetoric is consistently referred to as an art of *logos*. See William M. A. Grimaldi, *Aristotle, Rhetoric: A Commentary* (New York: Fordham U. Press, 1980), 1:6, 38–39, 93 for examples and analysis.

29. My thanks to Malcolm Schofield (the "skeptical interlocutor" of an earlier version of this chapter) for pointing to the significance of these passages.

30. Segal, "Gorgias," and Guthrie, *HGP IV*, 308–11.

31. Allen, *Dialogues*, 189; Dodds, *Plato: Gorgias*, 17–18.

32. Schiappa, *Beginnings*.

33. My thanks to David Sedley and George A. Kennedy for comments and criticisms of earlier drafts of the section "Did Plato Coin *Rhêtorikê*?"

34. A. W. Verrall, "Korax and Tisias, *JP* 9 (1880): 197–210; Richard C. Jebb, *The Attic Orators from Antiphon to Isaeos* (New York: Russell and Russell, 1962), 1:cxxi. I examine the ancient evidence for the Corax and Tisias myth in more detail in "The Beginnings of Greek Rhetorical Theory," cited above.

35. W. Rhys Roberts, "The New Rhetorical Fragment in Relation to the Sicilian Rhetoric of Corax and Tisias," *CR* 18 (1904): 18–21; J. H. Freese, *Aristotle: "Art" of Rhetoric* (Cambridge, MA: Harvard U. Press, 1926), xii-xiv.

36. Bromley Smith, "Corax and Probability," *QJS* 7 (1921): 15.

37. Ibid., 16–18, 41.

38. D. A. G. Hinks, "Tisias and Corax and the Invention of Rhetoric," *CQ* 34 (1940): 61–69.

39. A. E. Douglas, "The Aristotelian Συναγωγή Τέχνων after Cicero, *Brutus* 46–48," *Latomus* 14 (1955): 536–39.

40. Donald Lemen Clark, *Rhetoric in Greco-Roman Education* (New York: Columbia U. Press, 1957), 25; Kennedy, *APG*, 58–61; Wilhelm Kroll, "Rhetorik," *RE* supp. 7 (1940): 1041–42; Donald C. Bryant, *Ancient Greek and Roman Rhetoricians* (Columbia, MO: Artcraft Press, 1968), 30–31; Guthrie, *HGP III*, 178–79; James J. Murphy, *A Synoptic History of Classical Rhetoric* (New York: Random House, 1972), 6–7. Cf. [ ] Aulitzky, "Korax 3," *RE* 11 (1922): 1379–81; and Willy Stegemann, "Teisias 6," *RE* 5A (1934): 139–49; Jacqueline de Romilly, *Les Grands Sophistes dans L'Athènes de Périclès* (Paris: Éditions de Fallois, 1988), 92–94.

41. Verrall, "Korax," 14; Jebb, *Attic Orators*, cxxi; Smith, "Corax," 15; Hinks, "Tisias," 62.

42. See William M. A. Grimaldi, *Studies in the Philosophy of Aristotle's Rhetoric* (Weisbaden: Franz Steiner, 1972), 104–15; Grimaldi, *Commentary*, 61–63.

43. Eric A. Havelock, "The Linguistic Task of the Presocratics," *Language and Thought in Early Greek Philosophy,* ed. Kevin Robb (LaSalle, IL: Hegeler Institute, 1983), 55; based on Bruno Snell, *The Discovery of the Mind* (Oxford: Basil Blackwell, 1953), ch. 10.

44. Smith, "Corax," 21–42; Hinks, "Tisias," 63.

45. Guthrie, *HGP III,* 178; emphasis added.

46. Clark, *Greco-Roman,* 25.

47. Garner, *Law and Society,* 39–48. See also Michael Gagarin, *Early Greek Law* (Berkeley: U. of California Press, 1986).

48. Eric A. Havelock, *The Liberal Temper in Greek Politics* (New Haven: Yale U. Press, 1957), ch. 8.

49. See Smith, "Corax," 19–20.

50. Harold Cherniss, *Aristotle's Criticism of Presocratic Philosophy* (New York: Octagon Books, 1935); Havelock, "Task."

51. D. O'Brien, *Empedocles' Cosmic Cycle* (Cambridge: Cambridge U. Press, 1969).

52. Helle Lambridis, *Empedocles* (University, AL: U. of Alabama Press, 1976), 25–26.

53. Guthrie, *HGP II,* 135.

54. M. R. Wright, *Empedocles: The Extant Fragments* (New Haven: Yale U. Press, 1981), 6–9.

55. Guthrie, *HGP VI, 55.*

56. O'Brien, *Cosmic Cycle,* 72.

57. Havelock, "Task," 57. Felix Heinimann's portrayal of a sophistic sense of *technê,* e.g., attributes a more developed technical vocabulary to the Sophists than the available evidence supports ("Eine vorplatonische Theorie der τέχνη," *Museum Helveticum* 18 [1961]: 105–30 = Classen, *Sophistik,* 127–69).

58. In Rosamond Kent Sprague, ed. *The Older Sophists* (Columbia: U. of South Carolina Press, 1972), 70–71.

59. Classen, *Sophistik,* 246–47; emphasis added.

60. George A. Kennedy, "The Earliest Rhetorical Handbooks," *AJP* 80 (1959): 170.

61. Bruce A. Kimball, *Orators and Philosophers: A History of the Ideal Liberal Education* (New York: Teachers College Press, 1986), 17.

62. Kennedy, *APG,* 26; emphasis added.

63. Gomperz, *SR,* esp. 35–49. Gomperz suggests that *all* of Protagoras' teachings radiate from what he call the "rhetorical center"—*rhetorischen Mittelpunkte,* (*SR,* 282).

64. "So verschiedene Gesichter nun die älteren Sophisten auch zeigen, so zieht sich doch ihre Tätigkeit als Redelehrer wie ein roter Faden durch die ganze sophistische Bewegung hindurch" (Kroll, "Rhetorik," 1043).

65. Kerferd, *SM,* 82.

66. Havelock, *Preface,* 41.

67. Ibid., 303.

68. Ibid., 47.

69. Michael Gagarin has argued that the dialogue *Protagoras* was intended to show that Socrates and Protagoras shared a common view of the importance of *sophia* and *epistêmê;* see "The Purpose of Plato's *Protagoras,*" *TAPA* 100 (1969): 133–64.

70. Guthrie, *HGP IV,* 227; C. C. W. Taylor, *Plato: Protagoras* (Oxford: Clarendon Press, 1976), 141–48.

71. Taylor, *Plato,* 141. On the Sophists' analysis of the poets, see also Rudolf Pfeiffer, *History of Classical Scholarship from the Beginnings to the End of the Hellenistic Age* (Oxford: Clarendon Press, 1968), 32–37.

72. Kerferd, *SM,* 93–100.

73. Cf. Segal, "Gorgias."

74. DK 84 A9; Plato, *Protagoras* 337a; *Euthydemus* 277e; Kerferd, *SM*, 68–77.
75. See Bruno Snell, "Die Nachrichten über die Lehren des Thales," *Philologus* 96 (1944): 119–28 (= Classen, *Sophistik*, 478–90); Kerferd, *SM*, 48–49.
76. Robert J. Connors, "Greek Rhetoric and the Transition from Orality," *PR* 19 (1986): 46–49.
77. Havelock, "Task," 9. For a detailed analysis of Gorgias' prose style, see chapter 6 of Schiappa, *The Beginnings of Rhetorical Theory in Classical Greece* (New Haven: Yale U. Press, 1999).

4

TOWARD AN UNDERSTANDING OF
SOPHISTIC THEORIES OF RHETORIC

Even though the available evidence suggests that the Sophists did not use the term *rhêtorikê* to describe their teachings, a recovery of their ideas about rhetorical theory is both possible and desirable. It is possible because the fifth-century Sophists' *logos* was an obvious predecessor to (even if it cannot be limited to) fourth-century *rhêtoreia* and *rhêtorikê*. It is desirable for historical reasons: to improve our understanding of what the Sophists accomplished and how their doctrines were subsequently interpreted or distorted.

In this chapter I want to further the process of recovering sophistic ideas and practices concerning discourse by distinguishing between two interpretive approaches toward sophistic rhetoric and by correcting what I believe are false starts toward achieving an historical understanding of the Sophists' contribution to the early history of rhetorical theory.

HISTORICAL RECONSTRUCTION AND
CONTEMPORARY APPROPRIATION

In the past three decades there has been a virtual explosion of interest in the Sophists and rhetoric. Heinrich Gomperz's 1912 classic *Sophistik und Rhetorik* recently has been reissued, and the first-ever full-length

64

study of the sophistic tract *Dissoi Logoi* has appeared.[1] Traditional Platonic disregard for the Sophists has partially given way to respect for the aesthetic and philosophical aspects of sophistic rhetoric. For example, the relationship between the Sophists' stylistic concerns and the Greek transition from orality to literacy has been explored, and the Sophists' influence in Aristotle's *Rhetoric* is in the process of being documented.[2] John Poulakos' seminal "Toward a Sophistic Definition of Rhetoric" attempted to identify a "sophistic view proper" of the art of rhetoric.[3] Several essays examine the philosophical aspects of specific Sophists' rhetoric, including that of Gorgias and Protagoras.[4] Other exemplary individualistic studies explore Antiphon's contributions to argument and legal advocacy, Gorgias' *Encomium to Helen,* and Protagoras' "stronger and weaker" *logoi* fragment.[5]

Part of the renewed interest in research on the Sophists has been directed toward incorporating sophistic insights into contemporary rhetorical theory. Robert L. Scott's influential "On Viewing Rhetoric as Epistemic" combined Stephen Toulmin with Gorgias and Protagoras to provide one of the most provocative theories of rhetoric in recent decades.[6] More recently the Sophists have inspired new perspectives on historiography, political theory, an existential "rhetoric of the possible," the "rhetoric of the human sciences," composition theory, the history of consciousness, and an ideological basis for cultural criticism.[7]

An important bit of conceptual orientation is in order concerning the interpretive approaches utilized in studies of sophistic rhetoric. To put it simply, I believe that we need to be clear about what we are doing when reading or writing a work concerning the Sophists, and we need to make sure our methods match our goals. Specifically, it is important for students of rhetoric to differentiate between two approaches to the study of the Sophists of ancient Greece. Those approaches can be described as the construction of neosophistic rhetorical theory and criticism, and the historical reconstruction of sophistic doctrines.

There is an important difference between appreciating sophistic thinking as contributing to contemporary rhetorical theory and criticism, and reconstructing specific sophistic theories or doctrines about rhetoric. While both activities involve interpretation, they differ in that the former activity involves modern application and extension of sophistic thinking, while the latter deliberates over matters of historical fact. Though both activities are worthwhile intellectual endeavors, our scholarship can profit by keeping the two distinct.

Richard Rorty has drawn a useful distinction between historical reconstruction and rational reconstruction (or "contemporary appropriation").[8] In the case of ancient philosophy, historical reconstruction requires some fidelity to the methods and practices of classical philology because it attempts to reconstruct past thinkers' ideas as much as possible in their own words and intellectual context. As described by Stephen Makin, "An *historical reconstruction* of some philosopher's thought gives an account of what some past thinker said, or would have said, to his [or her] *contemporaries*. The thinker is not treated as reeducated into our techniques and positions." On the other hand, "a *rational reconstruction* treats a thinker (in many cases, dead) as within *our own* philosophical framework. We might include in a rational reconstruction of a philosopher's thought principles that the philosopher never formulated."[9]

Contemporary appropriation and historical reconstruction differ in terms of goals and methods. Since the goal of historical reconstruction is to recapture the past insofar as possible on its own terms, the methods of the historian and, in classical work, the philologist, are appropriate. Since the goal of contemporary appropriation is to provide critical insight to contemporary theorists, the needs and values of current audiences justify less rigidity and more creativity in the process of interpreting how dead authors through their texts speak to live, contemporary audiences.

The differences between historical reconstruction and contemporary appropriation in rhetorical studies can be made readily apparent through a contrast between different approaches to Aristotle's *Rhetoric*. Works such as W. M. A. Grimaldi's *Studies in the Philosophy of Aristotle's Rhetoric* and his commentary on the *Rhertoric* clearly are aimed at bringing the modern reader closer to a historically grounded understanding of Aristotle's original thinking.[10] Though modernists generally eschew efforts to discover an author's "intentions," it is clearly the case that historical reconstruction aims at re-creating how the author and his or her contemporaries understood the text.

By contrast, Neo-Aristotelian theory and criticism adapts Aristotle to the present and hence is only partially committed to a historical understanding of Aristotle's *Rhetoric*.[11] Accordingly, Neo-Aristotelian rhetorical theory can be categorized as an effort toward contemporary appropriation for the purposes of rhetorical criticism. Though Neo-Aristotelian scholars sometimes feud over Aristotle's intentions, most agree that Aristotle never intended that his work be a guide for rhetorical criticism, and few neoclassical theorists feel bound to stick to the text of Aristotle's *Rhetoric* in their efforts to inform contemporary rhetorical theory and criticism.[12] No doubt Neo-Aristotelian theorists' works are influenced by a particular historical view of the *Rhetoric,* but the important point is that historical view is seldom, if ever, the basis for how the Neo-Aristotelian approach is *evaluated.* Edwin Black's critique of Neo-Aristotelian criticism is fueled only in part by a belief that Neo-Aristotelian critics have misread Aristotle; his most enduring challenge is that, as practiced, Neo-Aristotelianism no longer meets the needs of today's rhetorical theorists and critics.[13]

Just as one can distinguish between Neo-Aristotelian rhetorical criticism and the historically grounded reconstruction of Aristotle's theory of rhetoric, one can also distinguish between the development of neosophistic rhetorical theory and criticism, and the historical reconstruction of sophistic theories of discourse. For example, essays such as Michael C. Leff's "Modern Sophistic and the Unity of Rhetoric" or Susan C. Jarratt's "Toward a Sophistic Historiography" are clearly efforts to draw on sophistic thinking in order to contribute to contemporary theory and practice.[14] They are examples of contemporary appropriation to the extent that their value is measured more on creativity and modern utility than strictly on historical accuracy. By contrast, treatments of the Sophists as found in the works of Richard L. Enos, G. B. Kerferd, W. K. C. Guthrie, and George A. Kennedy are clearly efforts at historical reconstruction.

Historical reconstruction can be justified as both intrinsically and instrumentally valuable. It is intrinsically valuable because historical knowledge begins with an understanding of the uniqueness of particular people, places, or events. If the Sophists are worth studying, then they deserve study on their own terms as well as on ours. "It is useful to recreate the intellectual scene in which the dead lived their lives," declares Rorty, because there is "knowledge—historical knowledge—to be gained which one can only get by bracketing" one's own historical context as much as possible.[15] Properly done historical reconstruction "helps us recognize that there have been different forms of intellectual life than ours."[16] As a result, one can learn the difference between "what is necessary and what is the product merely of our own contingent arrangements," recognition of which is "the key to self-awareness itself."[17]

If the notion of history for history's sake leaves one cold, an instrumental rationale for careful historical reconstruction is identifiable as well. If the purpose for doing history is to enlighten our understanding of the present, then there is a better chance for enrichment if we treat the past seriously: "Thought is the prisoner of whatever place it is to be found [if] it cannot break the bonds of the present."[18] It is just those

67

historical problems that appear to be the least interesting from a contemporary perspective that can be the most revealing "because they contain the elements which were peculiar to an age and no longer inspire curiousity in later ages."[19] Before we can "use" history, we must first adequately understand it.[20]

I am not suggesting that historical reconstruction should be done to the exclusion of contemporary appropriation. With Rorty I believe that both ought to be done, but done separately.[21] Otherwise, historical accounts tend to become self-affirming discoveries of early anticipations of voguish philosophical theories. There has been a tendency, especially prevalent in the case of the Sophists, to enhance the prestige of current theoretical pieties by linking them to ancient Greek roots. Accordingly, the Sophists as a group have been seen as anticipating "anti-idealist positions, positivism, liberalism, materialisms whether dialectical or otherwise."[22] The case of Protagoras is particularly revealing, as he has been called everything from skeptic to positivist (see chapter 1). The example of Protagoras is powerful testimony to Bloom's claim that "if we were to study history according to our tastes, we would see nothing but ourselves everywhere."[23]

A further justification for renewed historical reconstruction of sophistic theories of discourse was noted in the previous chapter: the fact that the Greek word for rhetoric (*rhêtorikê*) was not coined until the early fourth century BCE. Accordingly, any historical claim concerning how rhetoric was defined or theorized about during the fifth century BCE (the era of the Older Sophists) must be considered suspect if the claim presumes rhetoric was clearly recognized as a conceptualized, discrete verbal art with a body of identifiable teachings.

The objection could be made that the absence of the word *rhêtorikê* means little. Even without the word *rhêtorikê*, the practice of self-conscious oratory existed, and can be meaningfully discussed today. The absence of a word for gravity in prehistoric time, as one critic has commented, obviously does not mean that in prehistoric time such a force did not exist. Certainly one can grant that a discursive practice now called "rhetoric" existed prior to the coining of the term *rhêtorikê*. While the absence of *rhêtorikê* in the fifth century does not prevent us from appreciating sophistic thinking from the perspective of modern rhetorical theory (via contemporary appropriation), the relatively late appearance of the term nonetheless must be dealt with in any serious historical account of early theorizing about language. As intellectual disciplines evolve, so do their conceptual vocabularies. Accordingly, any serious effort to reconstruct historically the development of early Greek rhetorical theory must reckon with the late coining of the Greek word *rhêtorikê*.[24] To demonstrate the point I now turn to the specifics of the sophistic definition of rhetoric advanced by John Poulakos.

POULAKOS' SOPHISTIC DEFINITION OF RHETORIC

In this section I examine one of the most recent and prominent treatments of sophistic rhetoric for the purpose of demonstrating the importance of keeping historical reconstructions and contemporary appropriations distinct.[25] My argument is that while several of Poulakos' works are praiseworthy as examples of neosophistic rhetorical criticism, those same works require correction if viewed from the standpoint of *historical reconstruction*. The obvious question is: Is it fair and appropriate to evaluate Poulakos' influential work on the Sophists as historical reconstruction? The question is important because the charge of anachronism is serious to historical studies but irrelevant to contemporary criticism. I think the evidence offered below is sufficient to make the case that Poulakos, at least part of the time, is engaged in historical reconstruction and hence is accountable to the methodological expectations pertaining thereto. At the very least, it will be make clear that Poulakos' work is in need of conceptual clarification as to what sort of claims are being advanced.

Poulakos states in his article "Toward a Sophistic Definition of Rhetoric" that "we must reexamine the surviving fragments of and about the Sophists and seek to articulate on probable grounds their view of rhetoric. This essay purports to do just that. More specifically, it purports to derive a 'sophistic' definition of rhetoric and to discuss some of its more important implications."[26] The essay is dominated by specific historical claims about what the Sophists taught, were aware of, and sought to do or demonstrate. The Sophists are said to have conceived of rhetoric in a particular manner. Claims are advanced about what specific Sophists did: Antiphon commented on style, Thrasymachus wrote, Gorgias persuaded, Prodicus embellished, Hippias enchanted, Critias spoke, and Protagoras held certain positions. The Sophists are claimed to have been "interested in the problem of time" and have given "impetus to the related concept of *to prepon*." Poulakos explicitly denies "introducing new ideas in the field of rhetorical theory," but rather describes his work as articulating and reinforcing the idea that "some of our contemporary concepts about rhetoric originate with the Sophists."[27] This particular essay by Poulakos is not offered as a hypothetical account of a modern version of sophistic theory, but rather contains a series of claims about what the Sophists sought to do and say about rhetoric in their own time. A related essay by Poulakos examines the historical and conceptual relationship between the Older Sophists and Aristotle. Here Poulakos identifies specific concepts or "notions" that the Sophists placed "at the service of rhetoric." These concepts were "developed" by the Sophists and "came to designate ... rules" for the construction of discourse.[28] Poulakos concludes that Aristotle was indebted to the Sophists both conceptually and historically. In light of the above evidence, I think it fair to hold Poulakos' description accountable as historical reconstruction. At the very least, there is sufficient equivocation to merit a discussion of aims and methods.[29]

Once it is approached as historical reconstruction, a critique of Poulakos' sophistic definition can be based on theoretical and evidentiary concerns. On a theoretical level, I believe Poulakos continues a conceptual tradition that is no longer appropriate for the study of early Greek thought. That conceptual tradition is described by Rorty as "doxography." Rorty complains that many historical accounts of philosophy treat their topics as givens or as conceptual constants. Rorty attributes such a tendency to a sort of natural attitude on behalf of philosophers toward the objects of their analysis: "The idea [is] that 'philosophy' is the name of a natural kind—the name of a discipline which, in all ages and places, has managed to dig down to the same deep, fundamental, questions."[30] Hence standard histories of philosophy consist of different philosophers' treatments or theories of X—where X may be epistemology, ontology, rhetoric, etc. Most histories of rhetoric approach their subject in a similar fashion. An example is George A. Kennedy's influential history of rhetoric, which identifies three traditions: technical, sophistic and philosophical. These three views of rhetoric are continuing strands in the long tradition of rhetoric which stretch "throughout the history of western Europe."[31] The obvious problem is that particular historical nuances can be underestimated by a too-strict application of Kennedy's tripartite scheme.[32] Similarities between the traditions are underemphasized and the felt needs of specific historical contexts can be missed.[33]

Poulakos' work challenges the sort of portrait of the Sophists that one finds in Kennedy, but does so in such a way that preserves the integrity of Kennedy's tripartite schematization. Poulakos continues the assumption that there is a distinct sophistic view proper of rhetoric which can be compared and contrasted to competing views of rhetoric.[34] In the comments that follow I intend to call into question the notion of a distinct "sophistic view proper" and question whether there could have been one of rhetoric per se. Sophistic theorizing about rhetoric is best understood not as a collective answer to the question "What is rhetoric?" but as a process of asking questions about *logos* and the world. Instead of assuming that the Older Sophists held in common a particular perspective toward the art of rhetoric, we should examine how the Sophists laid the conceptual groundwork for what later became identifiable as rhetorical theory. As Eric Havelock has commented, "Much of the story of early Greek philosophy so-called is a story not of *systems of thought* but of a search for a primary language in which *any system* could be expressed."[35] Accordingly, the Kennedy/Poulakos "doxographical" approach errs by presuming that a distinctive sophistic view existed and by treating *rhêtorikê* as a recognized and conceptually discrete art in the fifth century.

I do not mean to imply that it is impossible to generalize about sophistic views of persuasion and discourse. My position is simply that 1) individual studies of the Sophists are a logically prior task to that of constructing a general sophistic view, and 2) there is a subtle but historically significant difference between describing early sophistic efforts at theorizing about *logos* and the world, and later efforts to organize and improve discursive strategies as part of a discrete and clearly conceptualized art of rhetoric. Precisely how much difference can be demonstrated only after much more work is done. The remarks that follow are, I hope, suggestive of the productiveness of a careful historical approach.

Specifically, I think Poulakos makes a number of claims about historically held doctrines that cannot be supported by the available evidence. Poulakos advances the following as the sophistic definition of rhetoric: "Rhetoric is the art which seeks to capture in opportune moments that which is appropriate and attempts to suggest that which is possible." Poulakos' explication of sophistic theory has five distinct elements: "rhetoric as art, style as personal expression, *kairos* (the opportune moment), *to prepon* (the appropriate), and *to dunaton* (the possible)."[36]

Poulakos claims that the "Sophists conceived of rhetoric primarily as a *technê,* or art." The problem with this characterization is that the term *rhêtorikê,* "art of the rhetor," is of fourth-century origin, not fifth. Prior to the fourth century the key conceptual term for the Sophists was usually *logos* and sometimes *legein*—terms broader in meaning than any ancient conception of *rhêtorikê*. If the Sophists did not conceive of their teachings as an art of rhetoric, then Poulakos' claim that the Sophists believed that rhetoric's "medium is *logos*" and its "double aim is *terpsis* (aesthetic pleasure) and *pistis* (belief)" is misleading as history because there is insufficient evidence to conclude that for the Sophists *rhêtorikê* was a discrete art with conceptualized means and ends. Accordingly, efforts to construct an authentic sophistic definition of rhetoric must be considered a contribution to the development of a modern neosophistic rhetorical theory rather than a contribution to the history of the Sophists.

The second element of Poulakos' sophistic theory of rhetoric concerns the issue of style. Poulakos is correct in insisting that the Sophists were "highly accomplished linguistic craftsmen." His assumption that stylistic decisions by the Sophists were based on aesthetic considerations requires a minor qualification. Robert J. Connors' essay "Greek Rhetoric and the Transition from Orality" demonstrates that the highly poetic style of the Older Sophists was a direct reflection of the oral modes of composition of fifth-century Greece.[37] If the Sophists' discourse seems highly stylized to the modern reader (or even to those reading it in the more literate fourth century), it is because predominantly oral (mythic-poetic) modes of thinking and speaking are foreign to us. Connors points out that there is a direct correspondence between the rise of book-oriented literacy and the decline of the "grand style" of the Older Sophists. Hence sophistic stylistic innovation was closely related to the changing syntax, word meanings, and modes of expression that mark the transition between the mythic-poetic and the rationalistic, literate ways of life.

Friedrich Solmsen's analysis of the different styles of discourse found in Thucydides provides a useful way of understanding the stylistic contributions of the Sophists.[38] Solmsen describes three stylistic devices as intellectual experiments of the late fifth century: antithesis, careful word choice, and the use of neuter forms. The development of different forms of antithesis parallels competing ways of conceptualizing about opposites—a dominant theme in early Greek philosophy.[39] Innovative antithesis can be found in sophistic fragments as well as in the fragments and works of the Presocratics, Isocrates, and Plato. With respect to word choice and the use of neuter forms Solmsen's analysis supports the claim that the evolving style was a direct result of growing abstraction and more formal approaches to argument. Accordingly, a historical approach to the Sophists must be cautious of form and content distinctions with respect to the texts of the late fifth century since form and content were so closely related. Describing the Sophists as self-conscious stylists can potentially obfuscate the issue.[40]

Poulakos' third element of sophistic rhetorical theory is the concept

of *kairos,* or "the opportune moment." Of the five elements of Poulakos'
sophistic rhetorical theory, *kairos* is the term with the most support in
the *ipsissima verba* of the Sophists. *Kairos* can be found in the surviving
texts of Gorgias and Isocrates, and there is a link to Protagoras—the
reliability of which is confirmed by the treatment of *kairos* in the Pro-
tagorean-influenced tract *Dissoi Logoi.* As Poulakos acknowledges, the
concept of *kairos* can be traced back to the poets and the tragedians.[41]
The evidence is a bit thin to suggest that all Sophists used *kairos* in a
technical sense. The evidence *is* adequate to say that certain Sophists
were the first to "professionalize" the term in its application to oral
prose. In light of the fact that Sophocles used the term in a technical sense
with direct reference to a *logos,* it can be safely concluded that the term
was professionalized by the last quarter of the fifth century.[42] Prior to
the Sophists *kairos* had a wide range of meanings rendered in context as
"due measure," "proportion," or "fitness." Thus, the meaning of "opportune time" found in the Sophists represented an abstraction which
advanced the term's analytic usefulness. Though it is clearly modernistic
to assert that the sophistic "notion of *kairos* points out that speech exists
in time," *kairos* is a term that can be safely identified as belonging to the
early conceptual development of rhetorical theory.[43]

The fourth element of Poulakos' sophistic definition of rhetoric is the
concept of *to prepon,* "the appropriate." There is less textual evidence
from fifth-century Sophists to support the notion that *to prepon* was a
consciously held theoretical concept than there is for *kairos.* Certainly
neither *kairos* nor *to prepon* was part of a sophistic theory that explicitly
deemed them "the two most fundamental criteria of the value of speech,"
as Poulakos claims.[44] There is simply no evidence that suggests that the
Sophists, as a group, had advanced a theory of discourse to the level of
abstraction implied by Poulakos. As noted previously, a shift in syntax
from using a word as an adjective or adverb (such as *prepontos*—"fitly,"
"meetly," or "gracefully") to use of a generic article in the neuter singular paired with a neuter adjective or adverb (such as *to prepon,* "the
fitting") is an important linguistic indication of the emergence of an
abstract technical sense of a term that signals its professionalization.[45]
A good indication of the status of sophistic theorizing would be the
occurrence of *to prepon* in fifth-century fragments or texts. The neuter
singular construction *to prepon* appears only in Gorgias' writings prior
to Isocrates and Plato. Accordingly, though *to prepon* provides insight
into the level of sophistication of Gorgias' theorizing, it cannot be safely
regarded as part of a general fifth-century sophistic rhetorical theory. I

73

do not deny the fact that both *kairos* and *to prepon* may be appropriate terms to describe choices made by sophistic speakers in *practice*. What is at issue here is whether the Sophists advanced *theorizing* about discourse to the point that such terms were used in a technical or professional sense such as that found in Aristotle's *Rhetoric*. The available evidence points to a sophistic theory of *kairos,* but not *to prepon.*

Perhaps it is enough praise of the Sophists' originality to say that they raised issues and sparked ideas that would later become codified into recognizable rhetorical theory. It is neither necessary nor supportable at this point to imply that there was an identifiable "sophistic view proper" of the art of rhetoric in the fifth century.[46] As Poulakos admits, sophistic approaches to discourse "come down to us as a story, a legacy" rather than as a completed treatise or text.[47] It should be added that their legacy does not include an identifiable sophistic definition of rhetoric, but rather a variety of incipient theories regarding discourse.

The final element of Poulakos' sophistic theory of rhetoric is the concept of *to dunaton,* which Poulakos renders as "the possible." In his essay "Rhetoric, the Sophists, and the Possible," Poulakos advances three arguments: first, that Aristotle's rhetoric "privileges the actual over the possible"; second, that "sophistical rhetoric exhibits a preference for the possible over the actual"; third, that the desirability of a "rhetoric of possibility" can be found, in part, in the writings of Martin Heidegger.[48] Poulakos' Heideggerian reading of the Sophists is potentially valuable as neosophistic rhetorical theory. However, no matter how creative and provocative Poulakos' portrayal of a sophistic rhetoric of possibility may be, there are good reasons to reject any historical claim that the Sophists held anything remotely similar to a doctrine of *to dunaton.*

Poulakos offers no sophistic *ipsissima verba* suggesting that any fifth-century Sophist ever used the neuter singular construction *to dunaton* (cf. DK 87 B 44, col. 2). Further, even if some Sophists used the word *dynamis* as "power" or "ability," there is no evidence that it was used in contrast to *energeia* ("actuality"). Prior to Aristotle *dynamis* and *energeia* were not considered polar terms. In fact, the word *energeia* apparently was coined by Aristotle himself, and even in his works some of the possible meanings of *dynamis* and *energeia* overlapped.[49] The philosophical pairing of potential and actual as opposites originated with Aristotle roughly a century after the acme of the Older Sophists.[50] In short, not only is it unlikely that the Sophists maintained *to dunaton* as part of a rhetorical theory, it is quite impossible that they consciously maintained a doctrine which exhibited an explicit preference for the possible over the actual.

One can imagine a defender of Poulakos saying that even if the Sophists did not maintain *to dunaton* at the level of doctrine, their discourse can be reconstructed to articulate a perspective, a rhetoric of the possible, which can be usefully contrasted to Aristotle's rhetoric of actuality. If there were sufficient textual evidence for such a contrast, such a defense would be plausible. But close examination of the evidence for the "possible" and "actual" readings of the Sophists and Aristotle respectively suggests that the defense is inadequate if approached historically. Accordingly, such a defense necessarily would involve a contrast between modern defenders of Neo-Aristotelian and neosophistic theories, but would tell us little of the historical clash between the Sophists and Aristotle.

Poulakos' evidence of a preference for actuality in Aristotle is a series of passages: one concerning *energeia* and *dynamis* in the context of Aristotle's metaphysics, and another with respect to the art of rhetoric. After noting that Aristotle says that actuality is prior to potentiality in definition, time, and essence, Poulakos concludes that for Aristotle "*dynamis* is inferior to *energeia*."[51] This characterization subtly distorts Aristotle's metaphysics, in which *dynamis* and *energeia* are inextricably related. What is "actual" is realized "potential": "they are only two ways of looking at the same thing."[52] Elsewhere Aristotle says, "Matter is potentiality, form actuality" (*On the Soul* 412a9–10). In Aristotle's metaphysical theory one does not find *energeia* without *dynamis*. Hence, even if one is considered prior to the other, it does not follow that one is inferior to the other in the sense implied by Poulakos. The passages cited by Poulakos with regard to rhetoric do not make the case any stronger. While the passages cited do, in fact, indicate that Aristotle uses forms of the word *energeia* to advocate that speakers ought to make their cases using facts, the context of the passages does not support a reading that Aristotle preferred a rhetoric of actuality *as opposed to* a rhetoric of possibility. Rather, the passages suggest 1) that speakers should know the facts concerning the subject of which they would speak, 2) that facts make one's case easier to prove, and 3) that speakers in the law courts ought to restrict themselves to the facts. The first two propositions would probably be assented to by fifth-century Sophists, provided that the propositions were translated into fifth-century terminology. In fact, the author of the sophistic *Dissoi Logoi* wrote, ca. 400 BCE, that speakers need to have "knowledge of every subject," including the laws, what is just, and "the facts."[53] In the case of the third proposition, it is straining the text to interpret it as implying that Aristotle opposed some sort of visionary rhetoric. A more plausible reading would be that he was responding to the well-known excesses of the law courts in which juries were bribed, totally irrelevant evidence introduced, and frivolous charges abounded.[54]

Sophistic and Aristotelian views of the aims of discourse have more in common than is implied by Poulakos here.[55] The comparison ought not be between Aristotle's advice on message construction (means) and the purpose espoused in sophistic rhetoric (ends); such a comparison is bound to make Aristotle's *Rhetoric* appear ethically inferior. In fact, Aristotle and at least some Older Sophists would have agreed that rhetoric ought to be used to bring about change for the better. Protagoras advocated substituting a desirable *logos* for an undesirable *logos*.[56] Aristotle advocated making the potentially virtuous person actually so (*Nicomachean Ethics* 1103a23–b2).[57] No doubt the philosophies of the Sophists differed significantly from Aristotle's, but not in the way suggested by Poulakos. When Poulakos claims that "the Sophists privilege the possible over the actual because in the sphere of actuality they usually find pain, misery and suffering; conversely, delight, joy and happiness are to be found in the region of possibility," surely he does not expect one to believe Aristotle favored the former over the latter.[58]

The preceding analysis has attempted to demonstrate the importance of maintaining a clear line between doing history and creating a theory of rhetoric. Though Poulakos' essay on the Sophists and "the possible" suggests that the line between historical reconstruction and contemporary appropriation can become rather fuzzy, that fact should not imply that the distinction between the two need not be made. Instead, such fuzziness reinforces the need to keep one's goals and methodologies clear and distinct. Viewed as historical reconstruction, Poulakos' argument that the Sophists maintained a doctrinal preference for a rhetoric of the possible is clearly problematic. If the argument is amended and viewed as an effort toward an existentialist, neosophistic theory of rhetoric, a more favorable verdict is possible.

I also do not mean to suggest that contempoary appropriations are completely unrestrained by the available historical record. A critic obviously can undercut his or her credibilty by making historical claims that cannot be supported. Makin suggests that good "rational reconstructions" depend on valid historical reconstructions, but I think he underestimates the value of creative, productive readings of historical texts.[59] Consider the example of Richard Weaver's reading of Plato's *Phaedrus*.[60] Though Weaver's essay has been criticized as historically unfaithful, few fair-minded readers would deny that the essay succeeds as an essay on contemporary rhetorical theory. Weaver makes the *Phaedrus* alive and relevant to the issues of his day in a way that would be difficult if the dialogue were examined from a strictly historical perspective. Accordingly, despite the flaws in his treatment as history, I believe his essay demonstrates the utility of a Neo-Platonic reading of the text.

Similarly, Poulakos' "Sophistical Rhetoric as a Critique of Culture" is clearly an example of a creative, productive neosophistic rhetorical criticism.[61] Here Poulakos weaves together lessons from the history of the Sophists with themes from contemporary theorists in order to make an argument concerning how critics ought to view discourse, power, and culture. The aim of the essay is to oppose the strictures of academic disciplines, not contribute to them by writing a traditional historical or philological account of the Sophists. As was the case with Weaver, historians might squawk over details—but there is little question that Poulakos' neosophistic critique is provocative.

TOWARD INDIVIDUALISTIC STUDIES OF THE SOPHISTS

To summarize the preceding section, Poulakos' historical description of sophistic rhetorical theory is in need of amendment. Though the Sophists were obviously interested in *logos,* it is historically inaccurate to say they held a common theory concerning the art of rhetoric. Furthermore, *to dunaton* played no documentable role in sophistic thinking, and sophistic style was part of the cultural shift from mythic-poetic to more rationalistic modes of expression. *To prepon* may have been a part of Gorgias' rhetorical theory, but the evidence is insufficient to claim it was part of a commonly held sophistic theory of rhetoric. *Kairos* as "the opportune moment" represents a genuine conceptual development by the Sophists toward a fifth-century theory of *logos.*

Since virtually no rhetorical doctrine can be identified that is common to all fifth-century Sophists, it is more appropriate to speak of the "world view" or "educational movement" of the Older Sophists than of a specific sophistic definition or theory of rhetoric. The best way to recover distinctly sophistic contributions to the historical development of rhetorical theory is to augment general studies of the Sophists as a group by examining the Older Sophists individually, acknowledging that not

77

one but many incipient rhetorical theories were developed during the fifth century.

A careful reading of Poulakos' work suggests that his portrayal of a sophistic theory of rhetoric draws most heavily from the surviving texts of Gorgias. Poulakos' sophistic definition of rhetoric and his description of five distinct elements of a sophistic theory of rhetoric would be much harder to challenge if two changes were made; namely, that the scope of the historical claims was narrowed to Gorgias and the word *rhêtorikê* was withheld from the description. The amended claims better fit the extant historical evidence, and it must be acknowledged that it is possible that the Sophists had little doctrine or theory in common. It is more appropriate to speak of the various philosophies, practices, and doctrines of the Sophists than of a specific sophistic theory of rhetoric. Accordingly, a close examination of the individual Sophists is a logically prior task to that of constructing a general sophistic view of discourse.

The conventional list of Older Sophists—Protagoras, Gorgias, Prodicus, Thrasymachus, Hippias, Antiphon, and Critias—is used by Poulakos in his essays concerning sophistic rhetorical theory.[62] Even within this limited group of fifth-century thinkers one finds a good deal of variety in doctrine. A brief review of the testimony about the seven Older Sophists will demonstrate the breadth and diversity of their thought.[63]

All seven theorized on matters one would now call scientific—both physical and biological. Protagoras, Antiphon, and Hippias showed interest in mathematics, and the latter two made original contributions to geometry. Protagoras, Gorgias, Prodicus, and Thrasymachus are reported to have discussed the emotions. Critias, Antiphon, Protagoras, and Gorgias left fragments directly pertaining to Eleatic philosophical doctrines. At least Protagoras, Prodicus, and Critias offered anthropological explanations of religion. All seven Older Sophists continued the efforts of earlier presocratic philosophers to reform use of language and to privilege prose over poetic forms of discourse; yet, like other Presocratics, they were constrained by the expectations and the linguistic resources of a predominantly oral culture. The result was a hodgepodge of discursive practices and theories such that a single theory of discourse or rhetoric cannot be easily extracted.

There was considerable variety among the Sophists concerning matters of style. The fragments from Protagoras suggest that he wrote highly memorable aphorisms, and, if Plato's portrayal in the *Protagoras* is accurate, he also made use of myth and narrative. Protagoras is also credited with a variety of "firsts" in discourse: the first to use the Socratic method, the invention of eristic, the first to utilize question and answer, and the first to use debate or "antilogic." Gorgias' highly poetic grand style is well known; he is also credited as the inventor of extemporaneous oratory. Prodicus emphasized correct speech (*orthoepeia*)—a clear example of the new rationalistic approach of *logos*—but his speech "The Choice of Heracles," as retold by Xenophon, shows obvious affinities with the mythic-poetic tradition. Of Thrasymachus there remain only secondhand reports which suggest he had a "good mix" of plain and grand style, while other reports say he had a "condensed diction." Hippias apparently wrote in a variety of formats, including poems, epics, tragedies, and prose. There is also good evidence that Hippias used written prose in novel ways, including the first doxography, the first list of Olympic winners, and possibly the first etymological study. Antiphon was the first to compose written speeches for others to use in the law courts. He was famous for coining new words, and he may have been the first to use discourse for what would now be called counseling or therapeutic purposes. Critias wrote in both verse and prose, and he may have written dramas as well. A book of aphorisms is attributed to him, and he, like Antiphon, was well known for coining new words. In sum, the Sophists excelled in all common forms of discourse, and each contributed to the development of new genres. Given that fifth-century Athens was in transition between mythic-poetic and rationalistic traditions, their divergence in styles reflects differences in the manner and extent to which each Sophist advanced *logos* over poetic *mythos*. For example, Protagoras, Gorgias, and Critias analyzed and possibly critiqued the epic poets, but there is no solid evidence that the other four Sophists did the same.

The diversity among Sophists is no less clear concerning clearly rhetorical matters. For example, Protagoras, Gorgias and Critias may have discussed *kairos* in connection with public speaking, but there is no clear evidence that other Sophists did so. There are scattered reports of Sophists publishing "commonplaces," but it is unlikely that they were called such in the fifth century. The closest to a book of commonplaces may have been Antiphon's set introductions to speeches for use in the law courts.

There has been a tendency to assume that because Aristotle divided rhetoric into forensic, deliberative, and epideictic, sophistic teachings concerning discourse can also be discussed within those categories. Once again, however, the originality of each Sophist is missed by imposing such an anachronistic schematization on sophistic works. For example, a variety of sources, both ancient (though post–fifth century) and modern have claimed that the Sophists were interested primarily in forensic rhetoric. Stanley Wilcox has thoroughly answered such claims by citing evidence of sophistic teaching and practice that fit the other Aristotelian categories.[64] The shortcoming of Wilcox's rebuttal is that he still accepts the applicability of fourth-century categories to fifth-century thought and practice. The confusions introduced by applying fourth-century rhetorical categories to fifth-century Sophists can be illustrated by summarizing the several Sophists' different concerns with what would later be called forensic rhetoric.

There is no surviving fragment from Protagoras that refers to the courts. It is true, however, that Protagoras and Pericles were acquainted and that Pericles was highly successful in advancing his career by successful lawsuits. Plato's portrayal of Protagoras suggests that success in the courts may have been part of an overall civic *aretê* taught by Protagoras. But none of this evidence indicates that Protagoras had or promulgated a theory of forensic speaking or even thought of legal pleading as a special type of discourse.

The only evidence concerning Gorgias and the law courts is similarly indirect and without implication that Gorgias thought of pleading as a special type or form of *logos*. There is suspect evidence from Plato in the *Gorgias*. There is also the extant "Defense of Palamedes"—the precise role of which in Gorgias' teaching is unknown. There is no evidence directly connecting Prodicus or Hippias to the teaching of forensic rhetoric, and there is, at most, uncorroborated evidence from Plato connecting Thrasymachus to forensic rhetorical practice. Antiphon and Critias were the only Older Sophists from Athens and hence able to speak in the law courts. Critias probably did, at least to defend himself before his death, but any further forensic rhetorical theory or practice by Critias is unproved. Antiphon was the first to compose speeches for others to deliver in court, and he spoke in court as well. Several of the Sophists reportedly wrote on the subject of justice, though there is no evidence of attempts at systematic definition prior to Plato.[65]

To characterize sophistic teaching as concerned primarily with forensic discourse is a misleading oversimplification. The various Sophists' interests in *logos* differed, and categorizations of rhetorical forms were missing from their treatments of discourse. To identify each of the Older Sophist's central theme or focal term illustrates the variety of their interests in the nature of *logos* and the differing directions that *incipient* rhetorical views were taking:

Protagoras	*Dissoi Logoi*
Gorgias	*Logos* as *apatê*
Prodicus	*Orthoepeia*
Hippias	Polymathy
Antiphon	*Antilogiae*
Critias	*Logos* and thought
Thrasymachus	*Logos* and power

These admittedly speculative identifications of the various Sophists' special interests show how difficult it is to describe sophistic rhetorical thinking in any single way. The object of sophistic studies should not be to redeem or condemn the Sophists, any more than the study of any ancient Greek philosopher should be to redeem or condemn a given class of thinkers. The object should be a thorough and comprehensive recovery of each Sophist's thinking as far as the available evidence permits. Selective interpretation of data to create a favorable picture of the Sophists as a class is as wrong as selectively interpreting the data to do the opposite. What is needed are more data and an effort to understand sophistic thinking in its own context as best one is able. As Kerferd argues, individualistic studies are the best way to overcome the negative legacy much of history has bequeathed to the Sophists:

> Perhaps too much attention has been given in the past to attempts to arrive at general characterisations of the Sophists and the sophistic movement. This is not so because general characterisations are in themselves in any way improper. But they must be based on detailed studies of the actual evidence concerning individual Sophists. Such evidence is often deficient, inadequate and difficult to interpret. But the same is true of the Presocratics generally, yet in their case detailed scholarly investigations and reconstructions can hardly be said to have been seriously deterred. A similar detailed approach to individual Sophists is now demanded, since only in this way will it be possible to go behind traditional Receptions.[66]

Poulakos carefully distinguishes between fifth-century Sophists and fourth-century Sophists—a distinction C. J. Classen points out is present in Aristotle's writings as well.[67] Such a distinction accepts the premise that not all Sophists were alike and hence adds support to the conclusion that individualistic studies of the Sophists are now needed. The following chapters exemplify such a method by analyzing the extant fragments of Protagoras and summarizing his contributions to early Greek philosophy and rhetoric.[68]

81

NOTES

1. T. M. Robinson, *Contrasting Arguments: An Edition of the Dissoi Logoi* (Salem, NH: Ayer, 1979).
2. Robert J. Connors, "Greek Rhetoric and the Transition from Orality, *PR* 19 (1986): 38–65; Richard L. Enos, "Aristotle's Disservice to the History of Rhetoric" (Paper presented at the Speech Communication Association Convention, Washington DC, 1983), and "Aristotle, Empedocles, and the Notion of Rhetoric," *In Search of Justice: The Indiana Tradition in Speech Communication,* ed. R. Jensen and J. Hammerback (Amsterdam: Rodopi, 1987), 5–21; John Poulakos, "Aristotle's Indebtedness to the Sophists," *Argument in Transition: Proceedings of the Third Summer Conference on Argumentation,* ed. David Zarefsky, Malcolm O. Sillars, and Jack Rhodes (Annandale, VA: Speech Communication Association, 1983), 27–42.
3. John Poulakos, " Toward a Sophistic Definition of Rhetoric," *PR* 16 (1983): 35–48.
4. Richard A. Engnell, "Implications for Communication of the Rhetorical Epistemology of Gorgias of Leontini," *WJSC* 37 (1973): 175–84; Richard L. Enos, "The Epistemology of Gorgias' Rhetoric: A Re-examination," *SSCJ* 42 (1976): 35–51; Bruce E. Gronbeck, "Gorgias on Rhetoric and Poetic: A Rehabilitation," *SSCJ* 38 (1972): 27–38; David Payne, "Rhetoric, Reality, and Knowledge: A Re-Examination of Protagoras' Concept of Rhetoric," *RSQ* 16 (1986): 187–97. See also Michael Gagarin, *Antiphon the Athenian* (Austin: U. of Texas Press, 2002); Bruce McComiskey, *Gorgias and the New Sophistic Rhetoric* (Carbondale: Southern Illinois U. Press, 2002); Scott Consigny, *Gorgias, Sophist and Artist* (Columbia: U. of South Carolina Press, 2001).
5. Richard L. Enos, "Emerging Notions of Argument and Advocacy in Hellenic Litigation: Antiphon's 'On the Murder of Herodes,'" *Journal of the American Forensic Association* 16 (1980): 182–91; Michael Gagarin, "The Nature of Proofs in Antiphon," *CP* 85 (1990): 22–32; John Poulakos, "Gorgias' 'Encomium to Helen' and the Defense of Rhetoric," *Rhetorica* 1 (1983): 1–16; Alexander Sesonske, "To Make the Weaker Argument Defeat the Stronger," *JHP* 6 (1968): 217–31.
6. Robert L. Scott, "On Viewing Rhetoric as Epistemic," *CSSJ* 18 (1967): 9–16; Michael C. Leff, "In Search of Ariadne's Thread: A Review of Recent Literature on Rhetorical Theory," *CSSJ* 29 (1978): 73–91.
7. Susan C. Jarratt, "Toward a Sophistic Historiography," *Pre/Text* 8 (1987): 9–26; John S. Nelson, "Political Theory as Political Rhetoric," *What Should Political Theory Be Now?* ed. Nelson (Albany: SUNY Press, 1983), 169–240; John Poulakos, "Rhetoric, the Sophists, and the Possible," *CM* 51 (1984): 215–26; Michael C. Leff, "Modern Sophistic and the Unity of Rhetoric," *The Rhetoric of the Human Sciences,* ed. John S. Nelson, Allan Megill, and Donald N. McCloskey (Madison: U. of Wisconsin Press, 1987), 19–37; Richard L. Enos, "The Composing Process of the Sophist: New Directions for Composition Research," *Occasional Paper* (Berkeley: Center for the Study of Writing, 1989); Susan C. Jarratt, "The Role of the Sophists in Histories of Consciousness," *PR* 23 (1990): 85–95; John Poulakos, "Sophistical Rhetoric as a Critique of Culture," *Argument and Critical Practices: Proceedings of the Fifth SCA/AFA Conference on Argumentation,* ed. Joseph W. Wenzel (Annandale, VA: Speech Communication Association, 1987), 97–101.
8. Richard Rorty, "The Historiography of Philosophy: Four Genres," *Philosophy in History: Essays on the Historiography of Philosophy,* ed. Richard Rorty, John B. Schneewind, and Quentin Skinner (Cambridge: Cambridge U. Press, 1984), 49–75.
9. Stephen Makin, "How Can We Find Out What Ancient Philosophers Said?" *Phronesis* 33 (1988): 122; emphasis added.
10. William M. A. Grimaldi, *Studies in the Philosophy of Aristotle's Rhetoric* (Wiesbaden: Franz Steiner, 1972), and *Aristotle's Rhetoric: A Commentary,* 2 vols. (New York: Fordham U. Press, 1980, 1988). See also Keith V. Erickson, *Aristotle: The Classical Heri-*

tage of Rhetoric (Metuchen, NJ: Scarecrow Press, 1974), and *Aristotle's Rhetoric: Five Centuries of Philological Research* (Scarecrow Press, 1975).

11. Sonja K. Foss, *Rhetorical Criticism: Exploration and Practice* (Prospect Heights, IL: Waveland Press, 1989), 71–80. On the use and abuse of classical rhetoric in contemporary theorizing, see Kathleen E. Welch, "A Critique of Classical Rhetoric: The Contemporary Appropriation of Ancient Discourse," *Rhetoric Review* 6 (1987): 79–86.

12. See, e. g., G. P. Mohrmann and Michael C. Leff, "Lincoln at Cooper Union: A Rationale for Neo-Classical Criticism," *QJS* 60 (1974): 459–67.

13. Edwin Black, *Rhetorical Criticism: A Study in Method* (New York: Macmillan, 1965).

14. Jarratt, "Historiography"; Leff, "Modern Sophistic."

15. Rorty, "Four Genres," 50.

16. Ibid., 51.

17. Quentin Skinner, "Meaning and Understanding in the History of Ideas," *History and Theory* 8 (1969): 52–53.

18. Allan David Bloom, "The Political Philosophy of Isocrates" (Ph.D. diss., University of Chicago, 1955), 233.

19. Ibid.

20. Alasdair MacIntyre, *Whose Justice? Which Rationality?* (Notre Dame: Notre Dame U. Press, 1988).

21. Rorty, "Four Genres," 49.

22. Kerferd, *SM,* 13.

23. Bloom, "Isocrates," 233.

24. An analogy from the history of science can help clarify the significance of an evolving conceptual vocabulary from the different standpoints of historical and rational reconstruction. What to us is now oxygen was to phlogiston theorists in the eighteenth century "dephlogisticated air." From the standpoint of modern chemists, it does no harm to "rationally reconstruct" phlogiston theory using the concepts of modern chemical theory in order to understand what the phlogiston scientists were really doing. However, the transition from "phlogiston" to "dephlogisticated air" to "oxygen" is precisely what commands the attention of the historian of chemistry. One cannot fully understand the theoretical evolution of chemistry in a historically defensible manner by superimposing a later-developed conceptual vocabulary.

25. One measure of the importance of Poulakos' work on the Sophists and rhetoric is that it won a national research award: See "SCA Awards Presented at Annual Meeting," *SPECTRA Newsletter* 22:1 (Jan. 1986), 1.

26. Poulakos, "Toward," 35.

27. Ibid., 46.

28. Poulakos, "Indebtedness," 31.

29. An example of Poulakos' equivocation can demonstrate the tension between the historical and contemporary objectives in his work. In an essay on Gorgias' *Encomium to Helen,* Poulakos offered a series of specific historical grounds for believing that Gorgias' speech was intended to be a cleverly veiled defense of the art of rhetoric in the fifth century, yet he concluded the essay by shifting to the position that the speech may be read as such *now* regardless of Gorgias' intent. If I am correct about the dating of the term *rhêtorikê,* then Poulakos' historical claim that Helen represented the feminine art *rhêtorikê* (just as Penelope represented *philosophia* elsewhere in Gorgias' writings) is plainly false, though his attenuated claim that the speech can now be read accordingly is still intact. See Poulakos, "Gorgias," 4–7, 15–16.

30. Rorty, "Four Genres," 63.

31. George A. Kennedy, *Classical Rhetoric and Its Christian and Secular Tradition from Ancient to Modern Times* (Chapel Hill: U. of North Carolina Press, 1980), 3–17.

32. Edward Schiappa, *The Beginnings of Rhetorical Theory in Classical Greece* (New Haven: Yale U. Press, 1999).

33. Carole Blair and Mary L. Kahl, "Revising the History of Rhetorical Theory," *WJSC* 54 (1990): 149–52.

34. Poulakos, "Toward," 37.

35. Eric A. Havelock, "The Linguistic Task of the Presocratics," *Language and Thought in Early Greek Philosophy,* ed. Kevin Robb (LaSalle, IL: Hegeler Institute, 1983), 8; emphasis added.

36. Poulakos, "Toward," 36.

37. Connors, "Greek Rhetoric"; Tony M. Lentz, *Orality and Literacy in Hellenic Greece* (Carbondale: Southern Illinois U. Press, 1989).

38. Friedrich Solmsen, *Intellectual Experiments of the Greek Enlightenment* (Princeton: Princeton U. Press, 1975), 83–124.

39. G. E. R. Lloyd, *Polarity and Analogy* (Cambridge: Cambridge U. Press, 1966).

40. See Poulakos, "Indebtedness," 31–32; "Toward," 37–38. There are two senses in which one can be said to have a "self-conscious" aesthetic. 1) In a *general* sense, as Carroll Arnold pointed out to me, all language-users use informal rules of thumb of what "sounds right" to guide their oral and written compositions. If this is the sense Poulakos intends, then my earlier critique missed the mark (in "neosophistic Rhetorical Criticism or the Historical Reconstruction of Sophistic Doctrines?" *PR* 23 [1990]: 202–3). However, such a general sense would also have the effect of rendering Poulakos' comments trivial. If *all* speakers and writers are self-conscious stylists, then Poulakos is hard pressed to find a unique sophistic aesthetic. 2) A more *specific* sense of self-conscious style would present Poulakos with a different problem. As I have just argued, the stylistic changes in the prose discourse of the Sophists cannot be attributed to a sophistic appreciation of style that is divorced from content. We should not anachronistically assume that there were explicit aesthetic theories competing in fifth-century Greece in the sense that, say, rococo and minimalism could be viewed as competing choices today; see Barbara Hughes Fowler, *The Hellenistic Aesthetic* (Madison: U. of Wisconsin Press, 1989). My thanks to Wynne Wilbur for her assistance on this point.

41. Poulakos, "Indebtedness," 31, 41 n34. See also William H. Race, "The Word Καιρός in Greek Drama," *TAPA* 111 (1981): 197–213.

42. Richard C. Jebb, *Sophocles: The Plays and Fragments, Part 6* (Cambridge: Cambridge U. Press, 1894), 174–75.

43. Poulakos, "Toward," 40. On *kairos* as "the appropriate time" see Race, "*Kairos,*" 211–13.

44. Poulakos., "Indebtedness," 31.

45. Havelock, "Task," 55; Bruno Snell, *The Discovery of the Mind,* (Oxford: Basil Blackwell, 1953), ch. 10. Cf. Andreas Graeser, "On Language, Thought, and Reality in Ancient Greek Philosophy," *Dialectica* 31 (1977): 360.

46. Poulakos, "Toward," 37.

47. Poulakos, "Indebtedness," 30.

48. Cf. Manfred S. Frings, "Protagoras Rediscovered: Heidegger's Explication of Protagoras' Fragment," *JVI* 8 (1974): 112–23. For doubts about the usefulness of postmodern readings of classical rhetoric, see George A. Kennedy, "Some Reflections on Neomodernism," *Rhetoric Review* 6 (1988): 230–33, and Robert L. Scott, "Non-Discipline as a Remedy for Rhetoric?" *Rhetoric Review* 6 (1988): 333–37.

49. LSJ s.v. *energazomai* and *energos;* Daniel W. Graham, *Aristotle's Two Systems* (Oxford: Clarendon Press, 1987).

50. Guthrie, *HGP VI,* 119–29.

51. Poulakos, "Possible," 217–18.

52. Guthrie, *HGP VI,* 123.

53. Robinson, *Contrasting Arguments,* 137–41.

54. Richard Garner, *Law and Society in Classical Athens* (New York: St. Martin's Press, 1987), 59–71, 139.

55. Poulakos acknowledges Aristotle's debt to the Sophists on certain matters in his "Indebtedness."

56. See chapter 6 of this book.

57. Guthrie, *HGP VI*, 345–49.

58. Poulakos, "Possible," 221.

59. Makin, "How Can We?"

60. Richard Weaver, *The Ethics of Rhetoric* (Davis, CA: Hermagoras Press, 1953), ch. 1.

61. Poulakos, "Culture."

62. Poulakos, "Indebtedness," 40 n2; "Toward," 47 n1.

63. The following discussion of the Older Sophists is based on the texts and fragments preserved in DK and found in Rosamond Kent Sprague, ed. *The Older Sophists* (Columbia: U. of South Carolina Press, 1972). As is defended in Sprague's book, I assume that Antiphon the Sophist and Antiphon the Orator were one and the same.

64. Stanley Wilcox, "The Scope of Early Rhetorical Instruction," *HSCP* 46 (1942): 121–55.

65. Eric A. Havelock, *The Greek Concept of Justice* (Cambridge, MA: Harvard U. Press, 1978).

66. Kerferd, *Legacy*, 3. It might be objected that individualistic studies of the Sophists are at odds with modern efforts to restore sophistic thinking to its proper place in the history of philosophy. As Poulakos has pointed out, Aristotle typically attacks the Sophists as a class rather than individually, "and this allows the contemporary reader to regard any one member of the class as an exception or a qualified case" ("Possible," 215). The objection may be answered on several grounds. To begin with, there is no assurance that general treatments of the Sophists can avoid negative characterizations of the class as a whole. On the contrary, Kerferd has ably documented how a variety of efforts to describe a general sophistic philosophy have resulted in oversimplified and negative schematizations (*Legacy*, 1–6; *SM*, 4–14). Efforts at describing a common sophistic rhetorical theory similarly tend to contrast *a* sophistic rhetorical theory with those of Plato and Aristotle. Such efforts tend to favor sophistic details that provide contrast with Plato and Aristotle while minimizing points of similarity. The result is a loss of accuracy in favor of scope or, more commonly, a theory of rhetoric that appears wholly inferior to that of Plato or Aristotle. Additionally, individualistic treatments of the Sophists will appear to be exceptional only if not all of the Sophists are studied. After all, the conventional list includes only seven Older Sophists; hence it should not be difficult to assess the Older Sophists as a class after a series of individual studies have been done. Perhaps in the dialectic between general and specific studies both values of accuracy and scope can be optimized.

67. C. J. Classen, "Aristotle's Picture of the Sophists," in Kerferd, *Legacy*, 7–24.

68. For Poulakos' response to my comments, see his "Interpreting Sophistical Rhetoric: A Response to Schiappa," *PR* 23 (1990): 218–28. I have responded in "History and Neosophistic Criticism: A Reply to Poulakos," *PR* 23 (1990): 307–15.

PART II

ANALYSIS OF THE MAJOR
FRAGMENTS OF PROTAGORAS

5

THE TWO-*LOGOI* FRAGMENT

The Greek text of what I will refer to as the two-*logoi* fragment is the following: Καὶ πρῶτος ἔφη δύο λόγους εἶναι περὶ παντὸς πράγματος ἀντικειμένους ἀλλήλοις (DL 9.51). Osborne's concern that so-called fragments are often paraphrases has validity with respect to the two-*logoi* fragment.[1] After all, our source is over six centuries removed from Protagoras, and no fifth- or fourth-century BCE writer quotes the statement in the same way Protagoras' human-measure or "concerning the gods" statements are quoted. Nevertheless, I think there are good reasons to treat Diogenes Laertius' words as faithful to Protagoras' original ideas. Accordingly, I will follow the convention of referring to the statement as one of Protagoras' fragments.

Diogenes Laertius introduced the fragment with the words "and he was the first to say" (*kai prôtos ephê*), implying that what followed was well-known. The existence of something like a Greek commonplace concerning two *logoi* is suggested by Clement of Alexandria: "Every argument [*panti logoi*] has an opposite argument, say the Greeks, following Protagoras."[2] Similarly, Seneca reported that "Protagoras declares that one can take either side on any question and debate it with equal success" (*Epistles* 88.43).[3] A book titled "Contradictory Arguments" is also attributed to Protagoras, though there is no certainty he wrote such a work (DK 80 A1, B5).

For my purposes the important idea of the fragment is that there are two *logoi* in opposition about every "thing" (*pantos pragmatos*). Even

89

if Diogenes Laertius is paraphrasing, Protagoras' actual words must have included three key notions: *logoi,* opposition, and things (*pragmata*). Given Aristophanes' portrayal of the two opposing *logoi* in the *Clouds* and the resonance between the two-*logoi* and weaker/stronger *logoi* fragments, there is no reason to doubt that those three notions are authentically Protagorean. Accordingly, my analysis of the fragment will focus on the three notions and what they meant to fifth- and fourth-century audiences.

THE SUBJECTIVE AND HERACLITEAN INTERPRETATIONS

The available translations can be usefully grouped into two categories: the subjective interpretation and the Heraclitean interpretation. The subjective interpretation is used in such translations as Michael J. O'Brien, "On every issue there are two arguments opposed to each other"; R. D. Hicks, "There are two sides to every question, opposed to each other"; Theodor Gomperz, "On every question there are two speeches, which stand in opposition to one another"; Bromley Smith, "On every question there were two sides to the argument, exactly opposite to one another"; Lazlo Versényi, "There are two sides, opposed to each other, to every question"; and Guthrie, "There are two opposite arguments on every subject."[4]

Such translations reduce Protagoras' statement to the proposition that a debate is possible on any topic. Or, as Kennedy paraphrases, "Something can be said on both sides of every question."[5] Such readings are consistent with interpretations of Protagoras that reduce all sophistic teaching to rhetoric. While a pragmatic result of the two-*logoi* statement may have been an advancement of the practice we now call debate, a strictly "rhetorical" reading of the fragment understates the philosophical content of Protagoras' doctrines.

The difference between the subjective interpretation and the Heraclitean interpretation turns on the translation of two key words, *logos* and *pragmata*. In the subjective interpretation *pragmata* is translated with such words as "issue," "question," and "subject." These words anachronistically subjectify *pragmata* since issues and questions are obviously human creations. It is implied further that the two *logoi*—sides, speeches, or arguments—are created solely by the arguers rather than being aspects of an object of inquiry. In contrast to the subjective interpretation there are examples of what I call the Heraclitean interpretation. They include Untersteiner, "In every experience there are two *logoi* in opposition to each other"; Kerferd, "There are two *logoi* concerning everything, these being opposed to each other"; and Guthrie, "Of every thing two contrary accounts can be given."[6]

It is worth noting that Kerferd's translation of the fragment has changed over time. In 1949 he rendered the fragment "On every question there are two accounts opposed to one another," and in 1967 "There are two *logoi,* or accounts, to be given about everything."[7] In 1981 he substituted "argument" for "account" but otherwise maintained his 1967 translation.[8] The transition reflects a shift from the subjective to the Heraclitean interpretation and is based, I believe, on a growing awareness of the philosophical significance of the two key words *logos* and *pragmata.*

Instead of the semantically related terms "issue" or "question," *pragmata* is most often translated from documents in Protagoras' time as "things." There is no reason why the word should not be translated thus in Protagoras' fragment as long as it is kept in mind that "thing" can include a deed, event, or act (as in "it seemed the thing to do" or "did you go to that thing last night?"). The wide breadth of phenomena covered by the term *pragmata* is the reason Untersteiner translates it as "experience" (*esperienza*): "Protagoras turned his inquiring gaze and his critical energy in all directions: the more difficult questions concerning divinity and reality, as well as on those concerning men's political, social and ethical life and their theoretical and practical activity, fall under the dis-integrating power of the two *logoi* which invest all experience."[9]

It is clear that the subjective translation and interpretation of *pragmata* is misleading inasmuch as it implies a modern subjective sense of "issue" or "question." The modern philosophical dichotomy of subjective/objective was not yet clearly conceived in fifth-century Athens; if it had been, Protagoras would have included all sorts of "things" as *pragmata*—things we now might call subjectively created as well as those objectively given. As T. M. Robinson notes in his analysis of the *Dissoi Logoi* document, for Protagoras *pragma* meant "reality" in a general sense.[10]

Logos is such a difficult word to do justice to in a short translation that Untersteiner simply chose not to translate it, and Kerferd's last translation supplied the word "argument" in brackets but left the Greek word *logoi* in his translation. Such reluctance is understandable. *Logos* was a much overworked word during the sixth, fifth, and fourth centuries BCE, and its meaning must be derived from context. Even in a clear and specific context a single word of translation will fail if multiple meanings are intended, as Kerferd argues was the case when the Older Sophists used *logos:*

> These [meanings] are first of all the area of language and linguistic formulation, hence speech, discourse, description, statement, arguments (as expressed in words) and so on; secondly, the area of thought and mental processes, hence thinking, reasoning, accounting for, explanation (cf. *orthos logos*), etc.; thirdly, the area of the world, that about which we are able to speak and to think, hence structured principles, formulae, natural laws and so on, provided that in each case they are regarded as actually present in and exhibited in the world-process.[11]

Reinterpreted along the lines of the above qualifications Protagoras' claim is not only a description of human argumentative prowess, but also a claim about the world. "Reality" (*pragma*) is such that there are two opposing ways (*logoi*) to describe, account for, or explain any given experience. Hence, the first step in recovering the significance of Protagoras' two-*logoi* fragment is to set aside the subjective interpretation as an unfaithful rendering of *logos* and *pragmata.*

My argument is that Protagoras' two-*logoi* fragment is best read as a logical extension of the Heraclitean theses popularly referred to in modern times as his theory of flux and his "unity of opposites" doctrine. Further, both the two-*logoi* and human-measure fragments can be read productively as responses to certain Eleatic theories concerning human ability to comprehend and speak correctly about "what is."

Heraclitus' unity of opposites doctrine was one of many different sixth- and fifth-century theories that dealt with various sorts of opposing pairs. It is not surprising that humans, being a species with two eyes, two ears, two arms, two legs, and two sexes, have in most cultures given special status to pairs. The strength of the influence of twosomes might be attested to in ancient Greek culture by the fact that nouns, verbs, and adjectives had, at one time, three possible endings indicating number: singular, plural, and dual.

Twosomes in presocratic thought generally had two common characteristics. First, each pair was conceived of as in some sort of conflict or opposition, though both the degree and the kind of opposition varied. Second, usually one of the two things in opposition was considered in some way preferable to the other. Thus, in Hesiod's poetry night was in

92

conflict with day, and just as night blots out the light of day and the vision of men, death blots out human life (*Theogony* 748–57).

There is considerable disagreement over the evolution of presocratic theorizing about opposites. Aristotle claimed that all of his philosophical predecessors held some kind of theory privileging opposites.[12] But it has been argued that Aristotle exaggerated and oversimplified the role of the opposites in presocratic philosophy.[13] Since Aristotle was a major source of information concerning the Presocratics for both ancient and modern scholars, there is now little consensus on such issues as who originated what doctrines, when, at what level of generalization and abstraction, and with what examples.

An indisputable fact is that a number of Presocratics were concerned with opposites, including Anaximander, Anaximenes, Heraclitus, Parmenides, Anaxagoras, Empedocles, Alcmaeon, and Melissus. All were grappling with the task of rationalizing the mythic accounts of the world and with overcoming theistic patterns of explanation as perpetuated through the poetry of Homer and Hesiod. For example, the earliest philosophical presocratic fragment pertaining to conflicting pairs is by Anaximander: "For they give justice [*dikê*] and reparation to one another for their offense [*adikia*] in accordance with the ordinance of time."[14] There is little textual evidence to support the thesis that Anaximander developed a theory of opposites, as has been suggested by Guthrie and others.[15] A word for "opposites" appears nowhere in Anaximander, and there is little hint of abstraction in his extant fragments.[16] Anaximander was describing what we would now call physical alteration by referring to the concrete legal practice of reciprocity and by suggesting that reciprocal give-and-take is perpetual.[17]

Between the times of Anaximander and Protagoras, theorizing about opposites became more sophisticated and conceptual. By Protagoras' time it had been theorized that certain basic opposites such as fire and water came into being by a "separating out" of a more primary substance of which they were the constituents.[18] Primary opposing pairs which were initially identified as they were encountered in nature (e.g., fire and water) became more abstract concepts when described with neuter adjectives (e.g., hot and cold). By Protagoras' time the neuter adjectives had been coupled with a neuter generic article, as in "the hot" and "the cold," which permitted further conceptualization and analytical manipulation.[19]

The most significant and celebrated theorist of opposites was Heracli-

93

tus. No Presocratic identified the number and variety of opposites that Heraclitus did. His extant fragments identify anthropocentric as well as cosmic opposing pairs, including night and day, sea and earth, warm and cool, wet and dry, divine and human, disease and health, hunger and satiety, weariness and rest, just and unjust, mortal and immortal, young and old, up and down, winter and summer.[20] Heraclitus also was original in proposing the *unity* of opposites.[21] An exemplary fragment reads "The teacher of most is Hesiod. It is him they know as knowing most, who did not recognize day and night: they are one."[22] This is one of many passages in which Heraclitus suggested that recognized opposites were in some way united. It also documents the presocratic efforts to contrast new ways of thinking against the poetic modes.[23]

Aristotle (perhaps anachronistically) interpreted Heraclitus' unity of opposites thesis in terms as broad as Protagoras' two-*logoi* fragment: "The doctrine of Heraclitus [is] that *all things [panta] are and are not*."[24] Jonathan Barnes has suggested that Heraclitus' writings imply that "every pair of contraries is somewhere coinstantiated; and every object coinstantiates at least one pair of contraries."[25] Clearly, the unity of opposites theme in Heraclitus' writings bears a strong resemblance to the logic of Protagoras' two-*logoi* fragment which claimed, in Barnes' terminology, that every "thing" coinstantiates at least one pair of contrary *logoi*.

There is additional evidence from the ancients to support a Heraclitean interpretation of Protagoras' doctrine. Sextus reports that Protagoras held that "the reasons [*logoi*] of all the appearances [*phainomenôn*] subsist in the matter" (*Outlines of Pyrrhonism* 1.218). Clement of Alexandria wrote, "Every *logos* has an opposite, say the Greeks, following Protagoras" (DK 80 A20). The Protagorean *Dissoi Logoi* tract, written around 400 BCE, contains a number of ideas and word usages that imply Heraclitean influence. Moreover, when Plato discussed Protagoras' theory of knowledge in the *Theaetetus*, he cited Heraclitus (as well as Empedocles) as someone who would agree with the notion that "if you speak of something as big, it will also appear small; if you speak of it as heavy, it will also appear light; and similarly with everything."[26] Finally, Aristotle described an implication of Protagoras' doctrines which is nearly identical to the passage quoted earlier regarding Heraclitus: "It follows that the same thing both is and is not, and is bad and good, and that the contents of all other opposite statements are true" (*Metaphysics* 1062b).

It is reasonable to conclude, therefore, that the two-*logoi* fragment is a Protagorean development of Heraclitus' world view.

THE ADVANCEMENT OF HERACLITEAN THOUGHT

Protagoras provided a logical extension of Heraclitus' doctrines and played an important role in the development of thinking about the relationship between language and reality, and between things and their predicated attributes or qualities.

The history of presocratic philosophical thought is a history of the development of new kinds of questions and patterns of explanation. Julius M. Moravcsik has suggested that presocratic speculation "goes through three stages of explanatory patterns. These are: explanation solely in terms of origin, explanation in terms of stuff or constituency, and explanation in terms of entities and their attributes."[27] Before the Presocratics, explanations of origin were theistic and mythical. The birth of Western philosophy is widely thought of as the point at which certain Greeks began to offer natural or scientific explanations of origin as an alternative.

Moravcsik calls the second stage compositional explanation. The question "Where does it come from?" is succeeded by the questions "What is it made up of?" and "What is its stuff?" These questions require levels of analysis rarely undertaken in mythic-poetic cultures. Answers to these questions require new ways of thinking and speaking: "The schemata 'x is made of y' and 'everything is made of y' require that we construe the elements of nature that we investigate as complexes. They also require an extension of the vocabulary; for we must add kind terms, and terms denoting varieties of relations of constituency."[28]

There are many kinds of possible compositional explanations, and it is for this approach to nature that the Presocratics are most well known. The Presocratics are believed to have suggested a sundry of underlying "stuff" such as air or water; proposed processes of alteration involving, for example, rarification and condensation; and, of course, they offered opinions about opposites.

In the third stage things were analyzed according to what we would now call their qualities or properties. Moravcsik calls this the attributional level of analysis, and it is not clearly reached in Greek thinking until the writings of Plato and Aristotle.[29] For Plato attributes or qualities became the Forms themselves. A given entity under analysis is the sum of attribute instantiations. Hence an object is beautiful because it "participates" in the Form of absolute Beauty (*Phaedo* 100d). For Plato the opposites are not unified, but represent distinct Forms-in-themselves, regardless of how they may be instantiated in everyday experience (*Republic* 476a).

Aristotle's approach to attributes is described by Moravcsik as the coat-hanger view: "We think of attributes as attaching themselves to some underlying entity that is more than the mere sum of attribute instantiations. It is like a coat-hanger on which the 'coats,' that is, attributes, hang."[30] Furthermore, the "coats" can be changed. The opposites are explained by Aristotle as potential versus actual attributes coming-to-be for a particular entity: a young man being beardless but potentially growing one as he matures, or a man with a full head of hair potentially going bald. Aristotle's theory of four causes also provided an analytical framework with which to explain why things gain or lose attributes.[31] The most important aspect of Aristotle's approach was the analytical step of divorcing object or substance from quality or attribute, a step integral to his physical and metaphysical theorizing.

What Plato's and Aristotle's writings have in common is that they represent the "quantum-jump" in abstract conceptualization necessary for the move from stage 2 to stage 3 explanations.[32] It was not an easy step. Plato's *Theaetetus* makes it clear that both the name and the abstract concept of a quality is novel (182a), and the *Republic* makes it obvious that he does not expect the multitude to understand what the Forms are (493e). It is not difficult to understand his pessimism. To comprehend the notion of abstract attributes requires a radical break from the dominant practices of mythic-poetic thinking and speaking. Plato's innovative syntax was designed to contrast the abstract notion of the thing itself per se, which is one, and which is unseen, with the concrete and situational logic of the poetic life world.[33] Plato's theory of Forms was a break not only from the mythic-poetic mindset but also from the the presocratic philosophers whose thinking was still compositional. To most Presocratics the notion of abstract quality was still foreign: "What we call a quality was for all Presocratics a characteristic which could not be considered separately from that of which it was characteristic."[34]

Moravcsik has argued that Heraclitus played an important transitional role in moving Greek thought from stage 2 to stage 3 explanatory patterns. A case can be made that he has overstated Heraclitus' contribution and missed the contribution made by Protagoras. Moravcsik's first argument is that Heraclitus' implicit epistemology ranked rational insight and the intellect over sense perception.[35] Moravcsik's reading of Heraclitus on this point is both anachronistic and unsupported by the available evidence. The verb *aisthanomai* (to have physical sensation of) and the abstract noun *aisthêsis* (sensation) do not appear until after Heraclitus, and their philosophical use to express sensation, as opposed to intellect, is documented no earlier than Plato.[36] Contrary to the implication of Moravcsik's translation of one of Heraclitus' fragments, Heraclitus never used a word for perception or perceptible.[37] In fact, the fragment in question supports a conclusion contrary to Moravcsik's: "Whatever comes from sight, hearing, learning from experience: this I prefer."[38] As Charles Kahn points out, a surer interpretation is that experience is a better teacher than the hearsay of the poets—a theme common among the Presocratics.[39] The fact that Heraclitus said that "nature loves to hide" and wrote of opposites which were partly unobservable is no better evidence of a unique epistemological role for insight in his philosophy. As Moravcsik appears to admit, such arguments certainly were not limited to Heraclitus.[40]

Moravcsik's second argument concerns the relationship between language and reality. Moravcsik represents the consensus view when he points out that Heraclitus was a pioneer of conceptual thinking about difference and sameness. Many of his fragments posited a unity thesis about opposites, and his famous claim of being unable to step into the same river twice challenged thinking about persistence and difference.[41] But Moravcsik's claims exceed his evidence when he credits Heraclitus with challenging the one designatum theory of names/labels—that is, the belief that "each species term labels a single entity, with more generic terms labeling complexes made up of these simples."[42] Heraclitus' fragments are concerned with the inability of most people to understand the way of the world; namely, the flux of opposites. But he does not address language itself as an object of inquiry, and his negative inferences about the way people speak are extremely general. Any Heraclitean criticism of an implicit one designatum theory of language is latent at best.

A better case can be made that Protagoras was a transitional figure between stage 2 and stage 3 explanation. Protagoras was the first recorded Greek thinker to treat language per se as an object of study. He was credited with being the first person to articulate the tenses of verbs and to divide speech into its different modes or voices (DL 9.53–54). He was also the first Greek of record to have noticed and commented on the gender of word endings.[43] Additionally, there are several references to Protagoras having criticized Homer's use of language (DK 80 A29, 30). In light of Protagoras' well-attested interest in language and his obvious Heraclitean influences, it is reasonable to read his two-*logoi* fragment as an extension of Heraclitus' thought into the realm of what we would now call linguistic theory.[44] The two-*logoi* statement helped to make language per se amenable to analysis and theory. Returning to the fragment itself, the case for Protagoras as a transitional figure can be pressed further.

TRANSLATION AND INTERPRETATION

The fragment is clearly a claim about the relationship between language and the things of reality. Given Protagoras' interest in language, it is reasonable to assert that his two-*logoi* fragment is an early attempt at "technicizing" or "professionalizing" the word and concept *logos,* for it is clear that the fragment is as much a claim about *logos* as it is about *pragmata.* Most translations understate this fact by translating the phrase *duo logous einai* as "there are two *logoi.*" Such translations render *einai* as purely copulative, which is probably anachronistic.[45] If Protagoras used the word *einai* (and it is possible that he did not), its use would have been more likely to be locative, and hence the phrase should be translated "two *logoi* are present."[46] A secondary reading, less likely but still plausible, would be to read *einai* in light of Protagoras' use of the verb "to be" in his human-measure statement and hence to assume that its use here is veridical.[47] Such an interpretation would render the phrase "two *logoi* are true" or "are the case." Either reading establishes that the two-*logoi* fragment takes as its subject the status of the two *logoi.*

The two-*logoi* fragment posits that there are two opposing *logoi* concerning "things." Accordingly, Protagoras is a likelier candidate than Heraclitus for having been the first explicit challenger of a naïve name/designatum theory.

It is also possible that Protagoras conceived of the two conflicting *logoi* as a nascent version of the logical form P and not-P. Two arguments support such a hypothesis. The first derives from the examination of the human-measure fragment. Interpretation of the human-measure fragment makes it clear that Protagoras was familiar with the logical concept of negation, making it plausible to read the two-*logoi* fragment accordingly.[48]

The second argument is based on the meaning of the word *logos*. Of the word's many meanings, two related themes occur repeatedly: language and rationality.[49] Thus Heraclitus' opposites in Protagoras' use began to be treated in a noncompositional manner, in terms of contrariety and contradiction rather than as strictly opposing forces of nature. Put differently, nature began to be viewed in more abstract logical patterns such as "as-P" and "as-not-P." Seeing opposites as essentially linguistic (*logoi*) was a necessary step to a more abstract conceptualization, to their being seen as attributes that can be predicated with respect to "things." It cannot be proved that Protagoras went this far, though a passage in Aristotle suggests that he did: "It is equally possible to affirm [*kataphêsai*] and to deny [*apophêsai*] anything of every thing. . . . This premise must be accepted by those who share the views of Protagoras" (*Metaphysics* 1007b21–23). The subjective interpretation, which limits the fragment to a purely linguistic reading, should be seen as significant but not as the sum total of the fragment's meaning. Protagoras' two-*logoi* fragment nevertheless contains insights integral to stage 3 attributional explanation. As Moravcsik stated: "We can treat opposites in terms of the laws of logic, rather than merely in terms of causal laws, only when we construe these as abstract elements, or at least abstract features of natural entities. . . . It is a long leap from causal laws governing opposite forces to the logical laws of negation and contradiction."[50] Protagoras may have made just such a leap. At least he helped to provide the conceptual framework to facilitate it.

A final bit of evidence can be cited showing that Protagoras was a transitional figure between stage 2 and stage 3 types of explanatory patterns. His later commentators tend to alternate between stage 2 and stage 3 accounts of his doctrines. Sextus' report that Protagoras held that *logoi* "subsist in the matter" and Aristotle's "same thing both is and is not" suggest a compositional interpretation of Protagoras, while Clement's "Every *logos* has an opposite" and Plato's "If you speak of something as big, it will also appear small" tend to lend credence to an interpretation of *logos* as something *apart* from its referent—a predication or attribution.[51] Such interpretive variability suggests that Protagoras' text was, in fact, a contribution to a transition between two patterns of explanation, making it possible to cast it in either pattern according to the needs and interests of his commentators.[52]

In sum: the subjective interpretation/translation of the two-*logoi* fragment is, by itself, inadequate since it does not faithfully translate the key words *logos* and *pragmata*. The Heraclitean interpretation/translation of the fragment is preferable in light of the affinity between it and Heraclitus' unity of opposites thesis. The two-*logoi* fragment represents a logical extension of Heraclitus' thinking. Specifically, the fragment represents a claim about the relationship between language and reality. Protagoras' claim marks a transition between compositional and attributional patterns/logics of explanation. Finally, the two-*logoi* fragment can be translated usefully with either a locative emphasis or a veridical emphasis (the former is preferred). The locative emphasis yields: "Two accounts [*logoi*] are present about every 'thing,' opposed to each other." The veridical emphasis yields: "Two contrary reports [*logoi*] are true concerning every experience."

NOTES

1. Catherine Osborne, *Rethinking Early Greek Philosophy* (London: Duckworth, 1987), 1–9. See also William W. Fortenbaugh's useful comments about my discussion of the two-*logoi* fragment in his review of the first edition of this book (*AJP* 114 [1993]: 624–26).

2. DK 80 A20 reads Ἕλληνές φασι Πρωταγόρου προκατάρξαντος παντὶ λόγωι λόγον ἀντικεῖσθαι. H. Gomperz renders this as "Jeder Rede steht eine andere Rede entgegen" (*SR*, 130).

3. Richard M. Gummere, *Seneca ad Lucilium: Epistulae Morales* (Cambridge, MA: Harvard U. Press, 1920), 2:374–75: "Protagoras ait de omni re in utramque partem disputari posse ex aequo et de hac ipsa, an omnis res in utramque partem disputabilis sit."

4. In Rosamond Kent Sprague, ed. *The Older Sophists* (Columbia: U. of South Carolina Press, 1972), 4; R. D. Hicks in DL, 463; Theodor Gomperz, *Greek Thinkers* (London: John Murray, 1901), 1:462; Bromley Smith, "The Father of Debate: Protagoras of Abdera," *QJS* 4 (1918): 202; Lazlo Versényi, *Socratic Humanism* (New Haven: Yale U. Press, 1963), 18; Guthrie, *HGP III*, 182. Dupréel's translation is: "Sur chaque chose il y a deux discours en opposition l'un avec l'autre" (*Sophistes*, 38).

5. Kennedy, *APG*, 31.

6. Untersteiner, *Sophists*, 19; Kerferd, *SM*, 84; Guthrie, *HGP III*, 182n. Untersteiner's translation reads: "Per primo sostenne che intorno a ogni esperienza vi sono due logoi in contrasto fra di loro."

7. G. B. Kerferd, "Plato's Account of the Relativism of Protagoras," *Durham University Journal* 42 (1949): 20, and "Protagoras," *Encyclopedia of Philosophy* (New York: Macmillan, 1967), 6:506.

8. Kerferd, *SM*, 84.

9. Untersteiner, *Sophists*, 19.

10. T. M. Robinson, *Contrasting Arguments: An Edition of the Dissoi Logoi* (Salem, NH: Ayer, 1979), 90n. On Aristotle's use of *pragma* in his *Rhetoric* see William M. A. Grimaldi, "A Note on the ΠΙΣΤΕΙΣ in Aristotle's *Rhetoric*, 1354–1356," *AJP* 78 (1957): 188–92.

11. Kerferd, *SM*, 83.

12. Aristotle, *Physics* 188a19, 188b27; *Metaphysics* 1004b29, 1075a28, 1087a29.

13. Harold Cherniss, *Aristotle's Criticism of Presocratic Philosophy* (New York: Octagon Books, 1935), 354–70; Eric A. Havelock, "The Linguistic Task of the Presocratics," *Language and Thought in Early Greek Philosophy*, ed. Kevin Robb (LaSalle, IL: Hegeler Institute, 1983), 7–82.

14. DK 12 A9, B1, trans. Jonathan Barnes, *The Presocratic Philosophers* (London: Routledge and Kegan Paul, 1982), 29; cf. KRS, 106–8.
15. Havelock, "Task," 60, 72–73; see also Barnes, *Presocratic,* 29–34; Guthrie, *HGP I,* 78–83.
16. KRS, 120.
17. Eric A. Havelock, *The Greek Concept of Justice* (Cambridge, MA: Harvard U. Press, 1978), 263–64.
18. Guthrie, *HGP I;* Charles H. Kahn, *Anaximander and the Origins of Greek Cosmology* (New York: Columbia U. Press, 1960); G. E. R. Lloyd, "Hot and Cold, Dry and Wet in Early Greek Thought," *Studies in Presocratic Philosophy,* ed. David J. Furley and R. E. Allen (New York: Humanities Press, 1970), 255–80.
19. Bruno Snell, *The Discovery of the Mind* (Oxford: Basil Blackwell, 1953), ch. 10; Havelock, "Task," 55–56; Andreas Graeser, "On Language, Thought, and Reality in Ancient Greek Philosophy," *Dialectica* 31 (1977): 360.
20. Charles H. Kahn, *The Art and Thought of Heraclitus* (Cambridge: Cambridge U. Press, 1979), 28–85.
21. G. E. R. Lloyd, *Polarity and Analogy* (Cambridge: Cambridge U. Press, 1966), 17.
22. Kahn, *Heraclitus,* 37 (fr. 19).
23. Ibid., 107–10.
24. Aristotle, *Metaphysics* 1012a24–25; emphasis added.
25. Barnes, *Presocratic,* 70.
26. 152d, trans. John McDowell, *Plato: Theaetetus* (Oxford: Clarendon Press, 1973), 17.
27. Julius M. Moravcsik, "Heraclitean Concepts and Explanations," *Language and Thought in Early Greek Philosophy,* ed. Kevin Robb (La Salle, IL: Hegeler Institute, 1983), 134.
28. Ibid., 136.
29. Ibid., 137; see also Cherniss, *Aristotle's,* 367; Graeser, "On Language," 372.
30. Moravcsik, "Heraclitean," 137.
31. Guthrie, *HGP VI,* 119–29, 223–33.
32. Moravcsik, "Heraclitean, 138.
33. Eric A. Havelock, *Preface to Plato* (Cambridge, MA: Harvard U. Press, 1963), 256–57.
34. Cherniss, *Aristotle's,* 362.
35. Moravcsik, "Heraclitean," 142–47.
36. Havelock, "Task," 59; see LSJ s.vv. *aisthanomai* and *aisthêsis.*
37. See Moravcsik, "Heraclitean," 143, fragment B55.
38. Kahn, *Heraclitus,* 35.
39. Ibid., 106.
40. Moravcsik, "Heraclitean," 144.
41. Ibid., 147–50.
42. Ibid., 148.
43. Aristotle, *Rhetoric* 1407b; ridiculed in Aristophanes, *Clouds* 658.
44. Kerferd, *SM,* 71.
45. Charles H. Kahn, "The Greek Verb 'to be' and the Concept of Being," *Foundations of Language* 2 (1966): 245–65, and *Verb.*
46. Kahn, "Concept," 257; Havelock, *Justice,* 237–38.
47. Kahn, "Concept," 249–50.
48. Kahn, *Verb,* 367–68.
49. Ibid., 403.
50. Moravcsik, "Heraclitean," 139.
51. Cherniss, *Aristotle's,* 369. On the emergence of a new stage of thinking about

words and things in the fifth century initiated by sophistic theorizing about *logos* see Manfred Kraus, *Name und Sache, ein Problem im frühgriechischen Denken* (Amsterdam: Grüner, 1987). See also G. B. Kerferd's review of Kraus (*CR* 40 [1990]: 59–60).

52. Kurt von Fritz makes an argument similar to mine (concerning the difference between things and qualities among pre- and post-Protagorean philosophers) when he discusses how those differences were reflected in Plato's treatment of Protagoras' human-measure fragment; see his article on Protagoras in *RE* 23 (1957): 914.

6

THE "STRONGER AND WEAKER"
LOGOI FRAGMENT

The full Greek text of the stronger/weaker *logoi* fragment is found in Aristotle's *Rhetoric*: καὶ τὸ τὸν ἥττω δὲ λόγον κρείττω ποιεῖν τοῦτ' ἔστιν (1402a23). Stripped of the introductory "And this is [an example] what one means by ..." the remaining text reads *ton hêttô de logon kreittô poiein*. Two categories of translation and interpretation are identifiable. The first interpretation can be labeled the Aristotelian-pejorative (hereafter "pejorative") interpretation and the second the Heraclitean-positive (hereafter "positive") interpretation.

The most perverse version of the fragment appears in Lane Cooper's translation: "making the worse appear the better cause."[1] So interpreted, there are few better examples of what it means to be an unscrupulous rhetorician. In fact, the phrase has achieved that dubious status of a popular slogan allegedly representing the worst aspirations of the sophistic movement and perhaps of the art of rhetoric itself. Keith V. Erickson described the phrase as a "fundamental indictment of Sophistry" that represents "the most famous criticism of rhetoric"; Alexander Sesonske suggested that the phrase is an appropriate "summary of Plato's complaint against the Sophists"; and W. K. C. Guthrie suggested that Protagoras' promise was understood even in ancient time as "the very essence of sophistical teaching."[2] If one grants such assessments even partial credibility, then the moral purpose and pedagogical orientation of

103

sophistic training was encapsulated in Protagoras' so-called "promise." Accordingly, a proper understanding of Protagoras' fragment is indispensable to a thorough understanding of sophistic theory.

THE PEJORATIVE INTERPRETATION

The pejorative translation is inadequate on three counts. First, the choice of the word "cause" for *logon* falls short of suggesting the rich meaning of *logos*. Second, the insertion of the word "appear" is inappropriate. Cooper's translation requires the addition of a word that is not in the text (*phainetai* or *aisthanomai*), and it suggests a reality/appearance distinction that Protagoras would not have drawn.[3] Cooper, of course, is not the sole representative of the pejorative interpretation. J. H. Freese's "making the worse *appear* the better argument" and W. Rhys Robert's "making the worse argument *seem* the better" are improvements only in the substitution of "argument" for "cause."[4] Sesonske's essay on Protagoras' promise, "To Make the Weaker Argument Defeat the Stronger," consistently inserted the word "defeat" when discussing the fragment.[5]

The third problem with the pejorative translation is the questionable translation of *kreittô* and *hêttô* as "better" and "worse." While later use in Plato and Aristotle of *kreittô* and *hêttô* implies the moralistic translation of better and worse, it is unlikely that in Protagoras' time such was the meaning. Lexicons document use of both terms back to Homer. *Kreittô* appears in Homer typically in reference to battle, and it meant "stronger," "mightier," or "more powerful." *Hêttô* also appears as early as Homer, with the apparent meaning of "weaker." Other usages of *hêttô* include "giving way," "yielding," "unable to resist or contend with," and "weaker" than another. In addition, from the time of Homer to that of Plato one finds passages which document the use of *kreittô* and *hêttô* as paired terms meaning "stronger" and "weaker." In the *Iliad* Apollo compared the strength of Hector to that of other mortals using *kreittô* and *hêttô* (16.722). In the fifth century book *On Fractures,* the author used the same words to describe "a weaker person grasping a stronger one" (3.15), and Plato's *Timaeus* described the battle of elements with *hêttô* and *kreittô:* "the weaker is fighting against the stronger" (57a). The terms also were used in the fifth-century Hippocratic treatises as quantifiers: *hêttô* as less and *kreittô* as greater. But the

104

quantitative sense is not evident when the terms were used together, and usage clearly did not suggest the ethical tone of better and worse.

It would not have been unusual to use terms implying physical strength to describe a *logos*. Terms denoting physical combat, particularly wrestling, were often used in describing an argumentative interaction. Protagoras was said by some to have written a book called "On Wrestling" (DK 80 A1, B8), and when one of the two battling *logoi* in the *Clouds* scored an early point "it" said, "I've got you held round the waist in a grip you can't escape."[6] Given the history of *hêttô* and *kreittô*, especially as they appeared together, the best translation of the terms in Protagoras' fragment is "weaker" and "stronger."

It is no accident that almost every word of Protagoras' brief "promise" has been translated pejoratively, given the fragment's context in Aristotle.[7] The reference to Protagoras followed a section describing the spurious use of argument from probability. Hence E. M. Cope's commentary translates the phrase as "making the worse appear the better argument" and interprets it in light of the context Aristotle created: "that is, giving the superior to the inferior, the less *probable* argument, making it prevail over that which is *really* superior, and more probable."[8] The quotation is followed in Aristotle's *Rhetoric* with: "Hence people were right in objecting to the training Protagoras undertook to give them. It was a fraud; the probability it handled was not genuine but spurious, and has a place in no art except Rhetoric and Eristic" (1402a24–28). Aristotle's interpretation is the result of filtering Protagoras' doctrine through his own philosophical system. As I have said, Aristotle's descriptions always contrast the Sophists' doctrines with his own system, and they are made to appear inferior (in modern terms) epistemologically, ontologically, and ethically. The pejorative translation is consistent with how Aristotle himself may have understood the fragment, though there is no reason it must be assumed that his interpretation is either exhaustive or necessarily superior to alternative readings. Aristotle's interpretation is not irrelevant, since it provides valuable insight about how Protagoras' promise later came to be understood. Furthermore, since we have a fairly good understanding of Aristotle's attitude toward Protagoras and other fifth-century Sophists, it is possible to discriminate among Aristotle's understanding and earlier interpretations in order to trace the evolution of the fragment's meaning in the century between Protagoras and Aristotle.[9]

There are two pre-Aristotelian references to the stronger/weaker *logoi* fragment, though neither reference directly identifies Protagoras as the phrase's originator. In Plato's *Apology* Socrates lists as one of the implicit charges against him that he "makes the weaker argument defeat the stronger" (19b5–6). The Greek is almost identical to that appearing in Aristotle: *ton hêttô logon kreittô poion,* which Benjamin Jowett translated as "makes the worse appear the better cause" and which H. N. Fowler in the Loeb edition translated as "making the weaker argument stronger."[10] The charge in Plato's *Apology* is not one specifically brought against Socrates by his accuser Meletus but a popular slander which Socrates suggests originated with Aristophanes (19c). Socrates does not directly address the charge, so Plato's *Apology* is of interest here only because it confirms the integrity of the fragment *ton hêttô logon kreittô poiein.*[11] The reference to Aristophanes, on the other hand, is both useful and important.

Aristophanes' *Clouds* portrayed Socrates as a leading Sophist whose school taught two "logics" (*logoi*): the "worse" (*hêttôn*) and the "better" (*kreittôn*).[12] Most commentators agree that Aristophanes used Socrates as his central character for primarily dramatic purposes, and that his portrayal was not necessarily historically accurate.[13] Having lived his whole life in Athens, Socrates was well known to Athenian audiences, and on stage presented an unmistakable figure "with his snub nose, bulging eyes, rolling gait and continuous, insatiable questioning."[14] Furthermore, Socrates was well known for his association with other Sophists and for sharing their interest in a variety of subjects. It should not be surprising that Socrates was presented as a representative Sophist, but it does not necessarily follow that Socrates held a doctrine identified with the phrase *ton hêttô logon kreittô poiein.* At least there is no evidence other than that in Aristophanes suggesting that he did.

Aristophanes' play is noteworthy because it appears to be an account (albeit perverse) of Protagoras' two-*logoi* doctrine and of the stronger/weaker *logoi* "promise."[15] The *Clouds* speaks initially of two *logoi* which are, in turn, described as *hêttôn* and *kreittôn* (line 112). Most commentators have agreed that the reference here is to Protagoras.[16] B. B. Rogers suggested that it might have been considered rude to have a distinguished foreign visiting Sophist portrayed as the butt of an entire comedy, and hence Socrates was made the target instead. It is at least as likely that Socrates was selected because he was well known and easily caricatured.[17]

Once a better understanding of Protagoras' fragment has been provided, I will return to Aristophanes' *Clouds* to try to identify its authentically Protagorean elements. For the moment it is sufficient to note that the sources traditionally relied upon for interpretations of Protagoras' stronger/weaker fragment were hostile to the Sophists' doctrines, and hence cannot be considered wholly reliable as historians of Protagoras' thinking. The conservative Aristophanes opposed the Sophists' challenge to tradition and was writing a bawdy farce. Hence both his agenda and his medium were possible sources of distortion and exaggeration. Both Plato and Aristotle were seeing Protagoras through their respective philosophical "terministic screens," again with agendas apparently at odds with that of Protagoras.[18] Accordingly, it is understandable that the traditional interpretation of Protagoras' promise has been pejorative. However, armed with an awareness of Plato's and Aristotle's biases, and equipped with what appears to be the original Greek of Protagoras' promise, an alternative interpretation is possible.

THE POSITIVE INTERPRETATION

The category of translations I call positive renders the fragment "to make the weaker argument stronger."[19] Translating the fragment accordingly makes its interpretation far more comprehensible in terms of fifth-century thinking. Specifically, the stronger/weaker fragment is best understood as companion to the two-*logoi* fragment. Of the two *logoi* in opposition concerning any given experience, one is—at any given time—dominant or stronger, while the other is submissive or weaker. Protagoras claimed to teach the ability to make the weaker *logos* stronger; that is, to challenge the relationship of stronger and weaker between conflicting *logoi*.

A positive reading of the fragment is incompatible with the somewhat sinister reading found in Aristotle. The pejorative interpretation suggests a perverse motivation on Protagoras' part—to want purposely to select arguments he *knew* to be base in order to make them merely *appear* better. Giovanni Reale's translation of the fragment as "make the stronger argument weaker" reflects a belief in such motivation, but his (otherwise faithful) translation reverses the word order to fit his conception of Protagoras. Virtually everything known of Protagoras (including all of Aristotle's other references) suggests that ethically he was a conservative and a traditionalist. In both dialogues where he is a major figure Plato treats him with respect, despite Plato's general opposition to the Sophists.[20] Certainly if Protagoras had not been a person of high moral

107

character, or if his teachings had advocated an amoral relativism, his opponents would have seized the opportunity to rebuke him publicly.[21] On the contrary, Plato has Socrates note that Protagoras enjoyed forty years of uninterrupted success and that his reputation was untarnished (*Meno* 91e). In short, Aristotle's portrayal of Protagoras' stronger/ weaker *logoi* doctrine fails to square with Protagoras' known doctrines, the history of the words he used, and what is known of the historical Protagoras.

The most obvious influence on Protagoras' stronger/weaker fragment is Heraclitus. The connection between Protagoras' stronger/weaker fragment and Heraclitus' thinking is clearest when the former is juxtaposed with the Heraclitean notion of flux. According to Philip Wheelwright's reconstruction of Heraclitus' fragments, Heraclitus held that "everything flows and nothing abides; everything gives way and nothing stays fixed."[22] The most famous example of *panta rhei* in Heraclitus was his alleged claim that "one cannot step twice into the same river," for "as one steps into the same rivers, new waters are flowing on."[23] For Heraclitus the natural state of affairs was strife or conflict between opposites, which modern commentators have interpreted as an explanation of change: "To him every change is a knock-down battle between ontological opposites, and there is no referee—neither a Platonic higher Form nor an Aristotelian 'underlying substance'—that can be regarded as standing logically outside the process."[24] As Havelock has argued, interpreting Heraclitus' fragments as a doctrine concerning the process of change is somewhat anachronistic, since a term for "change" was not brought into currency until the time of Plato and Aristotle: "Elementary as the conception of change, or, for that matter, of process, in the abstract may seem, it would appear that its formulation presented some difficulty."[25] By Protagoras' time there was an embryonic conception of change as the shifting or swapping of opposites.[26] An exemplary Heraclitean passage indicating, *sans* verbs, his understanding of change is "cold warms up, warm cools off, moist parches, dry dampens."[27]

The idea that change (or interchange) was the result of a battle between opposites became a commonplace in Greek thought, including Plato and Aristotle. Influenced by Heraclitus, a variety of fifth-century medical writers believed that health was the maintenance of the proper balance of opposites. Illness was characterized as the dominance of the wrong opposite: "For example, hunger is a disease, as everything is called a disease which makes a man suffer. What then is the remedy for hunger? That which makes hunger to cease. This is eating; so that by eating must hunger be cured. Again, drink stays thirst; and again repletion is cured by depletion, depletion by repletion, fatigue by rest. To sum up in a single sentence, *opposites are cures for opposites*."[28] Similarly, another Hippocratic author described the "new" theory in medicine as prescribing the healer to "counteract cold with hot, hot with cold, moist with dry and dry with moist"; since the illness "was caused by one of the opposites, the other opposite ought to be a specific [cure]."[29]

The parallel between the logic of these writers and Protagoras is striking. Though none of the medical writers used quite the same words as Protagoras did, there is an affinity between their theory for cures and the idea of making a weaker opposite stronger. It is true that the medical writers were far from unanimous regarding the theory of opposite cures, just as the Sophists were far from unanimous in their approaches to *logos*.[30] Nevertheless, the texts of the fifth-century medical writers provide ample evidence that a Heraclitean interpretation of the stronger/ weaker fragment is plausible.

The evidence adduced so far suggests that what Protagoras had in mind with the stronger/weaker fragment was the strengthening of a preferred (but weaker) *logos* for a less preferable (but temporarily dominant) *logos* of the same "experience." Protagoras' apology in the *Theaetetus* is strong evidence for such an interpretation, and it reinforces the connection between Protagoras and contemporary medical writers:

> By a wise man I mean precisely a man who can change any one of us, when what is bad appears and is to him, and make what is good appear and be to him. . . . To a sick man his food appears sour and is so; to the healthy man it is and appears the opposite. . . . What is wanted is a change to the opposite condition, because the other state is better. . . . Whereas the physician produces a change by means of drugs, the Sophist does it by discourse [*logoi*] (*Theaetetus* 166d–167a).

The positive view of Protagoras' claim to make the weaker *logos* stronger has the support of several modern commentators. Kerferd has hypothesized that "it is possible that Protagoras associated with the two-*logoi* principle the prescription attributed to him by Aristotle 'to make the lesser (or "the weaker") argument the stronger.' This may have been what the Sophist was expected to do when altering a man's opinions for the better."[31] Untersteiner also interprets the fragment positively, as is reflected in his rendering of it as "to change the lesser possibility of knowledge into a greater possibility of knowledge."[32] Untersteiner's rendering is better characterized as a modern reformulation than as a translation. However, noting what is wrong with his reformulation is a useful heuristic: by overstressing an epistemological reading of the fragment, Untersteiner indirectly provided a warning against an overly ontological reading. Both readings are misleading, since for the Greeks "knowing" and "being" were intertwined notions.[33] Modern thinking tends to separate cognition, perception, and experience into different categories and hence risks missing the point that the idea of substituting one *logos* for another was applicable to a broad array of "treatments"—from changing a city's conception of what is just to a person's experience of food.

A. T. Cole's interpretation of Protagoras' fragment is positive as well. In his view making a weak *logos* stronger meant making one argument prevail over another and hence improving the situation. The link between *logos* as discourse and as account of the world is well documented. Cole supports the applicability of the two senses of *logos* in his interpretation of Protagoras with Protagorean-sounding examples from fifth-century drama: "In Euripides *Suppliants* 486–93 the Theban messenger complains that mankind knows peace as a better *logos* but prefers war instead; in *Phoenissae* 559–60 Jocasta speaks of a patriotic and tyrannical course of action as the two *logoi* which confront Eteocles."[34] Cole also cites the Sophist Prodicus' famous speech "The Choice of Heracles" (as reported by Xenophon), which contrasted the two *logoi* of pleasure and virtue: "Heracles' choice is between two arguments, but also between the two ways of life to which these arguments are linked."[35] In each instance the two *logoi* in conflict represent arguments as well as external situations (peace vs. war, for example) between which a choice must be made.

The multivocal character of *logos* was diminished in the decades following Protagoras, especially as Plato and Aristotle dramatically increased the quantity and specificity of philosophical terminology. As *logos* in Plato and Aristotle became understood as primarily linguistic, Protagoras' promise could be reduced from a theory closely linking speech, thought, and human condition to an apparently amoral argumentative boast.

THE EVIDENCE OF ARISTOPHANES' *CLOUDS*

A reexamination of Aristophanes' *Clouds* provides further evidence for a positive interpretation, and it suggests an explanation for how

110

Protagoras' doctrine could be reinterpreted as perverse. The chief dramatic vehicle of *Clouds* is a clash between two personified *logoi*, one representing traditional education and pieties, and one representing the new sophistic teachings. Some versions of Aristophanes' play have the two competing *logoi* named *Dikaios* and *Adikos*. W. J. M. Starkie translated these terms with their traditional Greek meanings of just and unjust, respectively, while Rogers translated them right and wrong, and Arrowsmith as philosophy and sophistry.[36] However, recent scholars have adopted the position that *Dikaios* and *Adikos* were later emendations of the text and were not the words used by Aristophanes.[37] The surviving scholia are in conflict, but at least three surviving manuscripts have the *logoi* named *kreittôn* and *hêttôn*, as found in Protagoras' fragment.[38]

Evidence internal to the text of *Clouds* also suggests that the two *logoi* were named *kreittôn* and *hêttôn*. The expression *dikaios logos* never appears in the dialogue, and references to the unjust *logos* are usually preceded by a reference to the two *logoi* as the *kreittôn logos* and the *hêttôn logos* (112ff., 882ff.). The two *logoi* refer to themselves and each other at three different times as *kreittôn* and *hêttôn* (893ff., 990, 1038), and other characters refer to the two *logoi* with the same words (1338, 1444, 1451).

In addition to textual evidence favoring *kreittôn* and *hêttôn* as the names of the two *logoi*, there is also reason to doubt the choice of *dikaios* and *adikos*. The unjust *logos* in Aristophanes was not as abstract as the concept of *dikaiosunê* (justice-as-a-virtue) as used in the Platonic dialogues. Aristophanes used the term in the traditional Homeric sense of paying what is due. Indeed, the *logos* sometimes referred to in the *Clouds* as unjust is consulted on precisely the issue of how to avoid paying one's debts. Aristophanes, though he was clearly attacking the Sophists, was not necessarily claiming that the Sophists represented a general abstract force of injustice, but rather that they were not really giving Athens what they advertised: knowledge and *aretê*.

Once it is accepted that the original names given by Aristophanes to the two *logoi* were *kreittôn* and *hêttôn*, two facts about Protagoras' teaching become clear. First, his point of view was obviously important and sufficiently well known to enable Aristophanes to use it as a central dramatic vehicle. Second, the portrayal of the two *logoi* gives some indication of the content of the viewpoint, as long as Aristophanes' dramatic intent is taken into consideration.

The famous contest between the two *logoi* is both a battle of words and a conflict between two ways of life. The dominant way of life (*kre-*

ittôn logos) is based on conservative pieties, the most relevant of which are respect for traditional music and poetry (964ff.), acceptance of mythology (902ff.), and respect for elders (963, 981ff., 993). The *hêttôn logos* seeks to defeat the *kreittôn logos* and thereby replace it. Innovation challenges musical tradition (969ff.), poetry is challenged by rational argumentation (passim, but especially 317ff., 942ff., 1003, 1058ff., 1109), mythology is challenged by agnosticism and cynicism (1048ff., 1080ff., 1470ff., 1506–9), and moral nihilism in general challenges traditional values (1020ff., 1039ff., 1061). If students follow the teaching of the *hêttôn logos,* they will become Sophists (1111, 1308–9), and the primary skill taught is that of persuasive speaking (239, 260ff., 1077). Through the power of persuasive speaking and correct analysis (*orthôs diairôn,* 742) the old way of life will be overthrown.

There are a number of textual clues indicating that Protagoras and his doctrines were targets of Aristophanes' bombast. Agnosticism is described in terms borrowed from Protagoras' famed "concerning the gods" aphorism (247, 367, 903). A number of phrases refer to two *logoi,* usually in opposition (112, 244, 882, 886, 938, 1336). There is a passage that makes fun of the ambiguity of *metron*—a key word in Protagoras' human-measure fragment (638ff.). Another passage pokes fun at Protagoras' apparently original analysis of gender-based word endings (659–93; cf. Aristotle, *Rhetoric* 1407b). There also are two passages that document the link between Heraclitus and Protagoras; one refers to presenting "whatever is foul to be fair, and whatever is fair foul,"[39] and another in which the discussion centers on whether the same person or day can be both new and old (1178–84). And, as was noted earlier, there are many references to Protagoras' *kreittôn logos* and *hêttôn logos.*

The method of the *kreittôn logos* and *hêttôn logos* represented by Aristophanes appears authentically Protagorean. Through persuasive speaking a dominant *logos* is supplanted by its opposing *logos,* which is the equivalent of swapping one way of life, experience, or state of being for another. The Protagorean promise to make *ton hêttô logon kreittô* is, however, dangerously vague. Although Plato's examples portray Protagoras as interested in making changes that were considered desirable by all, and despite the fact that in general the Greeks recognized one of each opposing pair as more desirable, Aristophanes' treatment links the weaker *logos* with unjust acts and hence gives a moral flavor to the terms *hêttô* and *kreittô.* The needs of most non–book-oriented audiences probably led Protagoras to craft his sayings using terms that were common and easily remembered, hence the homophonic *kreittôn* and *hêttôn.* But the very richness of possible meanings (Kahn's "linguistic density") of such terms also makes them susceptible to perverse reinterpretation. Hence one *logos* could be rendered as morally inferior (worse) as well as in relative existential submission to a *kreittôn logos,* as in Aristophanes. Or, a *logos* could be represented as less true or probable as well as less persuasive compared to a *kreittôn logos,* as in Aristotle. Aristophanes was able to be true to Protagoras' method while standing Protagoras' moral content on its head.

To summarize, the Aristotelian pejorative interpretation and translation is flawed, making sense only in conceptual frameworks such as Aristophanes' and Aristotle's, which prejudged Protagoras' agenda as morally bankrupt. Read in light of the two-*logoi* fragment and with careful attention to mid-fifth-century usage of *kreittô* and *hêttô,* the stronger/weaker *logoi* fragment is better translated according to the Heraclitean positive interpretation. Such a rendering understands "making the weaker account [*logos*] stronger" as advocating the strengthening of a preferred (but weaker) *logos* to challenge a less preferable (but temporarily dominanat) *logos* of the same experience.

PROTAGORAS' INFLUENCE ON PLATO AND ARISTOTLE

I want now to repeat and extend my earlier claim that Protagoras was a transitional figure between "compositional" and "attributional" patterns and logics of explanation. Plato's and Aristotle's explanation of objects' changing attributes was an obvious conceptual advance beyond Heraclitus' poetic descriptions of the shifting or swapping of opposites. In fact, the explanations found in Plato and Aristotle suggest a Protagorean influence.

During the fourth century *logos* took on a more exclusively linguistic connotation. Hence, Plato and Aristotle used different terms to describe an external situation or an object's attributes that, during the fifth century, might have been covered by the word *logos.* Their descriptions of how situations or objects change resonate with Protagoras' notion of stronger and weaker *logoi.* In the *Timaeus* (57a) Plato states that "in the transition" (alteration) of fire, water, and earth, "the weaker [*hêttôn*] is fighting against the stronger [*kreittoni*]." Aristotle describes the four basic qualities (hot/cold, dry/moist) as opposites in conflict. When fire becomes air and air becomes water, it is because the dry has been overcome by or prevailed over (*kratêthen*) the moist, and the hot by the

113

cold.[40] Aristotle describes that relative status of opposing qualities as prevailing (*kratein*) versus corrupted, destroyed, or ruined (*phthora*). Like Protagoras' *kreittôn* and *hêttôn*, *kratein* and *phthora* are metaphorical extensions of Homeric battle references, and the two sets of terms appear to function in parallel fashion to describe competing states of being.

A major part of Aristotle's solution to the problem of explaining change and "becoming" were his concepts of potential (*dynamis*) and actual (*energeia*).[41] Contrary qualities and attributes for both animate and inanimate objects were described as relating as potential versus actual. For example, both heavy and light are potentialities for an object, but only one is actual at any given moment (*On the Heavens* 307b31ff.), and knowing and not-knowing are described as actually knowing versus potentially knowing (*Physics* 255a35–b5). Aristotle used his actual/potential pair to describe a wide variety of different states of being (see *Metaphysics* 1071a), but when the pair was employed to explain the logical relationship between actual qualities and their potential opposites (called "privations"), there was clearly an indebtedness to Protagoras' notion of dominant and submissive *logoi*. The parallel is further bolstered by the fact that in Aristotle's view, as in Protagoras', there typically was little question about which of an opposing pair of qualities was to be preferred.[42]

It is not possible to prove that Protagoras was transitional in that his stronger/weaker *logoi* fragment directly contributed to the development of Plato's and Aristotle's thinking concerning contrary qualities and attributes. However, the evidence is adequate to establish that Protagoras' doctrine extended Heraclitean explanation in such a way that there remained only a small step between Protagoras' *logoi* and the Platonic/Aristotelian "qualities."

NOTES

1. Lane Cooper, *The Rhetoric of Aristotle* (Englewood Cliffs, NJ: Prentice-Hall, 1932), 177. On the quality of Cooper's translation see Thomas M. Conley, "The Greekless Reader and Aristotle's *Rhetoric*," *QJS* 65 (1979): 74–79.
2. Keith V. Erickson, *Plato: True and Sophistic Rhetoric* (Amsterdam: Rodopi, 1979), 10–11; Alexander Sesonske, "To Make the Weaker Argument Defeat the Stronger," *JHP* 6 (1968): 218; Guthrie, *HGP III*, 377.
3. Gregory Vlastos, *Plato's "Protagoras"* (Indianapolis: Bobbs-Merrill, 1956), xiii.
4. J. H. Freese, *Aristotle, "Art" of Rhetoric* (Cambridge, MA: Harvard U. Press, 1926), 335; Roberts' translation is in Jonathan Barnes, *The Complete Works of Aristotle*, (Princeton: Princeton U. Press, 1984), 2:2235.

5. Sesonske, "To Make," passim. Dupréel's paraphrase is: "Protagoras recommandait son art comme le moyen de faire en sorte que 'le discours le plus faible devînt le plus fort'" (*Sophistes*, 39).

6. Line 1047, trans. Alan H. Sommerstein, *Aristophanes: Clouds* (Warminster: Aris and Phillips, 1982), 111. On Protagoras' book "On Wrestling" see Ernst Heitsch, "Ein Buchtitel des Protagoras," *Hermes* 97 (1969): 292–96 (= Classen, *Sophistik*, 298–305).

7. Since the translator's goal to is to reflect the context Aristotle provided for Protagoras' "promise," it is not surprising that the resulting translation is pejorative. Few translators add the sort of qualification found in Freese, *Aristotle*, 334n: "This utterance of Protagoras gave particular offence as apparently implying that the weaker cause was really identical with the worse, so that to support it was to support injustice. But, considering the high moral character ascribed to Protagoras, it seems more probable to take the formula as a statement of the aim of all ancient orators—how to overcome stronger arguments by arguments weaker in themselves."

8. E. M. Cope, *The Rhetoric of Aristotle with a Commentary* (Cambridge: Cambridge U. Press, 1877), 2:321. For Cope's view of the Sophists see his articles in *Journal of Classical and Sacred Philology* 1 (1854): 145–88; 2 (1855): 129–69; 3 (1856): 34–80, 252–88.

9. C. J. Classen, "Aristotle's Picture of the Sophists," in Kerferd, *Legacy*.

10. Benjamin Jowett, *The Dialogues of Plato* (London: Macmillan 1892), 402; H. N. Fowler, *Plato* (Cambridge, MA: Harvard U. Press, 1914), 1:75.

11. Cf. Sesonske, "To Make."

12. B. B. Rogers, *Aristophanes* (Cambridge, MA: Harvard U. Press, 1924), 1:275.

13. Ibid., 263–64; W. Arrowsmith, *Aristophanes: The Clouds* (Ann Arbor: U. of Michigan Press, 1962), 3; K. J. Dover, *Aristophanes: Clouds* (Oxford: Clarendon Press, 1968), xxxii–lvii; Sommerstein, *Clouds*, 3. Cf. W. J. M. Starkie, *The Clouds of Aristophanes* (London: Macmillan, 1911), xlvi–l.

14. Guthrie, *HGP III*, 371.

15. Dover, *Clouds*, lvii.

16. Guthrie, *HGP III*, 371; Sommerstein, *Clouds*, 165–66; Starkie, *Clouds*, 37.

17. For Rogers' suggestion and Guthrie's reply, see Guthrie, *HGP III*, 371 n3.

18. Kenneth Burke, "Terministic Screens," *Language as Symbolic Action* (Berkeley: U. of California Press, 1966), 44–62.

19. A number of translations, including my own in the first edition of this book, supply what is believed to be an implicit second definite article: "to make the weaker argument *the* stronger." As Michael Gagarin argues, the weaker *logos* may overcome the stronger (is it does in Aristophanes' *Clouds*), but it is likely that Protagoras had a pedagogical interest in making the weaker *logos* stronger, regardless of whether it ultimately wins. See his *Antiphon the Athenian* (Austin: U. of Texas Press, 2002), 24–26. Cf. Michael J. O'Brien's translation in *The Older Sophists*, ed. Rosamond Kent Sprague (Columbia: U. of South Carolina Press, 1972), 21; Kathleen Freeman, *Ancilla to the Presocratic Philosophers* (Cambridge, MA: Harvard U. Press, 1978), 126. H. Gomperz translates the fragment as "die schwächere Rede zur stärkeren zu machen" (*SR*, 135).

20. Guthrie, *HGP III*, 37, 39n.

21. Theodor Gomperz, *Greek Thinkers* (London: John Murray, 1901), 1:473.

22. Philip Wheelwright, *Heraclitus* (New York: Atheneum, 1974), 29; see also Jonathan Barnes, *The Presocratic Philosophers* (London: Routledge and Kegan Paul, 1982), 65.

23. Charles H. Kahn, *The Art and Thought of Heraclitus* (Cambridge: Cambridge U. Press, 1979), 166–69 (fr. 50).

24. Wheelwright, *Heraclitus*, 34; see also Kahn, *Heraclitus*, 204–10.

25. Eric A. Havelock, "The Linguistic Task of the Presocratics," *Language and Thought in Early Greek Philosophy*, ed. Kevin Robb (LaSalle, IL: Hegeler Institute, 1983), 33.

26. Ibid., 33–37.

27. Kahn, *Heraclitus*, 165–66.

28. *Breaths* 1, trans. W. H. S. Jones, *Hippocrates* (Cambridge, MA: Harvard U. Press, 1923), 2:229; emphasis added.

29. *Ancient Medicine* 13, Ibid., 1:35.

30. Charles H. Kahn, *Anaximander and the Origins of Greek Cosmology* (New York: Columbia U. Press, 1960), 130–33.

31. G. B. Kerferd, "Protagoras," *Encyclopedia of Philosophy* (New York: Macmillan, 1967), 6:506. Though not explicitly discussing the stronger/weaker fragment, Adolfo Levi suggests that Protagoras maintained that "the function of the rhetor is to replace the less perfect by better laws" ("The Ethical and Social Thought of Protagoras," *Mind* 49 [1940]: 302).

32. Untersteiner, *Sophists*, 53. From the Italian: "ridurre la minore possibilità di conoscenza a una maggiore possibilità di conoscenza."

33. Guthrie, *HGP III*, 187n.

34. A. T. Cole, "The Relativism of Protagoras," *YCS* 22 (1972): 34.

35. Ibid.

36. Starkie, *Clouds*; Rogers, *Aristophanes*, vol. 1; Arrowsmith, *Clouds*.

37. Dover, *Clouds*, lvii–lviii; Sommerstein, *Clouds*, 95–117.

38. Dover, *Clouds*, lvii–lviii.

39. 1020–21, trans. Sommerstein, *Clouds*, 109.

40. Aristotle, *On Generation and Corruption* 331a-b.

41. Guthrie, *HGP VI*, 119–29.

42. G. E. R. Lloyd, *Polarity and Analogy* (Cambridge: Cambridge U. Press, 1966), 51–65; Guthrie, *HGP VI*, 121–22.

7

THE "HUMAN-MEASURE" FRAGMENT

The Greek text of the human-measure fragment is: Πάντων χρημάτων μέτρον ἐστὶν ἄνθρωπος, τῶν μὲν ὄντων ὡς ἔστιν, τῶν δὲ οὐκ ὄντων ὡς οὐκ ἔστιν (DK 80 B1). Given the fame of this doctrine and that it is widely quoted in virtually identical language, there is no reason to doubt it represents Protagoras' own words.[1] The world view implicit in the human-measure fragment is substantially the same as that posited by the two fragments already analyzed. In Kahn's words, the human-measure fragment *resonates* with the ideas expressed in the two-*logoi* and stronger/weaker fragments, hence viewing the three fragments together amplifies an understanding of each.

Of extant fragments by Older Sophists, perhaps none is as important and as difficult to interpret and understand as Protagoras' human-measure fragment. Modern commentators have described the statement as being the heart and soul of the sophistic movement, and one poet went so far as to say: "'*Pantôn anthrôpos metron*' 'Man is the measure of all things.' Twenty-five hundred years later we sometimes wonder whether Protagoras didn't after all summarize everything in just three words."[2] The statement's ambiguity has allowed it to be all things to all people, and it has a legacy of multiple and contradictory interpretations. Both the brevity of the fragment and the lack of corroborative elaboration by Protagoras have led to controversies over its meaning.[3]

117

RECONSIDERING THE STANDARD TRANSLATION

The most common translation of the human-measure fragment is: "Of all things the measure is Man,[4] of the things that are, that they are; and of the things that are not, that they are not." Rendering the human-measure fragment into English is a relatively simple task, but interpreting its doctrinal content is difficult. The first step is to ascertain the most likely meanings of the words in the fifth century. The second step is to identify possible novel usages and interpret them in light of probable conceptual antecedents.

The difficulty with the words *pantôn chrêmatôn* is similar to the problem of translating *pragmata* in the two-*logoi* fragment. The word *chrêmata* was common, and can be given a host of different meanings depending on context. The dominant sense of *chrêmata* is "things," though it can be used to indicate "goods" or "property" (concrete usage) and "matter" or "affair" (more abstract usage). "Things" is the best translation of the human-measure fragment because a generic meaning is indicated (since there are no other contextual clues), and because *chrêmatôn* is preceded by *pantôn* (all, every, manifold), suggesting that Protagoras had in mind the widest possible range of objects.

It is unclear whether Protagoras saw any difference between *pragmata* and *chrêmata*. Discussions of the human-measure fragment in Sextus, Plato, and Aristotle typically use *chrêmata*, though some paraphrases substitute *pragmata* (DK 80 A13, 14, 16). It may have been that Protagoras used the word *chrêmata* because it implied things that one uses or needs, such as goods or property, which derive their status as things from their relationship to humans.[5] Significantly, such use of *chrêmata* can be found in Heraclitus, who generally used *panta* by itself to convey the notion of "all things."[6] If *pantôn* were used here abstract-theoretically and *chrêmata* in the common and concrete sense of "things," then their juxtaposition in the statement may have been designed to underscore the breadth of "things" of which humans are the measure. On the other hand, it is possible that the choice of *chrêmata* over *pragmata* was based on acoustical, rather than semantic, criteria. Though it is not possible to know with precision the reasons for Protagoras' choice, it is sufficient to note that the construction *pantôn chrêmatôn* clearly conveys the widest possible range of things as the subject of the statement. Untersteiner was not far off the mark when he translated both *pragmata* and *chrêmata* as "experiences."[7]

Metron is usually translated as "measure." In addition to the obvious literal sense of assessing quantity, "measure" can also refer to appropriate proportion or ordering. There are three uses of *metron* (or derivations) in the fragments of Heraclitus, all of which equate measure with the balance and order of nature. One of them involves the regulation of opposites.[8] Hence, Protagoras' claim that humans are the measure of all things is provocative. The statement challenges its hearers to consider the ways in which humans are "measures." Sextus equated *metron* with *kritêrion,* meaning criterion or standard (DK 80 A14). Hermias paraphrased with the words *horos,* meaning standard or limit—later used by Aristotle to mean a logical term or definition—and *krisis,* meaning judgment or decision (DK 80 A16). Plato likewise suggested that by being "measures" humans are the *kritêrion* or the *kritês* (judge) of things (*Theaetetus* 160c, 178b–c).

The only classical evidence to challenge a broad reading of *metron* appears in a passage of Plato's *Theaetetus* in which the human-measure statement is given an exclusively perceptual interpretation (152). However, Plato later contradicted himself by relying on the judgmental sense of *metron* (*Theaetetus* 160c, 178b–c). The weight of the evidence suggests, therefore, that Protagoras was fundamentally concerned with the *judgments* of humans, in which perception plays only a part.[9]

Estin and *einai* have been used interchangeably by various classical doxographers of Protagoras' human-measure statement. Both are forms of *eimi* (to be) and are typically translated simply as "is" and "to be," respectively. It is an error, however, to assume that Protagoras' use of "is" here is either the "is" of identity, as in "human(ity) = measure," or a purely copulative use of "is," linking subject with predicate, as in "human(ity) is the measure." Charles Kahn and Eric Havelock have pointed out that such uses of the verb "to be" were not fully realized in fifth-century Greek.[10]

It is possible that the appearance of *estin* or *einai* in the human-measure fragment was either for the acoustical enhancement of the statement or to emphasize the status of *anthrôpos,* as in "of all things the measure remains human(ity)."[11] One possible intent was to make the first clause into what Kahn calls an "emphatic assertion," which can be rendered in English as "the measure is-truly human(ity)."[12] That *einai* is not crucial to the meaning of the first clause may be seen by the fact that the paraphrase *pantôn anthrôpos metron* makes perfect sense in Greek without it (cf. DK 80 A16).

Anthrôpos is traditionally translated as "man" and can refer to an individual human or to humanity as a collective. Despite Theodor Gom-

The Major Fragments of Protagoras

perz's insistence that "no unprejudiced reader" would deny that Protagoras meant anything other than humanity as a whole, most scholars agree either that he meant human in an individual sense,[13] or that he intended *both* meanings.[14] It is worth noting that when Plato and Aristotle wrote of the philosophical significance of the human-measure statement, they alternated between the individual and generic senses of *anthrôpos*.[15] Since Protagoras could have constructed the human-measure statement in such a way as to say explicitly all humans or any human, the most reasonable interpretation is to assume he intended the word *anthrôpos* to convey both senses.

The first clause of Protagoras' aphorism combined conventional terminology in a way that was (and is) both provocative and memorable. Though it can be rendered simply and literally into English as "Human(ity) is the measure of all things," some of the original power of the Greek is lost. A better, though more cumbersome, translation is: "Of everything and anything the measure [truly-is] human(ity)."

The remainder of the human-measure statement illustrates the claim of the first clause: *tôn men ontôn hôs estin, tôn de ouk ontôn hôs ouk estin.* The traditional translation is "of the things that are, that they are; and of the things that are not, that they are not." Such a translation assumes the word "things" is implied by the words *tôn men* and *tôn de.* The terms when paired are used to mark off correlative phrases, as in "the former ... the latter," "the one ... the other." In Protagoras' statement the pair can be read either as referring back to the *chrêmata* of the first clause, as in "of the things ..." or as generic articles, as in "that which. ..." Either reading can be used without seriously changing the meaning of the statement.

The relative adverb *hôs* is alternatively translated as "how" or "that." The pivotal issue is: Was Protagoras contending that humans are the measure of "how" things are (essence), or that humans are the measure that determines "that" they are (existence)? Both positions have avid supporters.[16] Untersteiner suggests a compromise that makes sense to a modern reader: "If *hôs* expresses *that* certain experiences exist, it cannot escape the inquiry concerning the *way* in which these make themselves recognizable: their existence implies their manifestation."[17] Unfortunately, the fact that Untersteiner's solution makes sense to modern readers does not mean Protagoras would have made the same gloss. The choice between reading the human-measure fragment with an existential "that" or an essentialist "how" creates a false, anachronistic dichotomy. A clear conceptualization of essence cannot be documented prior to

120

Plato's notion of the Forms, and renderings of the Greek verb "to be" as existential are questionable.[18]

Accordingly, the translation I favor is "that," but without the existential baggage usually attached. *Hôs* is used in the fragment as generically as are the paired terms *tôn men* and *tôn de*. The semantic content of *hôs* mirrors that of *tôn men* and *tôn de*. Hence if *tôn men* refers to "the things" implied in *chrêmata*, so would *hôs*. If *tôn men* and *tôn de* are generic articles, as I will argue shortly, *hôs* would also refer to "that which."

The remainder of the statement is dominated by four occurrences of the verb "to be." The most common translations imply a purely existential interpretation of *ontôn* and *estin*. That is, "Human(ity) is a measure of all things" in that humans gauge their existence. However, it is just such an existential rendering of the Greek verb "to be" that has come under attack in recent philological studies by Kahn and Havelock. Kahn has argued that the construction of "to be" in Protagoras' human-measure fragment is a prototypical case of the veridical use of *eimi*. The use of multiple forms of *eimi* (*ontôn* and *estin*), the symmetrical balance of affirmative and negative expressions of *eimi*, and the use of "to be" in conjunction with a verb of judging (understood from *metron*) are, to Kahn, signs that Protagoras' use of "to be" is philosophical and veridical.[19] Accordingly, phrases such as *hôs esti* are translated generically as "what is" or "that which is the case." This can refer to any proposition or fact whatsoever: "In the philosophic formula the verb occurs twice: once for the fact as such (*ta onta*), once for the fact as recognized and affirmed in human speech or cognition (*hôs esti*). In modern terminology we may say that here the participle *to on* represents an arbitrary fact; the finite verb *hôs esti* represents an arbitrary proposition (or the content of any judgment)."[20]

Accordingly, I translate the human-measure fragment as: "Of everything and anything the measure [truly-is] human(ity): of that which is, that it is the case; of that which is not, that it is not the case."

THE FRAGMENT AS A RESPONSE TO PARMENIDES

There is a strong consensus that Protagoras' human-measure aphorism and the book for which it was the opening line were in response to Eleatic extremism as spawned by Parmenides.[21] The most authoritative evidence comes from the ancient Porphyry, who claimed to have memo-

121

rized the passage from Protagoras' book in which arguments are made "against those who propose being as one" (DK 80 B2). Plato's and Aristotle's treatment of Protagoras' human-measure statement in *Theaetetus* and *Metaphysics* respectively also portray it as a response to Eleatic monism.

Evidence internal to the text of Protagoras' human-measure fragment further supports an anti-Eleatic interpretation. Kahn's study of the Greek verb "to be" found that it was exclusively the philosophers who used particular "generic-negative" (my phrase, not Kahn's) constructions of the verb, such as *ouk esti tauta*—"that is not so."[22] Kahn suggested that there was nothing ungrammatical or incorrect about generic-negative constructions of "to be," but they were "full of logical traps."[23] It was just such "logical traps" that were the subject of Parmenides' famous poem. In fact, much of what Parmenides wrote has been described as a systematic analysis of *ouk esti*.[24] Given the rarity of generic-negative constructions of "to be," it is noteworthy that Parmenides' construction *hôs ouk estin* is repeated by Protagoras at the end of his human-measure aphorism.[25]

To understand Protagoras' human-measure fragment, then, it is necessary to comprehend the point of Parmenides' poem. That task is complicated by the fact that there are different interpretations of Parmenides. A tentative synthesis of the interpretations is possible, however, and will make clear the influence of Parmenides on Protagoras.

Some commentators have focused primarily on what would now be called Parmenides' metaphysics. B. A. G. Fuller, for example, portrays Parmenides' poem as a defense of "the Real." Contrary to Presocratics who saw the Real as in flux—everchanging and "becoming"—Parmenides reasoned that Being "is one," all change is thus illusory, and if the senses indicate change, the senses are wrong and ought not be trusted.[26] John Burnet's *Early Greek Philosophy* treats Parmenides' poem as a defense of a monistic physical theory: "What *is*, is a finite, spherical, motionless corporeal *plenum*, and there is nothing beyond it. The appearances of multiplicity and motion, empty space and time, are illusions."[27]

More recent commentators tend to interpret Parmenides as being concerned not only with the nature of reality but also with the appropriate modes of thinking and speaking. G. S. Kirk, J. E. Raven, and Malcolm Schofield say that "Parmenides claims that in any enquiry there are two and only two logically coherent possibilities, which are exclusive—that the subject of the enquiry exists or that it does not exist."[28] On this reading the subject of the poem is not so much Being or Reality as it is any given subject of inquiry. Jonathan Barnes has claimed that Parmenides was concerned with defining the limits of rational discourse. He paraphrased Parmenides' starting point as saying "Whatever we inquire into exists, and cannot not exist."[29]

Two recent full-length studies of Parmenides accept the premise that Parmenides was chiefly concerned with the nature of rational inquiry, and they press the point a step further by claiming that Parmenides' target was the improper use of language. Partially based on Kahn's writings on the Greek "to be," A. P. D. Mourelatos has argued that Parmenides was not concerned with Being, Reality, or Existence as such but with distinguishing two modes of discourse and thought, one positive, which can be represented symbolically as "A is B," and one negative, which can be represented by "A is not B."[30] Parmenides condemned the latter and argued that only the first is comprehensible. Mourelatos' student Scott Austin has portrayed Parmenides' poem as dedicated to exploring the nature of logic. Parmenides is suspicious of most constructions of *ouk esti*, especially any use that could imply sentences of the form "A is B and A is not B."[31]

The later interpretations of Parmenides which deemphasize the strictly metaphysical reading of his poem and emphasize the attention paid to thinking and use of language are on solid methodological footing. The growing mistrust of Aristotle as a reliable historian of his predecessors' doctrines has motivated closer textual analysis and less reliance on commentators centuries removed from the Presocratics. Furthermore, Kahn's and Havelock's writings on the Greek "to be" have forced reconsideration of any interpretation of the Presocratics which imposes a strictly existential translation of *esti* and *ouk esti*.

Havelock's analysis of Parmenides has managed to tie together several lines of interpretation I have just summarized. For Havelock the object of Parmenides' attack (as well as that of most other presocratic philosophers) was mythic-poetic culture itself—the "Homeric state of mind."[32] The conflict between the common sense of the general populace and the presocratic philosophers was a conflict between two contrasting ways of thinking about and understanding the world—the mythic-poetic tradition and the more rationalistic tradition represented by certain Sophists and philosophers. As I suggested in chapter 2, the mythic-poetic state of mind was one whose thought and expression were additive more than subordinate, aggregate more than analytic, close to the human life world, empathetic and participatory more than objectively distanced, and situational more than abstract. Put another way, Homeric mythic-poetic discourse tended toward "additive-amplificatory" ways of thinking, while the new rationalistic prose discourse tended toward "analytical-partitioning" ways of thinking.

As Greek culture evolved, both the style and content of discourse changed. Presocratics such as Parmenides were "poised between literacy and nonliteracy. Their style of composition is a form of mediation between ear and eye. They expect an audience of listeners, yet look forward to a reception at the hand of readers."[33] As many commentators have mentioned, Parmenides' poetic style is awkward and his meaning often obscure. Such awkwardness is understandable once it is recognized that he was struggling to express abstract and analytical ideas using a vocabulary and syntax not geared for such rationalization.

Havelock's argument is that Parmenides and other Presocratics were trying to change the language and thought habits which had been inculcated by the demands of a wholly oral culture for centuries: "The target of [Parmenides'] polemic is not a rival school of thought ... but the commonality of mankind, whose language is erroneous, whose thought is therefore erroneous and whose total experience of the environment is therefore erroneous."[34] The lynchpin of Parmenides' critique of the prevailing, erroneous common sense was his analysis of *einai*, "to be." The mythic-poetic mindset was reflected in statements that were logically impossible to Parmenides. The world described by the poets and perpetuated by the general populace was one of constant change and contradiction where people and things were constantly "becoming" something different. In Parmenides' student Melissus' words the populace believed that "what is warm becomes cold, and what is cold warm; that what is hard turns soft, and what is soft hard; that what is living dies, and that things are born from what lives not; and that all those things are changed."[35] Such thinking was "two-headed" to Parmenides because it implied the same "thing" could both be and not be, it both *is* and *is not*. Parmenides described the general populace as "tossed about, as much deaf as blind, an undiscerning horde, by whom to be and not to be are considered the same and not the same—and the route of all is backward-turning."[36]

Read against a backdrop of what he considered to be intellectual chaos, Parmenides' poem appears as an effort to purify thought and language by demarcating the appropriate uses of *einai*. Though there is legitimate disagreement over precisely to what Parmenides would have

124

granted his approval, there is little doubt that he vigorously opposed certain—if not all—uses of *ouk esti* (is not). Parmenides opposed statements from which one could imply "A is B and not B" because he believed them to assert, incoherently, that A both *is* and *is not*. To understand the world and to talk about it coherently demanded a correct understanding of what "is" implied, and if there was one thing that "is" could not imply to Parmenides it was "is not."[37]

Barnes has described Parmenides' influence on later presocratic thought as "all pervasive."[38] Parmenides' arguments, especially as augmented by his followers, Zeno and Melissus, had to be reckoned with by anyone with pretensions of being a serious thinker in ancient Greece. Protagoras' clash with Parmenides struck at the very heart of the Eleatics' monism and distrust of common sense.

In spite of Parmenides' admonitions against *ouk esti*, Protagoras explicitly stated that people determine what is *not* the case (*hôs ouk estin*) as well as what *is* the case. The Eleatics had declared that people were "two-headed," allowing that "things" could both be and not be. Furthermore, the Eleatics said that the senses were not to be trusted, for the interchange of opposites implies passing from being to not-being, and since that is impossible, sensory evidence to the contrary must be ignored as illusion.[39] Protagoras, on the other hand, openly embraced a sense of not-being with his declaration that human(ity) measures *hôs ouk estin*. Additionally, when read in conjunction with his two-*logoi* and stronger/weaker *logoi* fragments, Protagoras maintained that it was perfectly acceptable and coherent to talk about the interchange of opposites. Parmenides' reasoning was either/or oriented. One could talk either about that which is or that which is not. The latter led to contradiction and incoherence, so only the first option was acceptable. Protagoras' reasoning was both/and oriented. Humans measure both what is and what is not.

While the respects in which Protagoras differed from Parmenides are clear, it is less obvious how Protagoras met Parmenides' objections to *ouk esti* and the problems associated with a Heraclitean ontology. The book for which the human-measure fragment was the opening line is no longer extant. Nonetheless, evidence can be marshaled to support an argument that Protagoras' solution to the conceptual problems associated with contradictory accounts of experience involved the first defense of relativity based on a rudimentary notion of frame of reference.

A DEFENSE OF RELATIVITY

There are several sources of information concerning Protagoras' conceptualization of frame of reference. One of the clearest is a well-known story related by Plutarch concerning a discussion between Pericles and Protagoras (DK 80 A10). A young man, Epitimus of Pharsalus, was killed accidentally with a javelin. Pericles and Protagoras supposedly spent an entire day trying to decide whether one should regard the cause of death as the javelin, the man who threw it, or the supervisor in charge of the grounds. According to Giuseppe Rensi, "In fact the answer to the problem could be any one of the three and be always right according to the point of view—and so according to the person to whom the problem has been submitted."[40] To a doctor the best answer (*orthos logos*) would be the javelin; to a judge in a law court the best answer would be the person who threw it; and to an administrator the best answer would be the supervisor. No single answer can be judged correct in any abstract or absolute sense but only relative to the needs and interests of people directly involved in the experience. The answer is not arbitrary nor merely conventional; it is "objectively correct" according to each frame of reference.

The most thorough exposition of Protagoras' conception of frame of reference is found in Plato's dialogues. Plato's accounts of Protagoras' relativism imply that Protagoras believed the "things" of the world "are" only *relative to* particular frames of reference. To the form "A is B" must be added the notion "for C." The wind may be cold for one person and not cold for another (*Theaetetus* 152b). In either case one can only speak of the wind's coldness relative to someone. The wind must be experienced before declarations of what is the case (*hôs esti*) are possible. Once experienced, or "measured," differing accounts (*logoi*) are possible.

In the dialogues *Protagoras* and *Theaetetus* a number of different accounts (*logoi*) and frames of reference are used as examples of Protagorean relativity. According to Versényi, "We see a diversity of 'things' (fairness, justice, goodness, utility, nourishment, and their opposites) relative to an equal variety of 'measures,' which may be more inclusive (state, species of animals) or less inclusive (parts of humans and things) than the individual."[41] In each case there is a thing–quality (A is B) and a frame of reference that constitutes a "measure" (A is B for C).

How reliable should Plato's account be considered? Plato made it clear in his text that the human-measure statement was a direct quotation from the opening of Protagoras' book *Alêtheia,* or "Truth." The number of other sources that repeat the aphorism verbatim is ample evidence of the accuracy of the human-measure statement. Beyond the statement Plato indicated through various qualifications made by Socrates in the dialogue that the explanation and defense of Protagoras' doctrines were not directly from Protagoras' own writings, but were what Plato imagined Protagoras would have said. Had Protagoras been alive, Socrates admits, "he would have supported his own doctrines on a much grander scale."[42]

How far did Plato stray from Protagoras' own words in his portrayal? No generalization is certain, but evidence can be adduced concerning the faithfulness of the pertinent passages. Plato's subject for the dialogue *Theaetetus* was the nature of knowledge and not Protagoras' "philosophy" as such (unlike the dialogue *Protagoras*). Hence, the reduction of Protagoras' concept of "measure" to perception alone has been widely recognized as a simplification designed to facilitate Plato's attack on those thinkers allegedly equating perception with knowledge.[43] However, Plato's treatment of the "Protagorean" theory of perception cannot be dismissed as merely an irrelevant argument. Plato's example (152b) of differing perceptions of the wind's coldness appears to be authentically Protagorean.[44] Furthermore, Plato's own theory of perception as advanced in the *Timaeus* is very similar to that posited by "Protagoras" in the *Theaetetus*. A number of scholars agree that Protagoras' "secret doctrine" is Plato's own theory of perception, which Plato found acceptable as a physical explanation for sense perception even if it did not satisfy his desire for a philosophical explanation of infallible knowledge.[45]

It is reasonable to infer that Plato's description of a Protagorean theory of perception was not purely a fiction to be discredited. The description could have been based on what Plato believed that Protagoras' doctrines implied. Such a hypothesis is even more plausible when the human-measure fragment is juxtaposed with the two-*logoi* and stronger/weaker *logoi* fragments. The evidence suggests that Protagoras was a transitional figure between compositional and attributional logics of explanation. While Parmenides denied the reality of contrary qualities, and Plato elevated qualities to Forms with their own independent essences, Protagoras' fragments suggest that qualities are directly perceived or experienced by humans and hence "are" not in an abstract sense but "are" relative to people.

Further evidence from the *Theaetetus* supports the argument that Plato's account of a Protagorean notion of frame of reference is reliable.

Throughout the portions of the dialogue discussing his doctrines Protagoras is treated with respect and seriousness. He is ranked with philosophers such as Heraclitus and Empedocles and is portrayed as a "philosophically inclined teacher."[46] Furthermore, Protagoras is treated as *the* representative of philosophers who oppose the doctrines of Parmenides and the Eleatics. According to Michael Gagarin, this is "quite an honor, for it shows that Plato considered the Sophist to be not only a serious thinker, but as important as any of the great philosophers of the past and perhaps even more important."[47]

Given Plato's apparent respect for the seriousness of Protagoras' thinking, it is significant that it is precisely on the matter of relative frames of reference that Protagoras' contribution is made distinctive in the *Theaetetus:* "Shall we say that the wind itself, taken by itself, is cold or not cold? Or shall we accept it from Protagoras that it is cold for the one who feels cold, and not for the one who doesn't?"[48]

In a later passage Plato provides a more detailed explanation of Protagorean relativism: "The object, when it becomes sweet or sour and so on, must become so *to someone:* it cannot become sweet and yet sweet to nobody."[49] The meaning of the passage is clear: thing qualities "are," or "are the case" only for those who "measure" them. Plato continues: "It remains only . . . that *it* and *I* should be or become . . . *for each other;* necessity binds together our existence; but binds neither of us to anything else, nor each of us to himself; so we can only be bound to one another" (160b5).

Most commentators have been content to point out that this passage continues the thesis that perception must be experienced relationally. Two additional points are worth stressing. First, this sentence and those that follow are not limited to sense perception, but to *einai*—"that which is" or "what is the case." Second, Plato's choice of language to describe the relationship between person and thing, subject and object, is revealing. The two are "bound" or "tied" together (from *sundeô*). In Protagoras' time there was not a Greek word for frame of reference or a clear word for relativity. The best that Protagoras and Plato could do was put common words to new metaphorical use to describe an emerging theoretical concept.

The passage continues: "Accordingly, whether we speak of something 'being' or of its 'becoming,' we must speak of it as being or becoming *for someone, or of something or towards something;* but we must not speak . . . of a thing as either being or becoming anything just in and by itself" (160 b–c). Commentators generally have agreed that this passage indicates that Protagoras denied the value of hypothesizing about "things-in-themselves."[50] It made sense to Protagoras only to discuss thing-attributes in relation to people's experience of them, which are by definition relative.

The final bit of evidence I wish to examine in support of the originality of Protagoras' relativism is found in the writings of Sextus Empiricus. Writing around 200 CE, Sextus in his report of Protagoras' philosophy focuses on the human-measure statement. After equating "measure" with "criterion" and *chrêmata* with *pragmata,* he suggests, "Consequently [Protagoras] posits only what appears to each individual, and thus he introduces *relativity.*"[51] Both R. G. Bury and Michael J. O'Brien translate "relativity" from the Greek *to pros ti.*[52] The advantage of such a translation is that it identifies the clearest modern concept implied by the phrase; however, it underestimates the difficulty involved with developing the concept of relativity. The Greek *to* usually translates as the definite article "the," *pros* as "toward," and *ti* as an indefinite pronoun. *Pros ti* is found in Plato's exegesis of Protagoras' doctrine in the passage from the *Theaetetus* quoted extensively above. In that passage (160b9) the phrase is translated as "towards" by Francis M. Cornford, and as "in relation to" by H. N. Fowler and John McDowell.[53] The phrase later appears in Aristotle's *Categories,* from which it is universally translated as the category of relatives: "All such things as are said to be just what they are, *of* or *than* other things, or in some other way *in relation to* something else" (6a36).

What must be recognized is that the phrase *to pros ti* (and its variants) evolved over time. In Plato's writings the phrase appears as a spatial metaphor intended to convey a relationship between thing-attributes and people: the wind is cold *in relation to* someone. Subject and object-quality are "bound" or "tied" together. "What is the case" (*hôs esti*) must be "measured" by *anthrôpos.* In Aristotle the notion that things "are" relative is limited to a specific class of objects called "relatives." By Sextus' time the conceptual vocabulary was far richer than it had been six hundred years earlier, and it was a simpler matter to use the precision afforded by Aristotle's analysis to identify Protagoras retrospectively as a person "introducing relativity."

The final question to be addressed is whether Protagoras' relativism represented radical subjectivism or a positive and objective ontology. The former has been the position of the Platonic and Hegelian traditions of scholarship concerning the Sophists. For example, Bury wrote that

Protagoras' human-measure statement implies that "falsehood has no meaning," hence "objective truth" and "the possibility of knowledge" were rejected by Protagoras.[54] Guthrie described Protagoras' position as "extreme subjectivism" which "logically" led to "moral and political anarchy," and Untersteiner at one point described the doctrine of Protagoras as phenomenalism, a relatively recent philosophical theory that reduces material objects to *sensa*—that which is sensed.[55]

Writers influenced by the scholarly tradition led by Grote tend to characterize Protagoras' relativism as "objective."[56] The objectivist reading takes into consideration the influence of Heraclitus on Protagoras: the wind is really and "objectively" *both* cold and not-cold even though only one of the two accounts (*logoi*) may be experienced by a single person at a given time. The objectivist reading makes the most sense of Plato's treatment of Protagoras in the *Theaetetus,* Aristotle's treatment in the *Metaphysics,* and Sextus' summary in *Outlines of Pyrrhonism.*[57]

If a choice has to be made, the arguments I have offered regarding the probability of Heraclitus' influence on Protagoras suggest that the "objective" label is superior.[58] However, it is important to note respects in which the subjective/objective dichotomy is inappropriate. There are no clear fifth-century Greek terms equivalent to modern notions of subjective and objective. The well-known "sophistic" dichotomy between *nomos* and *physis* cannot be reduced to a subjective/objective dualism; even if it could, there is no clear evidence linking Protagras to the *nomos/physis* controversy.[59] Even in modern times "subjective" can imply a host of meanings with different philosophical implications.[60] If the subject/object pair is reduced to the more concrete concepts of people and things, then Protagoras' answer is clear: the two are "bound," "things" can be "measured" by people in contrasting ways (*logoi*), and a dominant experience (*logos*) of a thing is potentially alterable as an interchange or swapping of opposites.

NOTES

1. Cf. DK 80 A13, 14, 16, 19, 21a. Dupréel translates the fragment as "L'homme est la mesure de toutes choses, de celles qui sont, qu'elles sont, de celles qui ne sont pas, qu'elles ne sont pas" (*Sophistes,* 15). H. Gomperz's "literal sense" translates it as "Das Unterscheidungsmerkmal von Allem ist der Mensch, des Wirklichen, daß es wirklich, des Unwirklichen, daß es unwirklich ist" (*SR,* 204). Untersteiner translates it as "l'uomo è dominatore di tutte le esperienze, in relazione alla fenomenalità di quanto è reale e alla nessuna fenomenalità di quanto è privo di realtà," which Freeman translates as "Man is

the master of all experiences, in regard to the 'phenomenality' of what is real and the 'non-phenomenality' of what is not real" (Untersteinen, *Sophists*, 42). On the authenticity of the fragment see also Michael Gagarin, "The Purpose of Plato's *Protagoras*," *TAPA* 100 (1969): 159 n52.

2. Milton C. Nahm, *Selections from Early Greek Philosophy* (Englewood Cliffs, NJ: Prentice-Hall, 1964), 212; Kerferd, *SM*, 85; Demetrios A. Michalaros, *Protagoras: A Poem of Man* (Chicago: Syndicate Press, 1937), 8.

3. For summaries of the controversies see Untersteiner, *Sophists*, 77–91; Guthrie, *HGP III*, 188–92; Dupréel, *Sophistes*, 14–25; Alfred Neumann, "Die Problematik des Homo-mensura Satzes," *CP* 33 (1938): 368–79 (= Classen, *Sophistik*, 257–70); Lazlo Versényi, "Protagoras' Man-Measure Fragment," *AJP* 83 (1962): 178–84 (= Classen, *Sophistik*, 290–97); Antonio Capizzi, *Protagora* (Firenze: G. C. Sansoni, 1955), 104–27. Capizzi provides nine well-known German and Italian scholars' translations of the human-measure fragment (*Protagora*, 126).

4. Traditions die hard, especially in classical scholarship. A good example is the continued habit of translating *anthrôpos* as "man." Protagoras did not use *anêr* or *andros* (man); he used *anthrôpos*, which can refer to individual human beings or to humanity as a whole (women included). There is no evidence to suggest that Protagoras was any less sexist than other mid-fifth-century males (see Eva C. Keuls, *The Reign of the Phallus: Sexual Politics in Ancient Athens* [New York: Harper, 1985]); but there is no compelling reason to continue the use of the generic "man," while there are good reasons to use more inclusive language in our scholarship. (For an introduction to the relevant arguments I recommend Wendy Martyna, "Beyond the He/Man Approach: The Case for Nonsexist Language," *Language, Gender and Society*, ed. Barrie Thorne, Cheris Kramarae, Nancy Henley [Rowley, MA: Newbury House, 1983], 25–37.) Lacking a nonsexist precedent in classical scholarship concerning the so-called "man-measure" fragment, I have chosen to refer to the fragment as the human-measure fragment. In translating *anthrôpos* I use "human(ity)" to remind the reader that Protagoras' *anthrôpos* can mean either an individual human being or humanity as a larger group.

5. Versényi, "Protagoras," 182.

6. Charles H. Kahn, *The Art and Thought of Heraclitus* (Cambridge: Cambridge U. Press, 1979), 46.

7. From *esperienze*. See Untersteiner, *Sophists*, 42, 77–79, and Capizzi, *Protagora*, 104–8.

8. Kahn, *Heraclitus*, 44–49.

9. See Sextus Empiricus DK 80 A15, B1; Aristotle, *Metaphysics* 1009a; Adolfo J. Levi, "Studies on Protagoras. The Man-Measure Principle: Its Meaning and Applications," *Philosophy* 40 (1940): 152; Joseph P. Maguire, "Protagoras—or Plato?" *Phronesis* 18 (1973): 115–23; Jonathan Barnes, *The Presocratic Philosophers* (London: Routledge and Kegan Paul, 1982), 541–45. See also the discussions of *metron* in Dupréel, *Sophistes*, 52; Capizzi, *Protagora*, 108–11.

10. Kahn, *Verb*; Eric A. Havelock, *The Greek Concept of Justice* (Cambridge, MA: Harvard U. Press, 1978), 233–48.

11. Cf. Havelock, Ibid., 234–40.

12. Kahn, *Verb*, 332, 355–62.

13. Levi, "Studies on Protagoras," 149–50; Theodor Gomperz, *Greek Thinkers* (London: John Murray, 1901), 1:451; Eduard Zeller, *A History of Greek Philosophy* (London: Longmans, Green, 1881), 2:445; Untersteiner, *Sophists*, 88; Nahm, *Selections*, 208–29; John Mansley Robinson, *An Introduction to Early Greek Philosophy* (Boston: Houghton Mifflin, 1968), 245; Guthrie, *HGP III*, 189.

14. Untersteiner, *Sophists*, 42; Gomperz, *SR*, 217; Kurt von Fritz, "*Nous, Noein*, and their Derivatives in Pre-Socratic Philosophy," *The Presocratics*, ed. A. P. D. Mourelatos (New York: Anchor Books, 1974), 68–69. Cf. Dupréel, *Sophistes*, 19.

15. Plato, *Theaetetus* 152ff., 161c, 167c; *Cratylus* 386ff.; Aristotle, *Metaphysics* 1062b.
16. See Guthrie, *HGP III*, 189–90. Stelio Zeppi has argued that the second part of the human-measure fragment delivers the philosophically crucial point of the saying in his *Protagora e la filosofia del suo tempo* (Firenze: La Nuova Italia, 1961).
17. Untersteiner, *Sophists*, 84.
18. Charles H. Kahn, "The Greek Verb 'to be' and the Concept of Being," *Foundations of Language* 2 (1966): 245–65.
19. Kahn, *Verb*, 367.
20. Ibid.
21. Dupréel, *Sophistes*, 23–28, 41; Guthrie, *HGP III*, 47; Kerferd, *SM*, 92; Scott Austin, *Parmenides: Being, Bounds, and Logic* (New Haven: Yale U. Press, 1986), 120; Michael Gagarin, "Plato and Protagoras" (Ph.D. diss., Yale University, 1968), 122.
22. Kahn, *Verb*, 366.
23. Ibid., 367.
24. Austin, *Parmenides*; A. P. D. Mourelatos, *The Route of Parmenides* (New Haven: Yale U. Press, 1970), 74–93.
25. See Parmenides' fragment 2, lines 3 and 5 in Austin, *Parmenides*, 158.
26. B. A. G. Fuller, *A History of Philosophy* (New York: Henry Holt, 1945), 61–65.
27. John Burnet, *Early Greek Philosophy* (London: Adam and Charles Black, 1930), 182.
28. KRS, 241.
29. Barnes, *Presocratic*, 163.
30. Mourelatos, *Route*.
31. Austin, *Parmenides*, 11–43.
32. Eric A. Havelock, "The Linguistic Task of the Presocratics," *Language and Thought in Early Greek Philosophy*, ed. Kevin Robb (LaSalle, IL: Hegeler Institute, 1983), 7–82.
33. Ibid., 9.
34. Ibid., 18. Cf. Richard Mason, "Parmenides and Language," *Ancient Philosophy* 8 (1988): 149–66.
35. DK 30 B8 trans. in KRS, 399.
36. Fragment 6 in Austin, *Parmenides*, 161.
37. Austin, *Parmenides*, 11–43; Havelock, "Task," 20–28.
38. Barnes, *Presocratic*, 155.
39. Ibid., 296–302. Plato continued a Parmenidean-like critique of the flux theory in the *Theaetetus*: see F. C. White, "The Theory of Flux in the *Theaetetus*," *Apeiron* 10 (1976): 1–10.
40. Giuseppe Rensi, *Introduzione alla scepsi etica* (Firenze: F. Perrella, 1921), 118 (trans. in Untersteiner, *Sophists*, 31).
41. Versényi, "Protagoras," 180.
42. 168c5 trans. John McDowell, *Plato: Theaetetus* (Oxford: Clarendon Press, 1973).
43. Maguire, "Protagoras," 115–38; Barnes, *Presocratic*, 541–45.
44. Gagarin, "Plato," 137.
45. F. M. Cornford, *Plato's Theory of Knowledge* (London: Routledge and Kegan Paul, 1935), 49; John Burnet, *Greek Philosophy: Thales to Plato* (London: Macmillan, 1964), 196.
46. Gagarin adds that "if we look at Socrates' interlocutors in other dialogues, no one (except perhaps Parmenides) has the stature of Protagoras" ("Purpose," 162). See also Gagarin, "Plato," 122.
47. Gagarin, "Plato," 122.
48. 152b trans. McDowell, *Theaetetus*.

49. 160b trans. F. M. Cornford, *Plato's Theaetetus* (Indianapolis: Bobbs Merrill, 1957). Unless noted otherwise, translations from the *Theaetetus* are from Cornford.

50. McDowell, *Theaetetus,* 155; Versényi, "Protagoras," 182; Gregory Vlastos, *Plato's Protagoras* (Indianapolis: Bobbs-Merrill, 1956), xiii.

51. Sextus, *Outlines of Pyrrhonism* 216; emphasis added.

52. R. G. Bury, *Sextus Empiricus* (Cambridge, MA: Harvard U. Press, 1933), 1:131; Michael J. O'Brien's translation is in *The Older Sophists,* ed. Rosamond Kent Sprague (Columbia: U. of South Carolina Press, 1972), 11.

53. Cornford's translation is in Edith Hamilton and Huntington Cairns, *The Collected Dialogues of Plato* (Princeton: Princeton U. Press, 1961); H. N. Fowler's is in the Loeb Library collection; McDowell, *Theaetetus.*

54. Bury, *Sextus,* 1:xiv. See also P. H. Epps, "Protagoras' Famous Statement," *CJ* 59 (1964): 223–26.

55. Guthrie, *HGP III,* 186–87; Untersteiner, *Sophists,* 48 (see note 1 above). On phenomenalism see R. J. Hirst, "Phenomenalism," *Encyclopedia of Philosophy* (New York: Macmillan, 1967), 6:130–35.

56. Kerferd, *SM,* 87n.

57. G. B. Kerferd, "Plato's Account of the Relativism of Protagoras," *Durham University Journal* 42 (1949): 20–26.

58. See Harold Cherniss, *Aristotle's Criticism of Presocratic Philosophy* (New York: Octagon Books, 1935), 85n, 159n, 166; Richard Bett, "The Sophists and Relativism," *Phronesis* 34 (1989): 166–68.

59. Martin Ostwald, *From Popular Sovereignty to the Sovereignty of Law: Law, Society, and Politics in Fifth-Century Athens* (Berkeley: U. of California Press, 1986), 260–66.

60. John P. Sabin and Maury Silver, "Some Senses of Subjective," *Explaining Human Behavior,* ed. Paul F. Secord (Beverly Hills: Sage, 1982), 71–91.

8

THE "IMPOSSIBLE TO CONTRADICT" FRAGMENT

Unlike the fragments I have already examined, there is nowhere a passage that represents the "impossible to contradict" statement un-equivocally as Protagoras' original words. However, some combination of the words occur sufficiently often in ancient discussions of Protagoras to convince most scholars that it was part of his philosophy. What is commonly referred to as the "impossible to contradict" fragment are three words: οὐκ ἔστιν ἀντιλέγειν. Diels and Kranz do not list *ouk estin antilegein* as an authentic fragment, and the two references (DK 80 A1, A19) under "Life and Teachings" differ somewhat. While it is true that other fifth- and fourth-century thinkers also claimed *ouk estin antilegein* (most notably Antisthenes), the best available evidence points to Pro-tagoras as the phrase's originator.[1]

When *ouk estin antilegein* is extracted from context and examined as part of Protagoras' doctrine, it is almost always translated as "impossible to contradict." *Antilegein* is the infinitive form of the verb "to contra-dict." *Ouk estin* in this construction, with the infinitive, means "is is not possible" or "it is impossible."

COMPETING INTERPRETATIONS OF *OUK ESTIN ANTILEGEIN*

Exactly what point Protagoras was making in claiming *ouk estin anti-legein* is difficult to ascertain. When mentioned by Diogenes Laertius

134

(9.53) and Isocrates (*Helen* 1), *ouk estin antilegein* is simply listed as one of the beliefs to which Protagoras subscribed. In Plato's *Euthydemus* and Aristotle's *Metaphysics, ouk estin antilegein* is discussed at greater length, but it is difficult to know how accurate these descriptions were, given that the authors' purpose was not simply to describe the fragment's history. Nonetheless, relevant passages provide significant information for constructing an approximation of Protagoras' agenda.

In the *Euthydemus* (286a), the Sophist Dionysodorus defends the proposition that *ouk estin antilegein* by gaining consent to the claim "one cannot speak of that which is not." If two people appear to contradict each other, they must be talking about different things, since the same thing would result in the same—not contradictory—*logoi*. Differing *logoi* suggest that different things are being talked about, not that there is a contradiction.

Without resolving the difficulties with this defense of *ouk estin antilegein*, Plato's Socrates mentions that Protagoras used it, and turns to the proposition that "falsehood is impossible" since that is the proposition Socrates believes *ouk estin antilegein* implies. Socrates does not refute the doctrine that falsehood is impossible as much as he makes fun of it by pointing out that if one opinion were as true as any other, the Sophists would be out of a job.

Despite the fact that Plato's Socrates mentions that the account given of *ouk estin antilegein* is that used by the followers of Protagoras (*Euthydemus* 286c), it is doubtful that Protagoras would have used the exact language portrayed by Plato. First, Protagoras would not have granted his consent to the suggestion that one cannot speak of what is not (*hôs ouk esti*) since his human-measure aphorism states otherwise. Second, Protagoras' two-*logoi* fragment explicitly states that the same thing is capable of two different *logoi*—even of the form X and not-X.

It is possible, however, to imagine Protagoras offering a slightly amended version of the defense in the *Euthydemus*. The same thing, such as the wind, is capable of being measured (or experienced) in different ways: cold or not-cold. To each person experiencing or measuring the wind it may be a different thing: a cold wind or a not-cold wind. Things as measured do not contradict; they are simply different.[2]

Since Plato's apparent target was not *ouk estin antilegein* but the proposition that falsehood is impossible, it is understandable that he would modify Protagoras' defense. The distinction between "things" and "things as experienced" is subtle but important, and Plato's treatment

135

of Protagoras in the *Theaetetus* (160b) suggests it is a distinction of which Protagoras was aware.

Aristotle nowhere directly identifies *ouk estin antilegein* as a Protagorean doctrine. He mentions the phrase in passing in the *Topics* (104b19–21) as an example of a "paradoxical belief" held by some philosophers, and again in the *Metaphysics* (1024b34) as a proposition implied by Antisthenes' linguistic theories. There is no doubt that Aristotle was aware of the status of "impossible to contradict" as a contemporary slogan. That he does not mention *ouk estin antilegein* in the context of his attacks on Protagoras is curious but not inexplicable. It is likely that the initial use to which Protagoras put *ouk estin antilegein* was no longer relevant, had been supplanted by Antisthenes' doctrines, or would have interfered with what Aristotle wanted to address.

An extended treatment of Protagoras in the *Metaphysics* occurs in book *Gamma,* which introduces Aristotle's science of being *qua* being. The centerpiece of the book is Aristotle's defense of what is now called the law of noncontradiction: "The same attribute cannot at the same time belong and not belong to the same subject in the same respect" (1005b19–20). As J. Lukasiewicz observes, Aristotle formulates the law of noncontradiction in three ways: as an ontological, a logical, and a psychological law—though Aristotle does not note the differences among them.[3] The ontological formulation quoted above is the most fundamental and also the most germane to the study of Protagoras.[4] The logical formulation applies the law to statements (*logoi*): "Contradictory statements are not at the same time true."[5] The psychological formulation is put forth not so much as a law as it was evidence for the ontological formulation: "For it is impossible for anyone to believe the same thing to be and not to be, as some think Heraclitus says."[6] Though Lukasiewicz demonstrates that the three formulations are logically distinct, Aristotle tended to slip back and forth among the different senses of the law of noncontradiction depending on the needs of his argument.

Protagoras is mentioned explicitly twice in book *Gamma.* The first reference is part of a refutation of the thesis that contradiction is possible on any subject, a thesis that appears to be a variation of Protagoras' two-*logoi* and human-measure statements: "If all contradictories are true of the same subject at the same time, evidently all things will be one. For the same thing will be a trireme, a wall, and a man, *if it is equally possible to affirm and to deny anything of anything*—and this premise must be accepted by those who share the views of Protagoras."[7] Aristotle develops his argument by reducing the thesis to absurdity: "For if it is true that a thing is man and not-man, evidently also it will be neither man nor not-man" (1008a4–6).

Immediately following an attack on the opinion that "things may be so and not so" Aristotle makes his second explicit reference to Protagoras. Aristotle attributes to Protagoras the belief that "all opinions [dokounta] and appearances [phainomena] are true," from which Aristotle believes one must conclude that "all statements must be at the same time true and false" since "many men hold beliefs in which they conflict with one another" (1009a6–10). For Aristotle such a doctrine meant intellectual anarchy where falsehood and error were impossible to judge: "If, then, reality is such as the view in question supposes, all will be right in their beliefs" (1009a13–15). To Aristotle such anarchy would have made scientific study impossible, hence he believed the law of noncontradiction was prerequisite to securing the philosophical status of science.

How reliable a witness of Protagoras' doctrines should Aristotle be considered? It is not possible to say with confidence whether Aristotle was attacking fourth-century uses of Protagoras by Aristotle's contemporaries (fourth-century "Protagoreans"?) or if Aristotle simply altered Protagoras' notions in order to make them an easier target.[8] In either case there are good reasons for not regarding Aristotle's treatment of Protagoras in the *Metaphysics* as faithful to the original. To begin with, there is no evidence that Protagoras ever considered statements (*logoi*) as a subset of things (*pragmata*), even if it seems reasonable to us for Aristotle to do so. Much of Aristotle's defense of the law of noncontradiction and of his attack on Protagoras implies a shift from the ontological formulation to the logical formulation. But there is considerable difference between saying some "thing" like the wind can be cold and not-cold, and claiming that all statements are equally true. Protagoras claimed that contrasting *logoi* are possible concerning things, not other *logoi*. There is no evidence that Protagoras treated *logoi* as things, though his followers may have.[9]

It is also unclear whether Protagoras ever espoused the belief that falsehood is impossible. In Plato's *Euthydemus* "speaking falsely" is equated with "speaking what is not"—*hôs ouk esti*—which the interlocutors agree is impossible. As I have said, Protagoras would not have conceded such a point. On the other hand, the human-measure fragment as described in the *Theaetetus* does in fact imply that each person is the judge of what is true or false for him or her. Accordingly, it is plausible that Protagoras would agree to the proposition that each statement (*logos*) is true for the person believing it. This is not the same as Aristotle's

137

implication that Protagoras' doctrines imply that all statements are true *without qualification* or reference to the relative "measure."

POSITIVE CONTRIBUTIONS OF *OUK ESTIN ANTILEGEIN*

Not only is it likely that Aristotle misrepresented Protagoras' doctrines in book *Gamma* of the *Metaphysics,* it is clear that Aristotle was indebted to Protagoras for some of his beliefs. As I have shown, Aristotle did not totally reject the notion of opposites or contrary attributes. Rather, he rejected the notion that two contraries could be equally present at the same time. Not unlike Protagoras' stronger and weaker *logoi,* Aristotle's "actual" and "potential" qualities alternate so that only one is "true" at any given time. The actual/potential pattern of explanation is repeated in the *Metaphysics* shortly after Protagoras is mentioned at 1009a6. Some people believe, Aristotle observed, that "contradictions or contraries are true at the same time" (1009a24–25). Aristotle admits that the "same thing can at the same time be and not-be—but not in the same respect. For the same thing can be *potentially* at the same time two contraries, but it cannot *actually*" (1009a33–35). There is no evidence suggesting that Protagoras would have claimed otherwise.

In fact, the law of noncontradiction espoused by Aristotle was, in a very preliminary way, anticipated by Protagoras. "A is B" and "A is not B" contradict, according to Aristotle, but "A is B to C" and "A is not B to D" do not. Likewise, "A is B at Time-1" and "A is not B at Time-2" do not contradict, according to Protagoras *and* Aristotle. Protagoras' doctrines required that Aristotle acknowledge that predications do not appear in a vacuum, but occur in a given context or "measure." Protagoras introduced a preliminary notion of contextual relativity, and Aristotle built upon the concept in formulating his law of noncontradiction.[10] Aristotle's careful phrasing made it clear that he was aware of how conflicting *logoi* may not contradict: "The same attribute cannot *at the same time* belong and not belong to the same subject *in the same respect.*"[11] Aristotle's law of noncontradiction apparently fleshed out the rationale underlying Protagoras' own statement *ouk estin antilegein.*

Even if Plato's and Aristotle's treatments of Protagoras' *ouk estin antilegein* are not accepted as wholly accurate, they provide clues as to the likely antecedents giving rise to the phrase. As the treatments suggest, there is a definite "odor of Eleaticism" about the phrase *ouk estin anti-*

legein.[12] Since it is well documented that Protagoras maintained anti-Parmenidean positions, it is not unlikely that *ouk estin antilegein* represented part of Protagoras' response to the Eleatics.

Parmenides was critical of the common linguistic usage of his time, in part because it seemed to embrace contradiction. He criticized the general populace "by whom to be and not to be are considered the same and not the same."[13] Parmenides distinguished between the "divine" route of truth and the "mortal" route which he described as *palintropos,* "backward-turning." *Palin* also implies opposition and can mean "contrary." Parmenides' prominent student Melissus distrusted the senses specifically because they result in beliefs that "do not agree with one another" (*ou ... allêlois homologei*): "We believe that what is warm becomes cold, and what is cold warm; that what is hard turns soft, and what is soft hard."[14] The Eleatic "school" can be characterized as opposed to common sense in large measure because common sense appeared to result in contradiction. Protagoras' doctrine, which can be characterized as an attempt to rescue common sense, introduced the concept of relative "measures" in order to demonstrate that it is impossible to contradict—*ouk estin antilegein.*

Austin has argued that Protagoras saw a distinction between logical contradiction and how statements could vary by context, a distinction not acknowledged by Parmenides and the Eleatics. Accordingly, Austin claims, "Protagoras' view is more sophisticated than that of Parmenides ... and it advances towards the sort of understanding of the law of the contradiction that was later to come to birth in middle-late Plato and Aristotle."[15]

The most plausible conclusion is, then, that *ouk estin antilegein* is a further articulation of Protagorean relativism as found in the two-*logoi,* stronger/weaker *logoi,* and human-measure fragments. Though a lack of authoritative evidence on the meaning and purpose of the fragment limits what can be positively asserted about it, the resonance between *ouk estin antilegein* and the better known fragments reinforces the general depiction of Protagoras that I have offered in earlier chapters.

NOTES

1. Guthrie, *HGP III,* 182 n2; Kerferd, *SM,* 89–90. The phrase was attributed to Prodicus in a fourth-century CE papyrus (probably by Didymus): see Gerhard Binder and Leo Liesenborghs, "Eine Zuweisung der Sentenz οὐκ ἔστιν ἀντιλέγειν an Prodikos von

Keos," *Museum Helveticum* 23 (1966): 37–43; revised in Classen, *Sophistik,* 452–62. Kerferd suggests that the papyrus "vindicates completely the attribution of the doctrine [*ouk estin antilegein*] to Protagoras and his followers" (*SM,* 90).

2. See Binder and Liesenborghs, "Zuweisung"; Kerferd, *SM,* 90–91; Andreas Graeser, "On Language, Thought, and Reality in Ancient Greek Philosophy," *Dialectica* 31 (1977): 363–64. Another way of describing the same point would be to call different "things-as-measured" different "situations" (see Françoise Caujolle-Zaslawsky, "Sophistique et scepticisme: L'image de Protagoras dans l'uvre de Sextus Empiricus," *Positions de la Sophistique,* ed. Barbara Cassin [Paris: Vrin, 1986], 158–59).

3. J. Lukasiewicz, "Aristotle on the Law of Contradiction," *Articles on Aristotle,* vol. 3, *Metaphysics,* ed. Jonathan Barnes, Malcolm Schofield, and Richard Sorabji (New York: St. Martin's Press, 1979), 50–51.

4. See also *Metaphysics* 1006b28–34, 1007b18–21.

5. Ibid., 1011b13–14; see also 1006b11–22, 1008a28–30.

6. Ibid., 1005b23–25; see also 1005b25–32, 1008b12–19.

7. Ibid., 1007b18–23; emphasis added.

8. Harold Cherniss, *Aristotle's Criticism of Presocratic Philosophy* (New York: Octagon Books, 1935), 77–79.

9. See, e.g., T. M. Robinson, *Contrasting Arguments: An Edition of the Dissoi Logoi* (Salem, NH: Ayer, 1979), passim. Cf. Manfred Kraus' discussion of Gorgias' *logos* in his *Name und Sache: ein Problem im frühgriechischen Denken* (Amsterdam: Grüner, 1987).

10. Scott Austin, *Parmenides: Being, Bounds, and Logic* (New Haven: Yale U. Press, 1986), 120–25. See also Richard Robinson's discussion of overinterpreting early hints of the law of noncontradiction: *Plato's Early Dialectic* (Oxford: Clarendon Press, 1953), 2–4.

11. *Metaphysics* 1005b19–20; emphasis added.

12. H. D. Rankin, "*Ouk estin antilegein,*" in Kerferd, *Legacy,* 25.

13. Fragment 6 in Austin, *Parmenides,* 161.

14. DK 30 B8 in KRS, 399.

15. Austin, *Parmenides,* 121.

THE "CONCERNING THE GODS" FRAGMENT

Next to the human-measure statement, the "concerning the gods" fragment is Protagoras' best-known saying. It is quoted in whole or in part by Diogenes Laertius (9.51), Hesychius (DK 80 A3), Sextus Empiricus (A12), Cicero (A23), and Eusebius (B4); it is mentioned or paraphrased by Philostratus (A2), Philodemus (A23), Diogenes of Oenoando (A23), and Plato (*Theaetetus* 162d).

The fragment consists of two sentences: 1) περὶ μὲν θεῶν οὐκ ἔχω εἰδέναι, οὔθ' ὡς εἰσὶν οὔθ' ὡς οὐκ εἰσὶν οὔθ' ὁποῖοί τινες ἰδέαν. 2) πολλὰ γὰρ τὰ κωλύοντα εἰδέναι ἥ τ'ἀδηλότης καὶ βραχὺς ὢν ὁ βίος τοῦ ἀνθρώπου (DK 80 B4). The first sentence can be given either an existential or veridical reading. Either places Protagoras clearly in the mainstream "philosophical" use of *eimi* ("to be"). The existential reading is very common and is even accepted by Kahn: "Concerning the gods I am unable to know, whether they exist or whether they do not exist or what they are like in form."[1] Since Kahn's extensive study of the Greek verb "to be" has proved influential, I repeat his discussion of the first sentence in its entirety:

> Here in what is perhaps the earliest surviving "technical" use of *eimi* as existential predicate we see that questions of existence are explicitly distinguished from what will later be called questions of essence. And we see also that the latter would typically be formulated by sentences with be as copula: *hopoioi eisi idean*. (Compare the standard Hellenistic doctrine which asserts that we can know *that* the gods are but not *what* or *what*

sort they are.) This distinction between the existence and the essence or nature of the gods corresponds in logical terms to the syntactic contrast between *esti* as existential sentence operator and as first-order copula.[2]

Kerferd remains unconvinced of Kahn's suggestion that the "concerning the gods" fragment was the first technical use of *eimi* as an existential predicate, and he translates *hôs eisin* and *hôs ouk eisin* as "that (or how) they are" and "that (or how) they are not."[3] Nonetheless, an existential reading is plausible. The construction of Protagoras' statement identifies two issues: the question of existence (*hôs eisin*) and the question of the gods' *idean*—"form," "nature," or "appearance." Even a veridical reading would juxtapose the question of whether "they are the case" or "they are not the case" with "what they are like in form." Clearly the existence/essence distinction is nascent if not explicit in such a juxtaposition.

In any event, the construction of the first sentence of "concerning the gods" was syntactically provocative. *Hôs eisin* and *hôs ouk eisin* were stripped bare of any possible qualification that otherwise might have signaled Homeric-age connotations of location or status.[4] The twin phrases force the hearer to address the issue of whether the gods are true or false, fact or fiction, independent of considerations of what the gods are like.

Significantly, this innovative question of existence or nonexistence was posed in a statement still guided by narrative form. Syntax still had not evolved sufficiently to address the question of whether and what gods *are* in purely abstract fashion; that task was left to Plato. Protagoras' inquiry was framed as a personal one, "concerning the gods I am unable to know," to which an elaboration is added, "whether they exist or whether they do not exist or what they are like in form," to which the second sentence is added as further elaboration. Protagoras' prose was still influenced by the additive form of oral narrative, though his innovative use of *eimi* marks a progression toward the more nuanced analysis found in Plato and Aristotle.

The second sentence of the fragment is appropriately translated as "For there are many hindrances to knowledge, the obscurity of the subject and the brevity of human life."[5] Jaap Mansfeld suggests that the first phrase may have been an idiomatic expression meaning "there is more than one thing in the way."[6] Mansfeld's suggestion is plausible given Protagoras' tendency to create memorable aphorisms, and it can be accepted without changing the point of the second sentence.

The claim that life is too short to gain knowledge of the gods had precedent in Empedocles' claim that life is too short to acquire knowledge of what Empedocles called "the whole."[7] For the Greeks the polar notions of gods and humans were mutually defining.[8] Hence the very immortality and power of the gods that distinguished them from humans made the gods a subject too vast to be mastered in the short life of mortals.

What Protagoras had in mind as "the obscurity of the subject" is difficult to say. *Adêlotês,* translated above as "obscurity," can also imply uncertainty, to be in the dark about, or not evident to sense. One can imagine a number of reasons why the gods are a "subject" too obscure to reason about confidently. For my purposes, Protagoras' precise defense is unimportant. More germane is his agenda: Why did Protagoras reject the theologizing of his predecessors? Later I shall address the "concerning the gods" fragment as part of Protagoras' epistemology, but first I want to focus on Protagoras' attitude toward religion.

AGNOSTICISM OR ANTHROPOLOGY?

The "concerning the gods" fragment is typically assumed to be no more than a simple expression of agnoticism, self-sufficient in that the expression of agnosticism and its rationale are both expressed and need no further elaboration. Often the first sentence is cited as prima facie evidence of a Protagorean theory of agnosticism.[9] Diogenes of Oenoanda was mistaken to suggest that Protagoras was atheistic because saying he did not know whether gods exist did not "amount to saying that he knows they do not exist."[10]

A number of ancient commentators said that the "concerning the gods" fragment led to Protagoras' demise. Diogenes Laertius reported that "because he began his book in this way he was expelled by the Athenians, and they also burned his books in the marketplace" (9.51–52). Philostratus continued: "The Athenians banished him from all their territory. Some say this was a court-judgment, others that he was merely the object of a voted decree. Between island and mainland he moved ... until a small vessel on which he was sailing sank."[11] The traditional story holds that Protagoras' book *Peri Theôn* ("On the Gods") began with the "concerning the gods" statements and went on to justify Protagoras' agnosticism, perhaps by comparing arguments for and against the existence of the gods. Protagoras' agnosticism combined with the relativism of the human-measure fragment apparently led to his being seen as a corrupting influence deserving banishment. The story in its most recent version is found in Giovanni Reale's work. Reale concludes:

> It is clear that as the principle of *man-measure* is strictly applied it inevitably leads to a more total scepticism and immoralism, and in this sense his attitude of marked agnosticism with respect to the Gods could have been carried to the point of denying the existence of the Gods. If Protagoras did not come to this conclusion, it only happened because he did not track out the consequences to which his premises through their internal logic ought or at least could lead.[12]

It has also been suggested that Protagoras was a target of anti-Periclean and antiprogressive elements of Athenian politics, as were other intellectual leaders.[13] Kerferd claimed that anti-Periclean politics probably played a part in attacks on Sophists closely identified with Pericles, such as Anaxagoras and Protagoras, and he cited Plutarch's mention of a decree of Diopeithes providing for public prosecution of those who did not believe in the gods.[14] Whether for religious or political reasons, the story links the "concerning the gods" fragment with charges of impiety leading to Protagoras' demise.

Despite its popularity, there are good reasons to doubt the truth of the traditional story. There are several recent analyses of the evidence that conclude the story is a fabrication.[15] Protagoras' alleged trial and banishment is not mentioned by a single fifth- or fourth-century writer. Aristophanes, Plato, Xenophon, Thucydides, and Aristotle are just a few of the sources we would expect to mention the so-called decree of Diopeithes if, in fact, one existed. None of these authors make mention of Protagoras' prosecution.

Given Plato's dislike of democracy, it seems highly improbable that he would not have mentioned the fact that the masses turned against Protagoras.[16] Indeed, in a dialogue concerning the teachability of *arete,* Plato had Socrates state that Protagoras practiced his art for forty years before his death, and that "his reputation has been consistently high" (*Meno* 91e). It would be incredible, says Socrates, if during that time Protagoras had managed to fool "the whole of Greece" about the value of his teachings. Anytus, Socrates' hostile interlocutor, is portrayed as bitterly disliking the Sophists, hence he certainly would have seized the opportunity to point out that Protagoras had been condemned if the trial had actually occurred. Accordingly, both the dramatic and philosophical force of this passage of the *Meno* would have compelled Socrates or

Anytus to point out the irony of Protagoras' death being caused by an ungrateful and unvirtuous public.

Diogenes Laertius provided a fairly detailed account of the first reading of "On the Gods" where it is specifically stated that "On the Gods" was "the first of his works he read publicly" (9.54). Yet he also claimed that Protagoras lived on as a highly successful and respected Sophist for forty years.[17] It is unlikely that Protagoras would have been unmolested for forty years if "On the Gods" had been considered dangerously heretical. It is significant that Diogenes Laertius also reported that Protagoras' books were ordered burned (9.52; see also DK 80 A3, A4). Such an unprecedented and unparalleled action would surely have been discussed by at least one fifth-or fourth-century source, but it was not. There are sufficient references to Protagoras' books by later writers to assure us that the book-burning never took place (Isocrates, *Helen* 2; Plato, *Theaetetus* 152a). Perhaps the origin of the book-burning myth was Aristophanes' flaming conclusion to the sophistic "thinkery" in the *Clouds*.

The origin of the whole trial story is impossible to determine, but it is plausible that—like the story of Anaxagoras' persecution—it was an attractive myth since it served as an antecedent to Socrates' trial.[18] Also, the stories would have been plausible to Plutarch in light of the occasional expulsion of Greek Sophists from Rome.

Over time, the opening of "On the Gods" was probably divorced from the rest of the book in popular discussion as it took on the status of a primarily orally transmitted slogan or aphorism. If such was the case, then it is understandable that the first sentence of "On the Gods" became the basis for the story of Protagoras' trial. At the same time, the possibility that *Peri Theôn* was not a treatise advocating agnosticism leaves the door open for an alternative theory concerning the rest of Protagoras' text "On the Gods."

An alternative theory concerning the content of "On the Gods" was first suggested by Werner Jaeger in a public lecture in 1936. Jaeger interpreted the opening lines as indicating that Protagoras was advocating turning away from previous philosophical treatments of theology— which focused on whether the gods were true and what the gods were like—and toward examination of religion "as an anthropological fact to be understood in the light of its meaning and function in human civilization and social structure."[19] Jaeger's theory was based on two assumptions. The first was that the "concerning the gods" fragment is an inappropriate beginning to an entire book espousing agnosticism. As I have noted, the fragment can be (and was) seen as a self-sufficient

145

maxim implying that nothing more need be said: "If, in spite of this, Protagoras could still devote an entire treatise to the problem of the belief in God, he must have been satisfied with a somewhat lesser degree of certainty as his work progressed."[20] Protagoras was pushing aside what now might be called questions concerning the ontology of gods in favor of more answerable questions concerning "the phenomenology of religion, the origin, evolution, and value of divine belief."[21] Corroboration of Jaeger's argument is found in Plato's *Theaetetus* where Protagoras takes neither a theistic nor atheistic position but expressly refuses to discuss the existence or nonexistence of the gods (162d5–e2).

The second assumption upon which Jaeger's theory rested is that Plato's Great Speech of Protagoras in the dialogue *Protagoras* (320c8–328d2) is, for the most part, an authentic reproduction of one of Protagoras' writings. The Great Speech uses a myth followed by an analysis (*logos*) to trace the history of humanity from creation to the establishment of cities. Human development is described in two steps: "belief in the pantheon comes first, in parallel with the acquisition of technology; cooperative action, the basis of civilized life, comes after and is made possible only through the presence (that is to say a developing consciousness) of *dikê*, justice, and *aidôs*, shame."[22] I will take up the Great Speech in more detail in a later chapter when I address its significance for understanding Protagoras' contribution to rhetorical theory, but for the moment it is sufficient to observe that the Great Speech, if authentic, is a good indication that Protagoras' interest in "On the Gods" was in the basis for human religious practice and not merely to espouse agnosticism.

The evidence for the authenticity of the arguments in the Great Speech and for Protagoras' anthropological approach to religion is threefold. First, there is evidence in the text itself:

> The many indications of pre-platonic style in it, and the many parallels in style and content to other writers of the fifth century . . . indicate that the speech must go back to a fifth-century source, and it seems hardly likely that Plato would have looked to any source but Protagoras himself. These factors and the inner unity and cohesion of the speech, moreover, indicate that this is probably not a patchwork creation from several of his writings.[23]

Gagarin also points out that the Great Speech stands apart from the bulk of the arguments in the dialogue "in a way that is unusual, if not unique, in Plato."[24] Socrates raises no objections to the arguments of the Great Speech, but "sets out at the end of it on what is essentially a new course."[25] Plato could have broken up portions of the Great Speech in order to make the dialogue flow in the usual manner of his works. That he did not, according to Gagarin, suggests that the Great Speech was inserted intact from some work by Protagoras.

Second, there is evidence from two of Protagoras' associates, Prodicus and Pericles, of an anthropological approach to religion akin to the views expressed in the Great Speech. Prodicus is known to have expressed a theory that humans deify that which benefits them: first the objects of nature on which survival depends, then the skills (*technai*) which contribute to human welfare.[26] Pericles declared in his famous funeral oration that those who died in the Samian War had become immortal like the gods: "the gods themselves, we cannot see, but from the honours which they receive, and the blessings which they bestow, we conclude that they are immortal."[27] Pericles' statement reflects Protagorean influence by implying that direct knowledge of the gods is impossible and that they are "measured" in the same manner as fallen mortals: by inference and by their benefits.[28]

Third, there are unrelated bits of information about Protagoras that make sense if one assigns some level of authenticity to the Great Speech, or at least to the thesis that Protagoras took an anthropological approach to religion. Diogenes Laertius lists two relevant titles of works by Protagoras: "On the Original Order of Things," from which Plato might have extracted the Great Speech, and "On Those in Hades," about which there is no other reference but the very listing of which casts doubt on whether "On the Gods" advocated simple agnosticism. Plato relates the story that Protagoras allowed clients to challenge his fees if they would swear an oath in a temple as to how much they felt his teaching was worth (*Protagoras* 328b). Such a practice did not require Protagoras to believe in gods, only that he believe in the power *belief* in gods could have in practice.

Finally, there has been a case recently made by Ira S. Mark that Protagoras may have played a substantial role in collaboration with Pericles and the sculptor Pheidias in the design of the east frieze of the Parthenon.[29] Mark demonstrates how the arrangement and portrayal of the gods represented on the frieze closely follow how they were viewed by sophistic theology, especially that of Protagoras as portrayed in the Great Speech.

Despite the qualms of certain scholars, the most recent consensus is that the arguments of the Great Speech (if not the actual words) are largely authentic and hence provide a valuable source for information about Protagoras.[30] If the general authenticity of the Great Speech is accepted, Jaeger's alternative theory concerning the content of "On the Gods" becomes more plausible. "Concerning the gods" did not begin a text refuting traditional religion by defending agnosticism, but rather served as an introduction to a different approach to religion, best described in contemporary terms as anthropological. Humans worship those skills (*technai*) and virtues (*aretê*) that benefit them most, and in Protagoras' analysis the capacities most worthy of praise are those furthering *politikê technê*—the art of living in the *polis*. As Protagoras shifts from myth to *logos* in his Great Speech, divine gifts become qualities of human behavior: "In place of *dikê*, justice, comes *dikaiosynê*, a capacity for justice"; for *aidôs*, shame, comes "*sôphrosynê*, the capacity for [self] control, and *to hosion einai*, piety."[31] In Protagoras' view theology was comprehensible only in human terms.[32] Religion was understood by Protagoras as a social practice that furthers the goals of civilized people.

Two other points deserve mention here. First, Protagoras' contribution to the historical development of theological thinking is significant and provocative:

> The crisis of the philosophical idea of God has [with Protagoras] arrived. Any attempt to solve it will have to start from the side where it has at last become most plainly evident and bodes the most serious consequences; and this is the problem of the goal of human life and action, the problem of the Good that Socrates and his followers will soon be compelled to attack. In speculative theology no less than in philosophy as a whole, this moment marks the beginning of a new epoch.[33]

Second, the "concerning the gods" fragment and two other fragments provide additional evidence of Protagoras' preference for common sense over purely theoretical speculation. The gods as a subject of inquiry are obscure and inaccessible. There are *ta kôlounta eidenai*, "obstacles that impede knowledge," that make further study relatively fruitless. Accordingly, philosophers ought to turn away from useless speculation concerning Zeus and Prometheus, Anaximander's *apeiron* with its "divine attributes," and Parmenides' revealing goddess or his "god-like ball of 'what-is.'"[34] As Mansfeld notes, "As soon as an important thinker says that the notion of 'gods' is epistemologically irrelevant as far as he is concerned, this cannot but have far-reaching consequences for his notion of 'man.'"[35]

TWO MORE PROTAGOREAN FRAGMENTS

There are two other passages that provide testimony to Protagoras' anti-Eleatic, pragmatic attitude toward "knowledge." The first is found in Aristotle's *Metaphysics* in a section in which geometry is being differentiated from surveying. The former deals with objects of pure theory, while the latter deals with sensible objects: "For neither are perceptible lines such lines as the geometer speaks of—for no perceptible thing is straight or curved in this way; for a hoop touches a straight edge not at a point, but as Protagoras said it did in his refutation of the geometers" (997b35–998a4). Of Protagoras' refutation nothing more is known; apparently the refutaton was sufficiently well known that Aristotle assumed readers would be familiar with it. Diogenes Laertius lists "On the Subjects of Learning" as the title of one of Protagoras' books (9.55), and Plato portrayed Protagoras as scorning the advanced study of geometry and calculation (*Protagoras* 318e). Furthermore, Philodemus reported that Protagoras said of mathematics, "The subject matter is unknowable and the terminology repugnant."[36]

From these pieces of information it may be inferred that Protagoras refuted the geometers by recourse to common sense; a straight edge's contact with a hoop would obviously touch at many more than one infinitely small point. Untersteiner claimed that Protagoras criticized geometry "in order to rob the subject of scientific certainty and universal value."[37] It cannot be so concluded with certainty, but the similarity of Philodemus' report to the language of the "concerning the gods" fragment suggests that Protagoras did in fact distrust intellectual pursuits too far removed from concrete experience and practical utility.[38] It is relevant to note that Aristotle reports that some Sophists ridiculed mathematics for taking "no account" of "better or worse," "goods and evils."[39]

The last fragment to be examined for evidence of Protagoras' epistemological pragmatism (in modern terms) is the alleged "new" fragment unearthed during World War II. In the fourth-century CE works of Didymus the Blind, the following is attributed to Protagoras: φαίνομαι σοὶ τῷ παρόντι καθήμενος; τῷ δὲ ἀπόντι οὐ φαίνομαι καθήμενος; ἄδηλον εἰ κάθημαι ἢ οὐ κάθημαι.[40] Paul Woodruff translates the fragment as: "It is manifest to you who are present that I am sitting; but to a person who is absent it is not manifest that I am sitting; whether or not I am sitting is non-evident."[41]

149

The authenticity of the fragment is sharply disputed. Jonathan Barnes perhaps rightly rejects the fragment altogether on the grounds that it "is full of Stoic terminology and has no authority."[42] Catherine Osborne's warning that fragments may suffer substantial distortion when transmitted from writer to writer seems particularly apt in this case.[43] Woodruff, for example, has to conjecture at great lengths to provide a basis for the fragment's authenticity:

> A chain of reasonable but risky suppositions yields this hypothesis: Didymus took the passage from another post-Hellenistic writer (that would explain the spelling), who had it from an eclectic enemy of Skepticism (that would explain the use of *adêlon*), whose ultimate source could have been Democritus' attack against Protagoras (that would explain why the account does not square with Plato's). Each stage in this story would account for one of the many distortions the evidence has sustained.[44]

Jørgen Mejer accepts the authenticity of this fragment and suggests that it is proof of a sort of Protagorean positivism: "The only certain measure for deciding about the world is 'man' (individually or generically)—as we get beyond the level of sense impressions it is in vain to discuss the nature of things 'in themselves.' "[45] However, the evidence for Protagoras' accepting *only* the evidence of the senses is exceedingly weak and mostly based on questionable testimony from Plato and Sextus.[46] As I have shown, wide ranges of ideas, issues, and things are judged and measured by humans, not just the objects of sense perception.

Mansfeld accepts the judgment that the fragment is probably not in Protagoras' own words, but he suggests that it still contains a "Protagorean nut" that can be separated from its Skeptic "shell."[47] Specifically, Mansfeld believes there is parallel logic between the "concerning the gods" fragment and the "new" fragment; namely, that both address epistemological obstacles. Not being in the same room is a barrier to knowledge of the room's contents in the same way mortality is an obstacle to knowledge of the immortal: "One not in the same room with Protagoras at time *t* has no more grounds for either affirming or denying that Protagoras is sitting than the great teacher himself, during his short life, had for either affirming or denying that there are gods."[48]

Barnes' caution expresses an appropriate attitude toward the "new" fragment. True, Protagoras is reported to have argued through analogies and examples (cf. *Theaetetus* and *Protagoras*), but the "sitting" example has more in common with later eristic (perhaps Stoic or second-generation Sophists as portrayed in *Euthydemus*) than with Protagoras' known

150

examples and analogies. While the "new" fragment reveals how Protagoras came to be understood by later Hellenistic philosophy, it cannot be taken as seriously as *ipsissima verba*.

NOTES

1. Kahn, *Verb*, 302. Dupréel translates the fragment as: "A l'égard des dieux, je ne sais ni s'ils sont ni s'ils ne sont pas ni comment est leur figure. Beaucoup de choses empêchent de le savoir, l'obscurité (de la question) et la brièveté de la vie de l'homme" (*Sophistes*, 58).
2. Kahn, *Verb*, 302.
3. Kerferd, *SM*, 165–67.
4. Eric A. Havelock, *The Greek Concept of Justice* (Cambridge, MA: Harvard U. Press, 1978), 233–48.
5. Translation adapted from that by Ira S. Mark, "The Gods on the East Frieze of the Parthenon," *Hesperia* 53 (1984): 318.
6. Jaap Mansfeld, "Protagoras on Epistemological Obstacles and Persons," in Kerferd, *Legacy*, 40n.
7. DK 31 B2 in KRS, 284–85.
8. Mansfeld, "Protagoras," 43.
9. DK 80 A2, A3, A23. Cf. Paul Beattie, "Protagoras: The Maligned Philosopher," *Religious Humanism* 14 (1980): 108–15.
10. DK 80 A23; cf. B4.
11. DK 80 A2; cf. A3, A12, A23.
12. Giovanni Reale, *A History of Ancient Philosophy: From the Origins to Socrates* (Albany: SUNY Press, 1987), 163.
13. Mark, "The Gods," 340.
14. Kerferd, *SM*, 21; Plutarch, *Lives* 3.32.
15. I. F. Stone, in his "Was There a Witch-hunt in Ancient Athens?" plausibly suggests that the so-called decree of Diopeithes outlawing impiety was originally part of a fifth-century comedy that later writers took as fact (*The Trial of Socrates* [New York: Anchor Books, 1989], 231–47). See also John Burnet, *Greek Philosophy: Thales to Plato* (London: Macmillan, 1964), 90–91; Carl Werner Müller, "Protagoras über die Götter," *Hermes* 95 (1967): 140–59 (= Classen, *Sophistik*, 312–40). K. J. Dover doubts that a decree of Diopeithes ever existed, but grants that some sort of unsuccessful action was taken against Protagoras ("The Freedom of the Intellectual in Greek Society," *Talanta* 7 [1976]: 34–41). Kerferd accepts the truth of the story (*SM*, 43), while Guthrie admits the story is "perhaps rightly" rejected (*HGP III*, 263 n2). For a recent argument that the trial story is probably true, see Martin Ostwald, *From Popular Sovereignty to the Sovereignty of Law: Law, Society, and Politics in Fifth-Century Athens* (Berkeley: U. of California Press, 1986), 532–33.
16. Cf. Plato's *Gorgias*, where Plato describes the fickleness of the masses concerning Pericles and other leaders. As Burnet pointed out, it is also reasonable to expect mention of Protagoras' fate in Plato's *Apology* (*Greek Philosophy*, 91). See also Müller, "Protagoras," in Classen, *Sophistik*, 326–27, 339–40; R. S. Bluck, *Plato's Meno* (Cambridge: Cambridge U. Press, 1961), 358–59.
17. DL 9.56, probably on the authority of Plato, *Meno* 91e.
18. On the questionable reliability of oral myths, see Rosalind Thomas, *Oral Tradition and Written Record in Classical Athens* (Cambridge: Cambridge U. Press, 1989).

19. Werner Jaeger, *Theology of the Early Greek Philosophers* (Oxford: Clarendon Press, 1947), 176.

20. Ibid., 189.

21. Mark, "The Gods," 319.

22. Summarized by Mark, ibid., 323.

23. Michael Gagarin, "Plato and Protagoras" (Ph.D. diss., Yale University, 1968), 90.

24. Ibid., 95.

25. Ibid., 93. Adolfo Levi suggests that the myth and *logos* in *Protagoras* are authentically Protagorean, but that what comes after in the dialogue should be considered suspect ("The Ethical and Social Thought of Protagoras," *Mind* 49 [1940]: 297).

26. Jaeger, *Theology*, 179ff.; Guthrie, *HGP III*, 238–42; Kerferd, *SM*, 168–69; Mark, "The Gods," 314–15.

27. Plutarch, *Pericles* 8.

28. Mark, "The Gods," 340–41.

29. Ibid., 289–342.

30. For arguments against accepting the authenticity of the Great Speech see Eric A. Havelock, *The Liberal Temper in Greek Politics* (New Haven: Yale U. Press, 1957), 407–9 (for a response see Guthrie, *HGP III*, 64 n1); Antonio Capizzi, *Protagora: le testimonianze e i frammenti* (Firenze: G. C. Sansoni, 1955), 259. Kerferd, *SM*, 125–26, accepts the speech as a historically reliable guide to Protagoras. For summaries of the debate over the Great Speech's authenticity see Gagarin, "Plato," 85–104; Gomperz, *SR*, 159–62; Guthrie, *HGP III*, 64 n1; Mark, "The Gods," 323 n159.

31. Mark, "The Gods," 324.

32. Müller, "Protagoras," in Classen, *Sophistik*, 312–40.

33. Jaeger, *Theology*, 190.

34. Mansfeld, "Protagoras," 40.

35. Ibid., 43.

36. See 80 B7a in Rosamond Kent Sprague, ed. *The Older Sophists* (Columbia: U. of South Carolina Press, 1972), 22.

37. Untersteiner, *Sophists*, 33.

38. Auguste Bayonas, "L'art politique d'après Protagoras," *Revue Philosophique* 157 (1967): 56–57; Guthrie, *HGP III*, 267; cf. Dupréel, *Sophistes*, 46–47.

39. *Metaphysics* 996a29-b1; cf. 1078a31-b6.

40. M. Gronewald, "Ein neues Protagoras-Fragment," *Zeitschrift für Papyrologie und Epigraphik* 2 (1968): 1; punctuated as amended by Mansfeld, "Protagoras," 51–52. A fuller context of the fragment is provided in Paul Woodruff, "Didymus on Protagoras and the Protagoreans," *JHP* 23 (1985): 484–85.

41. Woodruff, "Didymus," 485. An alternative translation is: "To you who are present, I appear as sitting; to one not present I do not appear as sitting, it is not clear (sc. to him) whether I am sitting or not sitting" (Mansfeld, "Protagoras," 52).

42. Jonathan Barnes, *The Presocratic Philosophers* (London: Routledge and Kegan Paul, 1982), 645 n16.

43. Catherine Osborne, *Rethinking Early Greek Philosophy* (London: Duckworth, 1987), 1–9.

44. Woodruff, "Didymus," 493. Another theory is that the fragment comes from a work of Democritus which attacked Protagoras and which was preserved by Epicureans (Fernanda Decleva Caizzi, "La tradizione Protagorea ed un Frammento di Diogene di Enoanda," *Rivista di Filologia* 104 [1976]: 435–42).

45. Jørgen Mejer, "The Alleged New Fragment of Protagoras," *Hermes* 100 (1972): 177 (= Classen, *Sophistik*, 306–11).

46. Though Woodruff believes that the fragment comes from sources independent of Plato and Sextus, I find this unlikely ("Didymus," 494 n21). The sentiment expressed

in the fragment is easily derived from Plato's *Theaetetus,* where perception is described as knowledge (152ff.), or from Sextus in *Outlines of Pyrrhonism* (1.216–19). I see nothing in Didymus' discussion that cannot reasonably be explained as initially derived from Plato or Sextus and later filtered through Skepticism. Woodruff's claim that Didymus' account is inconsistent with Plato's and Sextus' suffers from two flaws. First, it assumes that Didymus would have felt obligated to be true to Plato's or Sextus' readings. Nothing prevented Didymus from taking an understanding gleaned from, say, Plato and putting it to use in his analysis of later doctrines of the Protagoreans. Second, I think Woodruff's unpacking of the logical entailments of the fragment ("Didymus," 494) attributes to Didymus a more nuanced reading of Protagoras than can be proven or safely assumed.

47. Mansfeld, "Protagoras," 51 n45.
48. Ibid., 52.

PART III

PROTAGORAS AND EARLY
GREEK PHILOSOPHY AND RHETORIC

10

PROTAGORAS AND
FIFTH-CENTURY EDUCATION

Clear-cut conceptual categories such as political theory, ethics, educational philosophy, and rhetorical theory were nascent at best in the mid-fifth century. Though any scholarly analysis of fifth-century thinking is bound to engage in a certain amount of oversimplification, it is possible to minimize the risk of misreading Protagoras' words. In such an inquiry scope and accuracy can be provided by moving from a broad view of the ontological and epistemological aspects of Protagoras' approach to *logos* (the goal, broadly speaking, of Part 2) to more specific views pertaining to what we now readily identify as educational philosophy, political philosophy, and rhetorical theory.

THE MYTHIC-POETIC TRADITION

Greek educational practices underwent dramatic changes between 450 and 350 BCE. By the fourth century formal schools with distinct curricula began to emerge and compete. There is a tendency (even in the fourth century) to assume that the same was true in the fifth century. However, there is no evidence of distinct and competing "schools" (except for children) prior to the time of Plato.[1] Further, the notion of an educational text that could be privately read and studied is primarily a fourth-century phenomenon. In the mid-fifth century serious thinkers might write down their thoughts, but it would be primarily with the intention of presenting them orally. A consistent readership for books did not emerge until around the last third of the fifth century, and even then books were very rare.[2] I believe that Protagoras' contributions to the advancement of the educational practices of his time involved changes in the predominant style and doctrine (keeping in mind that form and content are very much intertwined in this context). This being so, *how* Protagoras taught is at least as important as *what* he taught.

Protagoras was a good example of what Thomas S. Kuhn describes as a "revolutionary" pioneer in his field.[3] He was clearly influenced by and to some extent constrained by the mythic-poetic tradition he inherited, but he also played a significant role in changing that tradition. He did so by advancing different prose forms of discourse and by introducing (and popularizing) new patterns of explanation. Nevertheless, it is highly doubtful that Protagoras ever wrote a *technê*. The fifth-century manuals referred to in the fourth century were collections of exemplary speeches or, in some cases, perhaps general guidelines for speaking procedures in the law courts. In the case of Protagoras neither sort of text seems likely. Though his books appear to have been among the first written in prose, his surviving fragments bear the mark of aphorism: self-contained maxims designed for easy memorization.[4]

The oral characteristics of Protagoras' fragments may serve as a clue to the disparate treatments one finds, even in ancient times, of his ideas. I conjectured in the previous chapter that the first line of Protagoras' book *Peri Theôn* may have achieved a life of its own through oral transmission that was quite different than the original direction of the written text. The same could be true of other Protagorean sayings. Some later commentators state that they have actually read a book by Protagoras (DK 80 B2). But others talk about some of Protagoras' ideas in such a way that it is plausible they knew only what they had heard. Accordingly, when Plato discussed *ouk estin antilegein* in the *Euthydemus,* or when Aristotle conjectured about Protagoras' "promise" *ton hêttô de logon kreittô poiein* in his *Rhetoric,* it is entirely possible that they are responding to a primarily oral legacy—the *uses* to which later speakers (perhaps Euthydemus and Aristophanes, respectively) put Protagoras' notions. The more easily memorized Protagoras' comments were, the more likely they were to reappear in contexts quite different than Protagoras might have ever imagined.

158

In the case of the human-measure statement, memorization is encouraged through the use of antithesis, rhythm, and balanced phrasing—obvious in the English translation as well as in the original Greek. The two-*logoi* fragment is easily divided into three phrases: *duo logous einai / peri pantos pragmatos / antikeimenous allêlois.* The phrases are conceptually as well as acoustically distinct; they also build—each successive phrase amplifies the phrase before—again both conceptually and acoustically. The fragment may or may not be Protagoras' *ipsissima verba,* but the basic notion of paired *logoi* in opposition—*dissoi logoi* or *antilogoi*—became an unmistakably Protagorean legacy. The "concerning the gods" statement is preserved in nearly identical fashion by a number of sources. It has a rhythmic quality typical of an oral culture, yet its sense is more propositional and logical.[5] As Mansfeld points out, Protagoras justifies his position that he cannot know whether the gods exist or what they are like in form for the reason that the subject is obscure and life is short.[6] Furthermore, as an opening line of a book the statement logically implies that *since* the gods are unknowable, *then* the more appropriate subject of study is humanity.[7] The core of the stronger/weaker *logoi* fragment—*ton hêttô logon kreittô poiein*—was as memorable as it was infamous. The simple phrase *ouk estin antilegein* was well known in the fifth and fourth centuries. The phrase is noteworthy in the present context because it is possible that Protagoras was the first to coin the term *antilegein.* Even if he was not, he was clearly the first to provide *antilegein* with the logical sense of "contradict" as compared to the general sense of "cross-talk."

Cumulatively the fragments indicate several characteristics of Protagoras' writing style, and hence of his method of teaching. First, unlike his predecessor Parmenides or his contemporary Empedocles, Protagoras wrote in prose rather than in verse. His prose probably resembled that of Democritus, Zeno, or Melissus: a series of aphorisms modeled to create a continuous argument. Like those of all fifth-century writers, his works were designed to be read in public. The human-measure and "concerning the gods" statements are provocative, yet they are cast in familiar language and easily remembered. They are also self-contained summations of arguments to follow. No doubt Protagoras was influenced by the aphoristic style of Heraclitus, but his statements are not nearly as oracular. For the most part Protagoras' choice of words favors traditional vocabulary; he does not seem to have been the prolific inventor of new philosophical terminology that some Presocratics and Soph-

159

ists were. But what he said is revolutionary nonetheless, and his use of *einai* is sufficiently novel to place Protagoras on the cutting edge of fifth-century philosophical thinking.

What made Protagoras revolutionary is his preference for a humanistic *logos* over traditional *mythoi*. Here I am using *mythos* as shorthand for the mythic-poetic tradition that dominated Greek educational practices even into the fourth century. It was only in the last third of the fifth century (after the acme of Protagoras' career) that the teaching of writing became standard practice in Greek schools. Prior to that time oral recitation of the poets performed to music was the dominant teaching method.[8] Like other Presocratics, Protagoras was trying to discover and practice the abstract and analytical thinking characteristic of philosophical reasoning.[9] The new humanistic spirit of rationalism, facilitated in part by spreading uses of literacy (such as books), is represented by the term *logos*—named and praised as the source of great power and identified as the art and subject of fifth-century sophistic teaching.

It is unclear whether most fifth-century intellectuals associated specific cognitive skills with acquiring literacy. After all, writing was regarded with some suspicion during the fifth and fourth centuries.[10] There is anecdotal evidence that Protagoras believed that literacy was advantageous and took actions to promote the skill. While serving as "lawgiver" in the colony of Thurii, Protagoras apparently proposed that the sons of all citizens be taught to read and write at the public's expense.[11] Previously, publicly financed education had been provided only in rare instances, such as for war orphans or for refugees, hence Protagoras' proposed law was a radical departure from tradition. The account of Protagoras' proposed law is provided by Diodorus, who follows his description with an encomium of literacy (12.13). The encomium ends with an aphorism that J. V. Muir believes is by Protagoras: "So it must be considered that life is the gift of Nature, but the good [*kalos*] life is the gift of education which results from literacy."[12] Muir admits that his evidence is speculative at best, but since Protagoras is reported to have authored a text called *Peri tôn Mathêmatôn,* "On the Subjects of Learning" (DL 9.55), Muir's "tempting conclusion" is at least a possibility.

What distinguished the philosophical literati from the majority of Greeks was both what they said and how they said it. Protagoras' contribution to the revolution in educational practices can, accordingly, be distinguished by the teaching methods he introduced and by the subject matter or disciplines he introduced—recognizing, of course, that the

160

advancement of method and content was coterminous; the two are separable now only with the benefit of hindsight.

As I have said, Protagoras continued and expanded the presocratic innovation of critically analyzing the epic poets. This practice was revolutionary because it made discourse an object of study. Protagoras' original insights regarding *logos,* the gender of words, and the moods or modes of languge are noteworthy in two respects. First, they contributed to the formulation of a metalanguage: a set of terms appropriate for the analysis of language. Such language is obvious in the writings of Plato and Aristotle, wherein one finds most of the terms of grammar and logic familiar to a modern reader. But their technical vocabulary did not spring into place overnight; it came by a process of rapid evolution, and Protagoras was a principal founder. Of course, other Presocratics had previously criticized Homer and Hesiod, but Protagoras' method of analysis was different and original. When Heraclitus criticized the poets for failing to recognize that day and night are one (DK 22 B57), it was a matter of his *doxa* versus theirs. And after Parmenides offered an alternative description of "what is," it was defended in part as being the result of divine revelation. In both instances *logos* was understood as rationalized *mythos* and was set against a traditional *mythos.* In the case of Protagoras, *mythos* became an object of analysis—a text that could be analyzed, criticized, and altered. Furthermore, Protagoras created a vernacular capable of describing the process of comparing alternative accounts of the world (*dissoi logoi*) and of challenging one account with another (*ton hêttô logon kreittô poiein*). Plato's account of Protagoras' analyzing epic poetry is the earliest recorded instance of textual criticism, and it apparently started a practice that was continued by other Sophists at least through Isocrates' time (*Panathenaicus* 18).

Second, Protagoras' critical analysis of epic poetry contributed to the ascendancy of prose over poetry as the preferred vehicle of cultural knowledge. In this context the significance of Protagoras' explicitly calling himself a Sophist becomes more clear. In Plato's dialogue by the same name Protagoras is quite open about his profession of being a Sophist (316d–317c). Since other accounts refer to him as the first professional Sophist, Plato's account is probably based on historical fact (DK 80 A1, 2). In so naming himself Protagoras explicitly set himself up as successor to the mythic-poetic tradition. In retrospect the modern reader tends to find the succession obvious and noncontroversial. But Protagoras' claim was extremely provocative by mid-fifth-century

161

standards. In predominantly oral Greece the primary source of *sophia* was the poetry of Homer and Hesiod. Protagoras made the conflict between *logos* and *mythos* as the means to *sophia* more distinct than most of his presocratic predecessors. He did so by announcing himself as a Sophist, setting himself in commercial competition with the rhapsode, questioning the sagacity of the Muse, rejecting the possibility of knowledge of the gods, and declaring that *anthrôpos*—not the gods—is the master and measure of human experience. The way to wisdom was not divinely inspired poetry but contrasting human prose arguments. Protagoras' preference for *logos* can be understood as advocacy (through *praxis*) for a new way of thinking about the world, a way perhaps captured by the modern phrase "secular humanism."[13] Though freighted with contemporary controversy, the label is not so misleading as to be useless; he did, after all, evoke pious indignation for his anthropocentrism.

PROVIDING A *LOGOS* OF *LOGOS*

Protagoras is often cited as being the first grammarian and an early contributor to the history of semantics.[14] If we call Protagoras a secular humanist, it is fairly apparent how the label is to be understood—that is, in contrast to the religious orthodoxy of his time. But when such labels as "first grammarian" are used, the character of Protagoras' contributions can easily be missed. Some have assumed that "grammar" is a conceptual constant, a "given" which was in essence the same for Protagoras as it is for us today. Such an assumption is misleading. Protagoras' insights concerning the parts of speech, the gender of words, and what are now called grammatical moods were not part of a *grammatikê* per se and should not be so "reduced."[15] The first appearance of *grammatikê* to designate a specific verbal *technê* was in Plato in the fourth century (*Cratylus* 431e11; *Sophist* 253a12). Something of Protagoras' and Plato's contribution is lost if we describe them as "discoverers" or "inventors" of grammar.[16] What Protagoras was grappling with was the relationship of *logos* and the world; this much he had in common with his presocratic predecessors. But unlike them he also sought a rational account of discourse, a *logos* of *logos,* and in that sense he was the parent of all subsequent study of language—including logic, grammar, linguistics, and semantics.[17]

Protagoras is also credited with inventing the Socratic method, introducing the methods of attacking any thesis, originating the practice of arguing by questions, inventing eristic, and fathering competitive debate—*logôn agônas* (DK 80 A1, 3, 20). It must be remembered that the precise words designating specific and discrete verbal arts originated with Plato (such as *eristikê, dialektikê,* and *antilogikê*), but there is little reason to reject the historical plausibility of claims attributing such practices to Protagoras. Based on the extant fragments of Protagoras and various accounts in Plato, Kerferd has suggested the following as a useful schematization of the method of Protagoras: "(1) a formal expository style whether lecture or text-book, (2) the verbal exchange of a small informal discussion group, and (3) the antithetical formulation of public positions and the setting of party lines."[18]

To say that Protagoras first used a variety of useful educational practices is true enough, but the phrase implies a primarily mental (rationalistic or intellectual) activity. The task of the Sophist was to change people—to substitute one *logos* for another—and in fifth-century thinking such a process was not strictly mental or physical but *both*. In Gorgias' view the *logos* was a power that acted directly on the listener's psyche, and "the psyche exists on an equal level with the physical world and is closely related to it."[19] Though Protagoras' extant fragments are too few to show whether he had as fully developed a theory of *logos* as Gorgias' *Helen* reveals, our knowledge of mid-fifth-century thought concerning opposites and the role of the medical analogy in Protagoras' thinking suggests a close parallel. For Protagoras the task of the Sophist was to change the state or condition of the hearer for the better. For Protagoras *logos* referred not only to speech or discourse (hence the means of effecting change); it referred also to the competing "end-states"—competing ways of life (cf. Aristophanes' *Clouds*), choices of war or peace, judgments of just or unjust, etc.

Protagoras' *logos* thus referred to discourse *and* reality, and his process of making the weaker *logos* stronger could be described as psychophysical. Understood accordingly, Protagoras' place in the development of theories of discourse becomes clearer. While his efforts at rationalizing the *logos* seem simplistic by Platonic and Aristotelian standards, his fragments nonetheless reflect what were clearly seminal insights.

Orthoepeia (usually rendered "correct diction"), *orthotês onomatôn* ("correctness of names"), and *orthos logos* were doctrines often associated with fifth-century Sophists, including Protagoras.[20] The most explicit evidence concerning Protagoras is from Plato's *Cratylus,* which examines *orthotês onomatôn.* In the *Cratylus, onoma* is used to refer not only to names but to all parts of a sentence and even to a sentence as a

163

whole.[21] Early in the dialogue Hermogenes and Socrates discuss the best way to begin the investigation, and Socrates suggests they ask Callias to teach them "the correctness" (*tên orthotêta*) which he learned from Protagoras. Hermogenes rejects the suggestion since he rejects Protagoras' book *Truth* of which the lesson is part (391b–e).

Detlev Fehling and Charles Segal hypothesize that Protagoras wrote a separate work titled *Orthoepeia*.[22] Fehling suggests that the work may have begun by critiquing Homer's misuse of language (gender and mood), hence all three of Aristotle's discussions of Protagoras' views on language may have been derived from the same source (DK 80 A27–29). Segal adds the suggestion that Plato's portrayal of Protagoras' discussion of the poem by Simonides (*Protagoras* 339a7–d9) and Aristophanes' lampoon of semantic analysis in *Clouds* (659–93) and *Frogs* (1119–97) may have been derived from the same Protagorean text: "Such a work would have opened with a brilliant demonstration of multiple errors in the well known beginning of a poem. . . . It would then have proceeded to a discussion of individual 'contradictions' in later sections of the poems."[23]

Lacking more direct evidence it is difficult to say what doctrine the historical Protagoras might have had concerning *orthos logos*. Kerferd suggests that the most likely possibility is that there was a connection between Protagoras' two-*logoi* and stronger/weaker *logoi* notions and the term *orthos*.[24] Choosing the right account of a thing or event was not a matter of mere semantics to Protagoras but a matter of giving an *orthos logos*—a straightforward or correct account. Such a meaning from a known relativist may sound strange, but it coheres with fifth-century usage of *orthos* and what is known of Protagoras.[25] Such an interpretation also resonates with the Greek of a book attributed to Protagoras by Diogenes Laertius: *Peri tôn ouk orthôs tois anthrôpois prassomenôn*, "On Errors in Human Affairs." Hence Protagoras' concern with *orthos logos* was not only a matter of speaking correctly in the sense an aristocrat might imply (proper enunciation or clever word choice); his concern was with a correct understanding of *pragmata* as reflected in discourse.

Kerferd has declared that *antilogikê*, the "art of antilogic," is the key to understanding "the true nature of the sophistic movement."[26] Though the term *antilogikê* almost certainly was coined by Plato, the roots of such an art can be confidently traced to Protagoras. Kerferd describes *antilogikê* as the practice of "opposing one *logos* to another *logos,* or in discovering or drawing attention to the presence of such an opposition in an argument or in a thing or state of affairs. The essential feature is the opposition of one *logos* to another either by contrariety or contradiction."[27] In view of Protagoras' claim that every thing (*pragma*) has two *logoi* in opposition concerning it and his "promise" to make the weaker *logos* stronger, it is reasonable to attibute the origin of *antilogikê* as a practice (if not as a term) to Protagoras.

It is difficult to estimate how Protagoras' notion of *antilogoi* functioned in educational practice in his time. A clue can be found in how the notion of *dissoi logoi* evolved from the mid-fifth century into the *antilogikê* of Plato's *Phaedrus*. In Protagoras' time *antilogoi* were conflicting choices or judgments—judgments on Antiphon's forensic cases pro and con and Aristophanes' famous conflict between new and old educational practices. The story "Choice of Heracles" and various Greek dramas from the fifth century also provide examples of conflicting *logoi* with clear objective or external referents.[28] In each of these cases different speakers are portrayed as representing each *logos* and, with the possible exception of Antiphon's *Tetralogies,* one *logos* is implied or stated to be preferable to the other. In the 400 BCE treatise *Dissoi Logoi* the author identifies conflicting *logoi* concerning the same "thing," but generally attributes the conflicting *logoi* to other people and makes clear the author's preferred position. It is not until Plato's *Phaedrus* that it is implied that *one* person might deliberately advocate conflicting positions. Describing *antilogikê,* Plato claims that the Sophist's art is one that "can make the same thing appear to the same people now just, now unjust, at will" and that "he can make the same things seem to the community now good, and now the reverse of good" (261c–d). Plato does not appear to be describing fifth-century educational practice in the passage; hence his treatment of *antilogikê* in the *Phaedrus* and elsewhere is not a reliable guide to Protagoras' practices. Nevertheless, a brief explanation of Plato's critique of *antilogikê* is useful for understanding how Protagoras' notion of *dissoi logoi* evolved and was understood by Plato.

Plato criticizes *antilogikê* on two grounds. First, he implies that it is easy to abuse: the practice of *antilogikê* can be for the mere purpose of defeating an opponent through tricks in argument. It then becomes eristic—*eristikê*—which Plato blames for misology.[29] Plato associates such practices directly with fourth-century Sophists, not fifth, though he implies that the seeds for such abuse were sown by the Older Sophists. His second criticism is of the implicit ontology of the *antilogikê:* opposites exist only in the phenomenal world, thus they participate only imper-

165

fectly in the Ideal Forms. Hence, as long as Sophists are tied to the fickle *doxa* of the public—claiming that an act is now just, now unjust, etc.— their art will always be inferior to the art of discovering the true nature of reality: dialectic.[30]

Presented with the problem of rationalizing conflicting *logoi* of the form "X is p" and "X is not-p," Protagoras explained the differences according to the situational logic reflected in Homeric syntax: "X is p for Y" and "X is not-p for Z." After at least fifty years of progress in analytical thinking and revision of mythic-poetic vocabulary and syntax by his predecessors, Plato and possibly Socrates addressed the same problem by dropping the conflicting predicates and relative contexts in order to seek the unchanging essence of X; hence the Socratic/Platonic question "What *is* X?"[31]

Two passages in the dialogues of Plato connect the *logos* of Protagoras with fifth-century medical thinking.[32] The first is in the *Protagoras* where the title character is illustrating the relativistic nature of "good" through a tour de force which demonstrates the breadth of his experience:

> I know of plenty of things—foods, drinks, drugs, and many others— which are harmful to men, and others which are beneficial, and others again which, so far as men are concerned, are neither, but are harmful or beneficial to horses, and others only to cattle or dogs. Some have no effect on animals, but only on trees, and some again are good for the roots of trees but injurious to the young growths. Manure, for instance, is good for all plants when applied to their roots, but utterly destructive if put on the shoots or young branches. Or take olive oil. It is very bad for plants, and most inimical to the hair of all animals except man, whereas men find it of service both to the hair and to the rest of the body. So diverse and multiform is goodness that even with us the same thing is good when applied externally but deadly when taken internally. Thus all doctors forbid the sick to use oil in preparing their food, except in the very smallest quantities, just enough to counteract the disagreeable smell which food and sauces may have for them (334a–c).

Michael Gagarin believes that this passage is taken directly from a published work of Protagoras.[33] Given the consistency of the "X is P for Y" logic throughout the passage and the similarity between it and section 1 titled "On Good and Bad" of the *Dissoi Logoi* treatise (ca. 400 BCE), the authenticity of the passage is at least a good possibility.

The easy movement among what would now be called different fields, such as medicine, horticulture, and animal husbandry, was common in

166

fifth-century discourse. As G. E. R. Lloyd observes, there was no clear distinction drawn between the professional medical practitioner and the professional Sophist or philosopher.[34] Even in the fourth century Plato's and Aristotle's interests included such matters as the origins of disease and animal reproduction.[35] The absence of a clear demarcation between medical and sophistical arts during the fifth century is an important fact to recognize when interpreting passages in which the two practices are mentioned. Such a passage is found in Protagoras' "apology" in the *Theaetetus:*

> By a wise man I mean precisely a man who can change any one of us, when what is bad appears and is to him, and make what is good appear and be to him.... To the sick man his food appears sour and is so; to the healthy man it is and appears the opposite.... What is wanted is a change to the opposite condition, because the other state is better.
>
> And so too in education a change has to be effected from the worse condition to the better; only, whereas the physician produces a change by means of drugs, the Sophist does it by discourse.... When someone by reason of a depraved condition of mind has thoughts of a like character, one makes him, by reason of a sound condition, think other and sound thoughts.... And as for the wise, my dear Socrates, so far from calling them frogs, I call them, when they have to do with the body, physicians, and when they have to do with plants, husbandmen. For I assert that husbandmen too, when plants are sickly and have depraved sensations, substitute for these sensations that are sound and healthy, and moreover the wise and honest public speakers [*rhêtoras*] substitute in the community sound for unsound views of what is right. For I hold that whatever practices seem right and laudable to any particular state are so, for that state, so long as it holds by them. Only, when the practices are, in any particular case, unsound for them, the wise man substitutes others that are and appear sound (166d–167c).

Though the passage is filled with distinctions and terms Protagoras never would have used ("appears"/"is," "sensation"), it generally accords with the logic of the passage cited above from the *Protagoras.* Two further bits of evidence lend credence to a Protagorean analogy between medicine and discourse. The first is a consistent reference to Antiphon's using the power of discourse to aid the sick. A typical passage is that by Plutarch: "He composed a manual for the avoidance of troubles, on the analogy of the treatment of the sick by doctors.... He advertised that he had the power of curing those that were in trouble by means of

167

speech; and discovering the causes of their sickness by inquiry he consoled the sick."[36] The second is from Gorgias' *Encomium of Helen:*

> The effect of speech [*logos*] upon the condition of the soul is comparable to the power of drugs over the nature of bodies. For just as different drugs dispel different secretions from the body, and some bring an end to disease and others to life, so also in the case of speeches, some distress, others delight, some cause fear, others make the hearers bold, and some drug and bewitch the soul with a kind of evil persuasion (DK 82 B11 ¶14).

The analogy being drawn in these passages is a *literal* one: *Logos* is to the soul or psyche as medicine is to the body. Both arts involve someone skilled in effecting a change in someone else. In both, the sickness is part physical, part psychological. Substituting one *logos* for another (making the weaker *logos* the stronger) is to effect a change for the better. Whether the "patient" is a student, a jury, or a community, the process is the same.[37]

PROTAGORAS AND CIVIC *ARETÊ*

What has not yet been examined is the goal or objective toward which fifth-century education was directed. That objective was *aretê*. The goal of life as found in Homer is to display *aretê*: to be a teller of tales and a doer of deeds (*Iliad* 9.443), consequently helping one's friends and harming one's enemies. Though the concept of *aretê* underwent changes in the centuries following Homer, the basic aspiration to seek *aretê* continued throughout ancient Greek history.[38]

Aretê in Plato's dialogues often takes on the meaning of "virtue," specifically moral virtue. Prior to Plato the term had quite a different set of meanings associated with it. Three characteristics of the Homeric notion of *aretê* were as follows. First and foremost, *aretê* denoted skill and excellence: "Always be first and best, ahead of everyone else."[39] *Aretê* encompassed skills in a wide array of activities, including military, athletic, and intellectual.[40] Most of all it meant to best others in whatever *agôn* (contest) one competed. The competitive aspect of *aretê* remained dominant well into the fourth century.[41] Hence a common meaning of *agathos* ("good" in Plato) is to be good *at* aiding oneself and one's friends.[42]

Second, while Plato's notion of virtue was somewhat abstract, intangible, and unchanging, in Homer *aretê* was relatively concrete, tangible,

168

and relative to the situation. The *aretê* of a race horse was speed, of a cart horse strength.[43] If one could not aid one's friends by open means, cunning should provide deceitful means.[44]

Third, the Homeric conception of *aretê* equated it with nobility and high birth.[45] It is common in archaic cultures to assume that wealth, skill, and excellence are all a matter of one's lineage, and Greek culture under the influence of Homer was no exception. Prosperity is a sign of *aretê* and goodness because wealth benefits one's family and friends. In this connection it is important to note the relationship between *aretê*, wealth, and the physical defense of the *polis:*

> The primary function of any state is to survive, and to prosper as well as it may; and in a small state such as a Greek city-state, in competition with its neighbors for the produce of a not very wealthy land, this primary function can never be long out of mind. To ensure survival, the will and the ability to resist, coupled with good counsel, are the most evident necessities. In a hoplite-oligarchy, or any society in which the individual must buy his own fighting equipment, the most effective striking force is supplied by the rich; and, given the prestige derived from this in a society with the traditional Greek values, it is the rich who, even in a society which is a democracy in name, will give advice in the assembly and hold the most important offices.[46]

It is not surprising, then, that the nobility were considered those with *aretê* and were called the *agathoi,* since they most directly benefited the welfare and safety of the *polis.* The Homeric combination of elements—wealth, nobility, and *aretê*—preserved in the mythic-poetic tradition, helped to keep social control in the hands of the Athenian "first families."[47] Consequently, the fifth-century beginnings of a break from the Homeric tradition had revolutionary implications for the Athenian social-political order.

The change that took place in fifth-century Athens, of which the Sophists were a part, can be described as the democratization of *aretê.* Sometimes it has been implied that the Sophists were the cause of the change in attitude toward *aretê,* but such a claim does not give adequate credit to other important factors at work in the fifth century.[48] One such factor was the Athenian navy. "Liturgies" imposed on the wealthiest citizens financed the navy, providing the material means for poor men to prove their *aretê* in battle.[49] Furthermore, Athenian imperialism brought with it a host of practical managerial problems. The person able to aid the city's management exhibited a valuable *aretê.*[50] Under Periclean de-

169

mocracy a greater variety of people had opportunity to offer sound counsel in the assembly or to win fortunes in the popular courts, thereby proving their *aretê* and becoming *agathoi.*[51]

The sophistic contribution to this process of democratization was twofold. First, some Sophists helped to provide a theoretical justification for education and democracy itself.[52] Second, on a practical level the Sophists' secular theories and highly developed prose aided the break from the mythic-poetic tradition and the elitism associated with it. Protagoras was a pioneer with respect to both the theoretical and the practical aspects of advancing democracy.

It is virtually certain that Protagoras provided a theoretical justification for education and Periclean democracy.[53] His Great Speech in Plato's *Protagoras* is generally regarded as a moderately reliable index to his actual defense, and in it one finds an argument for the teachability of *aretê*—the underlying premise justifying education and Periclean democracy. Later I will examine some of the specific content of the Great Speech, but for present purposes it is not important *how* Protagoras justified democracy; it is significant *that* he did so. As A. W. H. Adkins put it, "The *aretê* of the *agathos politês* of the fifth century is a skill, a *technê.*"[54] Protagoras apparently claimed that this skill could be taught. It is a claim that one finds implicitly in Pericles' Funeral Oration, and it is explicitly defended in chapter 6 of the treatise *Dissoi Logoi*. Regardless of the argument's treatment by Plato, there is little doubt that Protagoras defended the radical thesis that *aretê* did not depend on birth or inheritance. Whether he was the first so to argue is difficult to say. The theme occurs in fifth-century drama, but it is impossible to ascertain who influenced whom. In any case Protagoras seems to have provided one of the first and most persuasive arguments on the teachability of *aretê*.

On the level of *praxis* the Sophists in general and Protagoras in particular contributed to the break from Homeric-age attitudes toward *aretê*. The ascendancy of a humanistic-rationalistic *logos* coincided with a decline in influence of Homeric patterns of thought; in this sense Protagoras' teachings were ideological in both function and content. Further, to whatever extent Protagoras taught individuals how to be more successful in the assembly and in court, his teaching aided the process of democratizing *aretê*. Skill is a prerequisite to success; *politikê technê* creates *agathos politês*.[55] The ordinary person can become *agathos politês*, "in the sense of becoming a politician skilled in word and action, to the ... end of promoting the prosperity of the city."[56]

The close relationship among the political, social, and theistic aspects

170

of the mythic-poetic tradition and the challenge it faced in the mid-fifth century is underscored by the importance of the rise of the secular courts. Periclean democracy in the 440s saw a tremendous increase in the construction and popularity of the *dikastêria* in Athens.[57] As the importance and power of prose discourse increased, the relative prestige and power of *mythos* was diminished: "The massive presence of the democratic courts went far to dissolve what remained of the close correspondence which had once existed between the city's social structure and the government and organization of the gods in traditional mythology."[58]

Poulakos has described the Sophists' lessons as subversive "in that they aimed to disempower the powerful and empower the powerless."[59] Accordingly, the Sophists' promise to make clever speakers who "could carry on the project of cultural critique" was popular "among the hitherto voiceless and marginalized."[60] Measured by contemporary standards, Poulakos' description is clearly an exaggeration. Even in its most radical form Athenian democracy limited citizenship to a minority of the adult population, retained the institution of slavery, and was thoroughly misogynist.[61] The "radical nature of Athenian democracy" is clear only when it is "measured against the standards of the age in which it developed."[62] As progressive as some fifth-century sophistic theories might have been, the Sophists were not strict egalitarians.[63] They provided their services for those who could afford them, hence "what the Sophists were able to offer was in no sense a contribution to the education of the masses."[64] Though Protagoras' doctrines contributed to the democratization of Athens and can be read as a justification for radical democracy, Ostwald is correct in concluding that "only the wealthy could afford Protagoras."[65]

In addition to the passages I have cited so far, three additional references connect Protagoras with the subject of education. They include: "Teaching requires natural endowment and practice," and "they must learn starting young" (DK 80 B3); and "Protagoras said that art [*technai*] was nothing without practice and practice nothing without art" (DK 80 B10). Since the references are far removed from Protagoras' time, their authenticity is difficult to determine. They are noteworthy for their novelty as early speculations about education. To say that "today the Greek system of higher education, as built up by the Sophists, dominates the entire civilized world" is to claim too much.[66] Nonetheless, Protagoras' contributions to fifth-century educational theory and practice place him as one of the more original and significant educators and philosophers of ancient Greece.

171

NOTES

1. William V. Harris, *Ancient Literacy* (Cambridge, MA: Harvard U. Press, 1989), 57–64. On rival philosophical schools see Eric A. Havelock, "The Linguistic Task of the Presocratics," *Language and Thought in Early Greek Philosophy,* ed. Kevin Robb (LaSalle, IL: Hegeler Institute, 1983), 42–82. For the development of Greek higher education see Frederick A. G. Beck, *Greek Education 450–350 B.C.* (New York: Barnes and Noble, 1964).

2. Rosalind Thomas, *Oral Tradition and Written Record in Classical Athens* (Cambridge: Cambridge U. Press, 1989), 19–20; Eric A. Havelock, *Preface to Plato* (Cambridge, MA: Harvard U. Press, 1963), 40. On the point that books remained rare well into the fourth century, see F. H. Sandbach, *Aristotle and the Stoics* (Cambridge: Cambridge U. Press, 1985), 1–3.

3. Thomas S. Kuhn, *The Structure of Scientific Revolutions* (Chicago: U. of Chicago Press, 1970). Throughout his work Kuhn notes how revolutionary scientists have one foot in the past tradition while contributing to the development of a new one; the result is that their work is sometime difficult to classify.

4. E. G. Turner, *Athenian Books in the Fifth and Fourth Centuries B.C.* (London: H. K. Lewis, 1977), 18; Eric A. Havelock, *The Muse Learns to Write* (New Haven: Yale U. Press, 1986), 92. See also Leonard Woodbury, "Aristophanes' *Frogs* and Athenian Literacy," *TAPA* 106 (1976): 349–57; F. Jacoby, "The First Athenian Prose Writer," *Mnemosyne* 13 (1947): 13–64.

5. Cf. Jonathan Barnes, "Aphorism and Argument," *Language and Thought in Early Greek Philosophy,* 91–109.

6. Jaap Mansfeld, "Protagoras on Epistemological Obstacles and Persons," in Kerferd, *Legacy,* 40.

7. Ibid., 43; cf. the Great Speech in Plato's *Protagoras.*

8. Havelock, *Preface,* 40.

9. Ibid., 286, cf. 290; and "Task."

10. See Plato's *Phaedrus;* Havelock, *Preface,* 40, 55 n14; Harris, *Ancient Literacy,* 30–33; Thomas, *Oral Tradition.* For two very different verdicts on the Older Sophists' written works, see Takis Poulakos, "Intellectuals and the Public Sphere: The Case of the Older Sophists," *Spheres of Argument: Proceedings of the Sixth SCA/AFA Conference on Argumentation,* ed. Bruce E. Gronbeck (Annandale, VA: Speech Communication Association, 1989), 10–14; and Tony M. Lentz, *Orality and Literacy in Hellenic Greece* (Carbondale: Southern Illinois U. Press, 1989), 109–21.

11. J. V. Muir, "Protagoras and Education at Thourioi," *Greece and Rome* 29 (1982): 20.

12. Ibid., 22.

13. Humanism is "any philosophy which recognizes the value or dignity of [humans] and makes [them] the measure of all things or somehow takes human nature, its limits, or its interests as its theme" (Nicola Abbagnano, "Humanism," *Encyclopedia of Philosophy* [New York: Macmillan, 1967], 4:69–70). On the role of prose in sophistic teaching see James L. Jarrett, *The Educational Theories of the Sophists* (New York: Teachers College Press, 1969), 16–18.

14. Norman Kretzmann, "History of Semantics," *Encyclopedia of Philosophy* (New York: Macmillan, 1967), 7:359.

15. Robert A. Kaster, *Guardians of Language: The Grammarian and Society in Late Antiquity* (Berkeley: U. of California Press, 1988). Cf. Saul Levin, "The Origin of Grammar in Sophistry," *General Linguistics* 23 (1983): 41–47.

16. See Havelock, "Task," 57.

17. Dupréel, *Sophistes,* 49–52; Kretzmann, "History," 359; Wilhelm Windelband, *History of Ancient Philosophy* (New York: Scribner's, 1924), 115.

172

18. Kerferd, *SM,* 34, adapted from Havelock, *The Liberal Temper in Greek Politics* (New Haven: Yale U. Press, 1957), 216.

19. Charles P. Segal, "Gorgias and the Psychology of Logos," *HSCP* 66 (1962): 106.

20. Kerferd, *SM,* 68–77. See also Ruth Scodell, "Literary Interpretation in Plato's *Protagoras,*" *Ancient Philosophy* 6 (1986): 25–37.

21. Kerferd, *SM,* 70.

22. Detlev Fehling, "Protagoras und die ὀρθοέπεια," in Classen, *Sophistik,* 341–47; Charles Segal, "Protagoras' *Orthoepeia* in Aristophanes' 'Battle of the Prologues' (*Frogs* 1119–97)," *Rheinisches Museum für Philologie* 113 (1970): 158–62.

23. Segal, "Protagoras' *Orthoepeia,*" 161. For the argument that Protagoras' written works may have included the analysis of Simonides' poem as portrayed by Plato (*Protagoras,* 339aff.), see Rudolf Pfeiffer, *History of Classical Scholarship from the Beginnings to the End of the Hellenistic Age* (Oxford: Clarendon Press, 1968), 32–33.

24. Kerferd, *SM,* 75–76. Pfeiffer perhaps justifiably concludes that "no plausible reconstruction of a true 'theory' of *orthoepeia* is possible" (*History,* 39).

25. See Richard Bett, "The Sophists and Relativism," *Phronesis* 34 (1989): 154–61. In what Kerferd calls an "audacious conjecture" (*SM,* 69), Italo Lana has suggested that one result of Protagora's theory of *orthos logos* was the unusual use of *dynamia* (feminine ending) instead of the expected *dynamis* in the Proem of the Laws of Charondes. See Italo Lana, *Protagora* (Torino: Università di Torino Pubblicazione, 1950).

26. Kerferd, *SM,* 62.

27. Ibid., 63.

28. DK 84 B2; Euripides, *Suppliants* 486–93; *Phoenissae* 559-60.

29. Kerferd, *SM,* 59–67; cf. Plato, *Phaedo* 89d-90c.

30. See G. B. Kerferd, "Le sophiste vu par Platon: un philosophe imparfait," *Positions de la Sophistique,* ed. Barbara Cassin (Paris: Vrin, 1986), 13–25, and *Legacy,* 5; *SM,* 66–67. See also Richard Robinson, *Plato's Earlier Dialectic* (Oxford: Clarendon Press, 1953).

31. Cf. Havelock, *Preface.*

32. On the importance of the relationship between philosophy and medicine see Michael Frede, "Philosophy and Medicine in Antiquity," *Human Nature and Natural Knowledge,* ed. A. Donagan, A. N. Perovich, Jr., and M. V. Wedin (Dordrecht: D. Reidel, 1986), 211–32.

33. Michael Gagarin, "Plato and Protagoras" (Ph.D. diss., Yale University, 1968), 96–98.

34. G. E. R. Lloyd, *Magic, Reason and Experience* (Cambridge: Cambridge U. Press, 1979), 96.

35. Plato, *Timaeus;* Aristotle, *Generation of Animals.*

36. [Plutarch] *Antiphon* 833c = DK 87 A6. J. S. Morrison renumbers this as 87 A3 ¶18 in R. K. Sprague, *The Older Sophists* (Columbia: U. of South Carolina Press, 1972), 117.

37. Auguste Bayonas, "L'art politique d'après Protagoras," *Revue Philosophique* 157 (1967): 57–58.

38. H. D. F. Kitto, *The Greeks* (Harmondsworth: Penguin, 1957); Werner Jaeger, *Paideia: The Ideals of Greek Culture* (New York: Oxford U. Press, 1945), 1:12.

39. *Iliad* 6.208, trans. Charles H. Kahn, *The Art and Thought of Heraclitus* (Cambridge: Cambridge U. Press, 1979), 12.

40. Cf. *Iliad* 15.642.

41. Alasdair MacIntyre, *After Virtue* (Notre Dame: Notre Dame U. Press, 1981), 129.

42. A. W. H. Adkins, *Merit and Responsibility: A Study in Greek Values* (Oxford: Clarendon Press, 1960), 37–38, 156–63.

43. Kitto, *The Greeks,* 172.

44. MacIntyre, *After Virtue,* 124.

45. Jaeger, *Paideia,* 3–14; see also T. A. Sinclair, *A History of Greek Political Thought* (London: Routledge and Kegan Paul, 1951), 44–46.

173

46. Adkins, *Merit,* 197.
47. Eric A. Havelock, *The Muse Learns to Write* (New Haven: Yale U. Press, 1986), 5.
48. G. B. Kerferd, "Sophists," *Encyclopedia of Philosophy* (New York: Macmillan, 1967), 7:486.
49. Adkins, *Merit,* 197.
50. Ibid., 225; Sinclair, *History,* 48.
51. Richard Garner, *Law and Society in Classical Athens* (New York: St. Martin's Press, 1987), 11–19.
52. Reimar Müller, "Sophistique et démocratie," *Positions de la Sophistique,* 179–93. Not all Sophists were enthusiastic supporters of radical democracy. We can safely describe those Older Sophists closely associated with the temporary overthrows of the democracy in the late fifth century as antidemocratic. See Martin Ostwald, *From Popular Sovereignty to the Sovereignty of Law: Law, Society, and Politics in Fifth-Century Athens* (Berkeley: U. of California Press, 1986), 229–50.
53. G. B. Kerferd, "Protagoras," *Encyclopedia of Philosophy* (New York: Macmillan, 1967), 6:506; "Sophists," 496.
54. Adkins, *Merit,* 244.
55. Cf. Plato, *Protagoras* 319a3–5.
56. Adkins, *Merit,* 226.
57. Garner, *Law,* 39–48.
58. Ibid., 43.
59. John Poulakos, "Sophistical Rhetoric as a Critique of Culture," *Argument and Critical Practices: Proceedings of the Fifth SCA/AFA Conference on Argumentation,* ed. Joseph W. Wenzel (Annandale, VA: Speech Communication Association, 1987), 99.
60. Ibid., 101.
61. Josiah Ober, *Mass and Elite in Democratic Athens: Rhetoric, Ideology, and the Power of the People* (Princeton: Princeton U. Press, 1989), 3–10; Eva C. Keuls, *The Reign of the Phallus: Sexual Politics in Ancient Athens* (New York: Harper, 1985); Eva Cantarella, *Pandora's Daughters: The Role and Status of Women in Greek and Roman Antiquity* (Baltimore: Johns Hopkins U. Press, 1987).
62. Ober, *Mass and Elite,* 7.
63. Ostwald, *Sovereignty,* 229–50; cf. Dupréel, *Sophistes,* 25–28.
64. Kerferd, *SM,* 17.
65. Ostwald, *Sovereignty,* 242.
66. Jaeger, *Paideia,* 317.

11

PROTAGORAS, *LOGOS*,
AND THE *POLIS*

I turn now to Protagoras' theory of *logos* and its implications for social-political theory. It has long been recognized that Protagoras' human-measure fragment presented a viewpoint supportive of Periclean democracy, but the political implications of Protagoras' general views and his theory of *logos* have not received adequate attention.

On one level or another, significant philosophical disourse always interacts with the discourse and mindset of the prevailing social-political order. The interaction need not be intentional; for his philosophy to be significant Nietzsche need not have intended the uses to which his philosophy was put by Nazi Germany.[1] Even modern academic philosophy, often apparently far removed from the vagaries of everyday political life, can function ideologically by making the "collective critique of the culture virtually impossible and the reproduction of the dominant culture virtually certain."[2]

The relationship between philosophical issues and social-political matters was even clearer in ancient Greece. Unduly influenced by the impression that Plato rejected life in the *polis* and advocated the quiet life of philosophical contemplation, many histories of early Greek philosophy fail to note the political orientations and activities of those we now call philosophers. Plato's writings are thoroughly ideological, and even Plato tried his hand at influencing politics—through the training of the would-be philosopher-king, Dion.[3] Plato's persistent rejection of Athenian democracy and his claim that only a few elite philosophers possessed the truth marked him, according to Karl Popper, as an enemy of democracy and the "open society."[4]

Virtually all of the presocratic philosophers were actively involved in the political affairs of their time. The notion of a professional philosopher as such did not emerge until Plato's writing.[5] Fifth-century Athens drew no clear lines between political, dramatic, and philosophical discourse: the audience and agenda for all three were one and the same.[6] Accordingly, there is an important sense in which all significant public discourse of the fifth century was both influenced by—and in turn sought to influence—the social-political life of the *polis*.

As I have shown at some length, Protagoras' fragments are at odds with the views of Parmenides and the Eleatics. To what extent was the conflict between Protagoras' and Parmenides' philosophies part of a larger struggle? A precise answer is impossible, but several facts from the fifth century provide clues. Parmenides is said to have been a lawgiver of Elea.[7] Though nothing is known of his laws, E. L. Minar has suggested that there was probably a connection between Parmenides' political views and social position and his philosophical views.[8] Given Parmenides' portrayal of knowledge as a gift of divinity and his description of mortals as wandering about deaf and blind in two-headed fashion, the obvious inference is that Parmenides favored a form of government more restrictive than democracy. Parmenides' follower Melissus of Samos attacked the views of other philosophers concerning opposites and of those who argued for the trustworthiness of the senses, "just as Parmenides and Zeno levelled their critiques against mortal opinions in general."[9] Melissus also battled Pericles head-on, as they were rival admirals of their respective navies; Melissus won at least one battle which has been dated at 441 BCE.[10] Given that the Sophists were actively involved with the political events of their time, any thorough treatment of sophistic theories of *logos* requires an examination of the probable interaction between *logos* and the *polis*.

PROTAGORAS AND PERICLEAN DEMOCRACY

Athenian democracy did not spring into place overnight. Its establishment was gradual and cautious. The beginnings of democracy are traditionally attributed to the reign of Solon, beginning approximately in 594

BCE. Prior to Solon there was a ruling class of wealthy and "high born" elites, later referred to as the *Eupatridai:* "It appears that *Eupatridai* effectively dominated the major magistracies and hence the government was largely or entirely controlled by the nobility."[11] By the late seventh century there was a growing group of individuals who were weathly but not noble born (sometimes called *kakoi*), as well as a large class of working poor—many of whom had fallen into debt and bondage to the wealthy. Due to rising social and political tensions between these groups, Solon was empowered to reform the process of governance.

Though the precise content of Solon's reforms remains a matter of controversy, two significant actions have been widely accepted as true: "the rectification of the position of Athenians who had fallen into debt-bondage and a change in the prerequisites for holding the major offices of the state."[12] The elimination of debt bondage in effect defined the Athenian citizenry, and made it impossible for Athenians to become slaves in their own *polis.* The change in membership of the ruling elite resulted in a fourfold class system defined strictly by wealth.[13] The archonships of the state were limited to those in the higher classes. *Thetes,* the lowest class, who constituted two-thirds of the citizen body, were not eligible.[14] The practical results of Solon's reforms for advancing democracy were, in retrospect, quite modest. But they at least opened the door to political mobility for those not of high birth, and they paved the way for later, more significant steps toward democracy.

Cleisthenes' reforms took place near the end of the sixth century. According to Martin Ostwald, Cleisthenes was "no ideological democrat but a practical statesman and politician concerned with eliminating the roots of internal conflict from the society in which he lived."[15] In part, his reforms were aimed at reconfiguring the organization of the state at the local level in such a way as to reduce the power of old aristocratic families in the Assembly and in the Council of Five Hundred.[16] Another significant change was the creation of ostracism laws, which increased public accountability and reduced persistent conflict among the aristocratic clans by exiling, in Josiah Ober's words, "any individual who threatened the national consensus, especially by publicly advocating ideas or acting in ways that threatened the values of political society."[17] It is important to note that "even after the reforms of Cleisthenes the upper class retained effective control of the organs of government."[18] Certain important political rights, such as membership on the Council of Five Hundred, were still available only to about one-third of the adult male population.[19]

A series of reforms associated with Ephialtes and Pericles at about 462 set the stage for "radical" democracy.[20] One set of reforms effected the transfer of certain powers from the noble-born members of the Areopagus to more democratically controlled bodies.[21] Jurisdiction over all crimes against the state and the *dokimasia* (scrutiny) of elected officials were put into the hands of the more democratic Council of Five Hundred and the popular people's courts known as the *dikastêria*.[22] Combined with the requirement that legislative measures be approved by the Assembly, the broad powers given the *dikastêria* meant that virtually all important state actions required the consent of the people. According to Ostwald, not until these reforms were in place could Athens be properly called a democracy:

> But only after Ephialtes removed from the Areopagus those powers that had given it guardianship over the state and distributed them among Council, Assembly, and the popular law court in a way that necessitated the establishment of *dikastêria* can we fairly call Athens a democracy. Although the upper classes still retained a virtual monopoly of the generalship, all magistrates were henceforth answerable for their conduct in office not to a small group drawn from the upper class but to those to whom they owed their election to office and those ultimately most affected by their official acts, the people as a whole.[23]

Ober has suggested that Athenian democracy was fully realized only after pay for jury duty was instituted during the 440s. Sponsored by Pericles, jury pay made active involvement in the *dikastêria* a practical possibility for the working classes. This effectively empowered the masses to be the legal judges of *all* citizens' actions. Full or "radical" democracy, therefore, initially flourished at the same time that Pericles became the de facto leader of Athens: "By the 440s, if not before, *dêmokratia* became the standard term to describe the Athenian form of government, and the demos indeed possessed the political power in the state."[24]

Pericles was the leading Athenian politician between 450 and his death in 429. He was reelected to a generalship each year between 443 and 429, "a record that demonstrates his continuing popularitry with the voting population."[25] The precise relationship between Protagoras and Pericles is impossible to ascertain, but there is no doubt that they knew and influenced each other. A variety of facts from the period provide clues concerning their mutual influence. Protagoras' visits to Athens roughly coincided with Pericles' political career.[26] As noted earlier, Plutarch reported that Protagoras and Pericles spent a whole day discussing the proper adjudication of an accidental death involving a man being struck by a javelin on a practice field. The discussion shows the intimate connection between Protagoras' relativism, the notion of *orthos logos,* and the practical administration of state justice (DK 80 A10). A fragment from Pericles' funeral oration of 440/39 BCE (during Protagoras' acme) contains passages that echo Protagoras' human-measure and "concerning the gods" fragments.[27] A variety of passages in fifth-century drama suggest mutual influence between Pericles and Protagoras.[28] The design of the sculpture on part of the Parthenon suggests the influence of Protagoras' new anthropocentric explanation of the gods.[29]

Around 444 BCE Pericles sought to establish a colony at Thurii. The exact political motivation behind this is in doubt, but it was certainly part of Athenian imperialism. Pericles' hope was that the colony would be "Athenian in its leadership and Panhellenic in its composition, and . . . might develop into a political and cultural centre establishing and extending Athenian influence far more efficiently than could be hoped for by any treaty of alliance."[30] In many ways Thurii was intended to be a model city, and its establishment attracted a number of fifth-century notables. Protagoras was given the task of creating the constitution or laws (*nomoi*) of Thurii (DL 9.50). Little is known of these laws, but they were essentially democratic, and they included a provision that no one was allowed to be elected general (*stratêgos*) twice within a period of five years (Aristotle, *Politics* 1307b7). Typically Greek city-states traced their legal codes back to divine lawgivers.[31] That the "agnostic" Sophist Protagoras was given such a task for an important new colony suggests how respected he was and how thoroughly he was involved in current political events.

Protagoras apparently was given charge of the training of Pericles' sons (Plato, *Protagoras*). When Pericles' sons Paralus and Xanthippus died, Protagoras praised Pericles' behavior:

> For though his young and beautiful sons had died within a period of only eight days he bore it without grieving. For he maintained his tranquility of mind, a fact which served him well every day by bringing good fortune, calming distress, and raising his reputation among the people. For at the sight of the manly way he endured his sorrows all judged him high-minded and brave and superior to themselves, knowing well their own helplessness in like circumstances (DK 80 B9).

Pericles died in 429. The traditional story held that sometime between 420 and 415 Protagoras was expelled by the Athenians on the grounds of impiety. That story may have been a fabrication. If he were expelled, his banishment was probably the direct result of his continued association with those still representing Pericles' anti-Spartan party.[32]

PROTAGORAS' VISION OF THE *POLIS*

The facts known about Protagoras' associations with Pericles underscore the necessity of understanding the social-political context in which his "theory of *logos*" appeared. In addition to the fragments already examined, the primary guide to Protagoras' political theory is found in Plato's *Protagoras,* most notably in the Great Speech (320c8–328d2). While the speeches put in the mouth of Protagoras by Plato should not be regarded as *ipsissima verba,* they probably represent his *ipsissima praecepta.* Plato's character Protagoras was asked to defend the thesis that *aretê* can be taught. Protagoras agreed, giving the audience the choice of a story (*mythos*) or a reasoned argument (*logos*). The audience encouraged Protagoras to make the choice, and he decided it would be more pleasant to tell a story. Protagoras' myth can be summarized as follows.

Once there were gods but no mortal creatures. When the time came for the gods to create mortal creatures, Prometheus and Epimetheus were charged with equipping the creatures and giving each suitable powers for survival. Different creatures received different skills, sizes, foods, and means of protection from the elements and from each other. However, Epimetheus had overlooked humans, whom Prometheus discovered naked and unready for survival. So from Hephaestus and Athena, Prometheus stole the "wisdom in the arts" (*tên entechnon sophian*) together with fire and gave them to humanity. Because humans "had a share in the portion of the gods," they alone of all creatures worshiped the gods. Further, through their skill humans discovered speech (*phônê*) and names (*onomata*) and provided themselves with life's necessities.

Nonetheless, humanity was nearly wiped out by wild animals because they lacked the art of politics (*politikê*). Zeus, fearing their total destruction, sent Hermes to impart to humans respect for others (*aidôs*) and for justice (*dikê*). Anyone incapable of acquiring *aidôs* and *dikê* must be put to death as a plague to the city.

Protagoras then shifted to his *logos,* his reasoned defense for the teach-

180

ability of *aretê*. In matters of political wisdom when individual virtues (*aretai*) such as justice (*dikaiosunê*) and moderation (*sôphrosunê*) are involved, all are expected to partake in the discussion. Without such skills the city could not long endure. The city's practices demonstrate that all agree that these skills are acquired by instruction (*didakton*). One such practice is punishment which is not undertaken for the sake of revenge but to deter future wrongdoing. If someone lacks *dikaiosunê*, *sôphrosunê*, or *hosiotês* (being holy) and cannot be taught, that person must be expelled or executed.

The process of education occurs throughout life. The family teaches the child to excel, then the schools do the same, then the state itself through its laws (*nomoi*). Those with sufficient wealth continue their sons' education as long as possible, which proves they believe *aretê* is teachable. It is true that some fathers turn out worthless sons, but that fact does not deny the teachability of *aretê*. Such sons would still show more justice than savages without comparable training. Everyone in the city is a teacher of *aretê*, just as everyone is a teacher of the Greek language. Protagoras proclaimed himself as better than many at helping men become noble and excellent (*kaloi k'agathoi*), and hence he had earned the career of Sophist.

At least three theses suggested in the Great Speech can be regarded as authentically Protagorean. The first is the teachability of *aretê*. This thesis was crucial to the justification of the career of a Sophist. The notion that someone can become *agathos* through means other than birth or inheritance was revolutionary for both educational practice and for the prevailing social-political order.

Protagoras' defense of the teachability of *aretê* was ingenious. Though his insistence that all citizens partake in the political art was essentially democratic, his claim that some people are more skilled than others left the door open both to the art of the Sophist and to the long reign of a capable leader such as Pericles. His defense was consistent with the defense of the human-measure statement in the *Theaetetus;* each person's judgments are true for that person, but that does not exclude the possiblity that someone else can provide a better judgment.

Some scholars have maintained that Protagoras' Great Speech represents a specific *moral* theory.[33] However, as I noted previously, Plato's use of *aretê* as "moral virtue" differs significantly from the Homeric sense of *aretê* as "excellence" in a competitive sense. What is the sense of *aretê* found in Protagoras? As Adkins has noted, late in the fifth century one finds evidence of a bifurcation of *aretai* into "competitive"

181

and "cooperative" excellences.[34] By Plato's time the virtues of *dikaiosunê, sôphrosunê*, and *hosiotês* were probably seen as cooperative virtues, but it is unlikely that they were seen as such in Protagoras' time. During Protagoras' time *aretê* denoted and commended "excellences deemed most likely to ensure the success, prosperity and stability of the group."[35] The excellences of justice, moderation, and holiness were not valued as intrinsically good but as being beneficial to the *polis*. Plato was interested in virtue in itself and the relationship among the virtues; the abstract idea of justice as an end in itself began with him.[36]

The meaning of *dikaiosunê* in Protagoras' time is important because it is possible that Protagoras wrote on the subject. Diogenes Laertius cited two sources who claimed that "almost the whole of [Plato's] *Republic* can be read in the *Controversies* of Protagoras."[37] On its face such a claim seems wildly improbable, but some scholars suggest that Book 1 of the *Republic* originally appeared as a separate dialogue.[38] Book 1 analyzes such competing conceptualizations of justice (*dikaiosunê*) as honesty, helping friends and harming enemies, the interest of the stronger, and whether justice or injustice is more profitable. It is plausible to imagine Protagoras exploring just such issues—not from the Platonic perspective of determining what justice itself "really is," but from the standpoint of evaluating differing conceptions of justice with respect to their benefit to the *polis*.[39]

If Protagoras did, in fact, write on the subject of *dikaiosunê*, it is likely that his treatment of justice differed from the treatment of his predecessors. *Dikê*'s traditional meaning was that of a process: "as 'paying back *dikê*' and 'giving *dikê*' or 'taking *dikê* (as a penalty) for something'."[40] In the writings of Herodotus—our best guide to Protagoras' likely usage—*dikaiosunê* began to mean "a possession of the individual who can use it, in short, a property of the person, a part of his character."[41] If Plato's representation of *dikaiosunê* in the Great Speech is authentically Protagorean, then Protagoras' contribution may have been to identify justice as an individual *aretê*, or skill, that is valuable to the *polis* and that can be taught. As noted by Havelock, it is quite possible that Protagoras was the first to coin the word *dikaiosunê*. If so, then he could be credited with advancing the concept of justice about as far as possible given the constraints of the syntax in use at the time.[42] The next major conceptual advancement did not take place until the writings of Plato.[43]

The second authentic Protagorean thesis of the Great Speech is his theory of punishment. The relevant text is as follows:

In punishing wrongdoers, no one concentrates on the fact that a man has done wrong in the past, or punishes him on that account, unless taking blind vengeance like a beast. No, punishment is not inflicted by a rational man for the sake of the crime that has been committed—after all one cannot undo what is past—but for the sake of the future, to prevent either the same man, or by the spectacle of his punishment, someone else, from doing wrong again. But to hold such a view amounts to holding that virtue can be instilled by education; at all events the punishment is inflicted as a deterrent. This then is the view held by all who inflict it whether privately or publicly. And your fellow countrymen, the Athenians, certainly do inflict punishment and correction on supposed wrongdoers, as do others also. This argument therefore shows that they too think it possible to impart and teach goodness (*Protagoras* 324a6–d1).

Trevor Saunders' close reading of the passage provides solid reasons for believing that these lines represent "the actual penology of the historical Protagoras."[44] Prior to Protagoras' time, punishment was seen as part of the process of *dikê*—retribution or vengeance for harmful acts. There is no doubt among scholars that Protagoras originated the notion that the more important social role of punishment is to deter future harms; crime itself is not a sufficient justification for inflicting punishment.

The significance of Protagoras' innovation should not be understated. His reconceptualization of punishment as an act of education is as analytically creative as it is humane. As Havelock has exclaimed, "What centuries of angry superstition are rolled back in this statement!"[45] Saunders adds: "At one blow, he severs the link between crime and punishment, injury and counter-injury, tit-for-tat, which was very strong in Greek thought and still is in ours."[46]

Though Protagoras' theory of punishment has been "justly celebrated" by various scholars, the "fit" of this theory with Protagoras' other known doctrine has not been stressed.[47] The notion that education and punishment can change human behavior is a break from previous notions of inherited guilt or god-sent sins.[48] The teachability of *aretê* and the human-measure fragment go hand in hand. Protagoras' suggestion that punishment can reform an individual (325a) resonates with his medical analogy and his weaker/stronger *logoi* fragments. These connections not only give further reason to regard the theory as authentically Protagorean, they also suggest that Protagoras held a fairly complete and coherent view of humanity, *logos*, and the *polis*.

The third Protagorean thesis found in the Great Speech concerns the role of *logos* (as "discourse") in the *polis*. The relevant passage occurs after Protagoras says that Zeus ordered the civic art to be given not just to some but to all. Proof of his myth is the fact that Athenians have a participatory democracy: "When the subject of their counsel [*sumboulê*] involves *politikê aretê* ... they listen to every man's opinion, for they think that everyone must share in this kind of *aretê;* otherwise the state could not exist" (322e2–323a3). From the standpoint of detecting a rudimentary theory of *logos,* the passage contains several important elements which recur in Protagoras' speeches and fragments: participation by the many—through discourse—in making judgments.

Various scholars have noted that in the above and similar passages Protagoras offers "for the first time in human history a theoretical basis for participatory democracy."[49] It should be acknowledged at this point that political participation was denied to the majority of the adult population: women, foreigners, and slaves. Nonetheless, as Ober has argued, the historical significance of Athenian democracy deserves recognition:

> We may deplore the Athenians' exclusivist attitude, but moral censure should not obscure our appreciation of the fundamental importance of the new democratic political order. For the first time in the recorded history of a complex society, *all* native freeborn males, irrespective of their ability, family connections, or wealth, were political equals, with equal rights to debate and to determine state policy.[50]

Accordingly, Athenian democracy has been described as the parent of all democracies, and Protagoras appears as the first reasoned defender.[51]

In a passage slightly earlier in the dialogue Socrates asks for an explanation of what Protagoras teaches. Protagoras responds that his discipline (*mathêma*) is *euboulia* concerning the management of household and state affairs, such that students can become *dunatôtatoi* (powerful, influential, or capable) in the city's management and in discourse (*legein;* 318e5–319a2). *Euboulia* in the fifth century generally meant good or wise counsel.[52] Translations of the *Protagoras* render *euboulia* in this passage variously as "prudence" (Ostwald), "good planning" (Hubbard and Karnofsky), "proper management" (Taylor), "proper care of ... affairs" (Guthrie), "good judgment" (Lamb), and "formation of correct decision" (Havelock).[53] The desirability of *euboulia* is described in Sophocles' *Antigone:* "How better than all wealth is sound good counsel" and "to reject good counsel is a crime."[54] In four different passages of the *Protagoras* the *means* of discursive participation by many is connected to the intended *end* of good judgment.[55] Hence the provocative

184

connection of sound discourse (*orthos logos*) and good judgment (*euboulia*) by Protagoras seems eminently plausible.[56] Pericles' Funeral Oration as reported by Thucydides includes the following passage: "We Athenians decide public questions for ourselves, or at least endeavor to arrive at a sound understanding of them, in the belief that it is not debate [*logôi*] that is a hindrance to action, but rather not to be instructed by debate before the time comes for action" (2.40.2). If the speech is authentically Periclean, it may reflect Protagoras' influence.[57]

Protagoras' implicit theory of *logos* becomes explicit in Aristotle's *Rhetoric* (1391b7): "The use of persuasive speech [*pithanos logos*] is to lead to *krisis* (judgement or decision)." William M. A. Grimaldi has argued that this sentence summarizes the *telos* of rhetoric in Aristotle: "The concept of the audience as judge is underlined throughout the *Rhetoric* by frequent references to the fact that all rhetoric is directed towards *krisis,* or judgment, as its final goal."[58] Protagoras' rhetorical theory, therefore, can be described as an early formulation or anticipation of just such a relationship between *logos* and collective judgment.

Far from entailing solipsism or absolute subjectivism, Protagoras' *logos* is an instrument aimed at *intersubjectivity*.[59] Consensus is expressed in fifth-century Greek by *homonoia* (sameness of mind) or *homologos* (agreement).[60] For Protagoras, a consensus induced through *logos* was the means of reaching good judgment.[61] The sophistic tract called *Rhetoric to Alexander* describes law (*nomos*) as the "common agreement of the community"—*homologêma poleôs koinon* (1422a). This description was a radical departure from notions of the law being laid down or "given" by tyrants or deities. It is reasonable to believe that Protagoras played an important role in advancing such thought.[62] An echo of Protagoras' thinking is found in an aphorism of Democritus: "By encouragement and persuasive speech one will prove a more powerful advocate of excellence [*aretê*] than by law and compulsion."[63] *Logos* is the means to excellence, consensually constructed law (*nomos*) being one manifestation.

A further suggestion of the manner in which the Sophists connected *logos* with the *polis* is found in a later exchange in the *Protagoras*. A dispute breaks out after Socrates requests Protagoras to keep his answers short. This occurs after Socrates has recognized Protagoras' competence in making speeches and in engaging in question and answer (329b1–5). Protagoras objects to Socrates' request: "What do you mean by 'make my answers short'? Am I to make them shorter than the subject demands?" To which Socrates responds, "Of course not." They agree that

185

the answers should be as long as necessary. To which Protagoras responds, "As long a reply as *I* think necessary, or *you?*" (334d6–e3). Mansfeld reasonably claims that this pasage is another Platonic illustration of Protagoras' human-measure principle.[64] It is also the first of several passages that display Protagoras and other Sophists laying down the ground rules for a speaking contest (see 335a4–338e5). The competitive nature of the Greeks turned almost every public speaking opportunity—whether in the assembly, the law courts, or even private gatherings—into an *agôn,* a competition of wits and speaking ability.

According to Diogenes Laertius, Protagoras was the first to conduct debates *(logôn agôn),* the first to introduce "eristic," and the first to intitiate the practice of questioning and the "Socratic type of argument" (DK 80 A1, A3). The term eristic *(eristikê)* is of fourth-century origin, and it is used by Plato to mean "seeking victory in argument."[65] Protagoras did not use the term, but Diogenes Laertius' attribution is consistent with his claim that Protagoras introduced contests of speaking. There is no way of confirming this, but Plato's testimony seems sufficient for us to conclude that such practices were in use during the fifth century. It is likely, then, that Protagoras' contribution may have been to help formalize various speaking activities.

Before Plato coined the term "dialectic" to formalize a process of discussion, the verb *dialegesthai* meant "to hold dialogue" or "to render and receive discourse."[66] Plato showed four different Sophists—Protagoras, Hippias, Prodicus, and Critias—participating in the discussion of how the dialogue between Socrates and Protagoras should proceed. Beneath the surface parody of the Sophists, Havelock believed, there is evidence of an authentic sophistic achievement in rationalizing the rules of *logôn agôn.*[67]

How plausible is the conjecture that certain Older Sophists, Protagoras in particular, helped to rationalize *logos* by formalizing procedures of public discourse? The *Topics* of Aristotle includes numerous passages demonstrating that dialectic in Aristotle's school was a carefully regulated activity; the duration was fixed, and questions were to be framed to elicit yes-or-no answers.[68] No doubt Aristotle's rules had predecessors. The quasi-technical character of the language used by Plato's Sophists in the *Protagoras* makes it clear that they were in the process of formalizing certain procedures.[69] Given the active involvement in political affairs by virtually all of the Older Sophists, and given the fact that Pericles selected Protagoras to write the laws at Thurii, it is reasonable to infer that some Sophists did, in fact, aid in the formulation of rules or principles governing the discourse of the assembly and the law courts.

NOTES

1. Robert C. Solomon, *From Rationalism to Existentialism* (New York: Harper, 1972), 105–38.

2. John Poulakos, "Sophistical Rhetoric as a Critique of Culture," *Argument and Critical Practices: Proceedings of the Fifth SCA/AFA Conference on Argumentation*, ed. Joseph W. Wenzel (Annandale, VA: Speech Communication Association, 1987), 97. See also Takis Poulakos, "Intellectuals and the Public Sphere: The Case of the Older Sophists," *Spheres of Argument: Proceedings of the Sixth SCA/AFA Conference on Argumentation*, ed. Bruce E. Gronbeck (Speech Communication Association, 1989), 9–14.

3. Guthrie, *HGP IV*, 17–32.

4. Karl R. Popper, *The Open Society and Its Enemies*, (London: Routledge and Kegan Paul, 1966); see also I. F. Stone, *The Trial of Socrates* (New York: Anchor Books, 1989). On the ideological aspects of Plato's theory of rhetoric, see Charles Kauffman, "The Axiological Foundations of Plato's Theory of Rhetoric," *CSSJ* 33 (1982): 353–66.

5. Eric A. Havelock, "The Linguistic Task of the Presocratics," *Language and Thought in Early Greek Philosophy*, ed. Kevin Robb (LaSalle, IL: Hegeler Institute, 1983), 56–57.

6. Alasdair MacIntyre, *After Virtue* (Notre Dame: Notre Dame U. Press, 1981), 129.

7. DL 9.23; see also Guthrie, *HGP II*, 2 n3.

8. E. L. Minar, "Parmenides and the World of Seeming," *AJP* 70 (1949): 41–53.

9. KRS, 400.

10. DK 30 A3; see KRS, 390–91; Guthrie, *HGP II*, 101.

11. Josiah Ober, *Mass and Elite in Democratic Athens: Rhetoric, Ideology, and the Power of the People* (Princeton: Princeton U. Press, 1989), 57.

12. Ibid., 60.

13. According to Ober, "Membership in each group was defined by an individual's wealth, based on a standard derived from annual agricultural production: *pentekosiome-dimnoi* (500 measures), *hippeis* (300), *zeugitai* (200), and *thêtes* (less than 200)" (*Mass and Elite*, 61).

14. Martin Ostwald, *From Popular Sovereignty to the Sovereignty of Law: Law, Society, and Politics in Fifth-Century Athens* (Berkeley: U. of California Press, 1986), 23.

15. Ibid., 16.

16. Ibid., 15–26.

17. Ober, *Mass and Elite*, 74.

18. Ostwald, *Sovereignty*, 26.

19. Ibid., 23.

20. Aristotle, *Politics* 1274a7; *Constitution of Athens* 27. The reforms were in the name of Ephialtes, but Pericles apparently played an important role. See also J. A. Davison, "The Date of the *Prometheia*," *TAPA* 80 (1949): 79n.

21. Robert W. Wallace, *The Areopagus Council, to 307 B.C.* (Baltimore: Johns Hopkins U. Press, 1989).

22. Ostwald, *Sovereignty*, 43–47.

23. Ibid., 78.

24. Ober, *Mass and Elite*, 81–82.

25. Ibid., 86.

26. See Appendix A. On Pericles and Protagoras see also D. Placido, "Protágoras y Pericles," *Hispania Antiqua* 2 (1972): 7–19, and "El pensamiento de Protágoras y las Atenas de Pericles," *Hispania Antiqua* 3 (1973): 29–68.

27. The fragment is from Plutarch's *Pericles* (8) and is not "the" Funeral Oration recorded by Thucydides. See Ira S. Mark, "The Gods on the East Frieze of the Parthenon," *Hesperia* (1984): 340–41.

28. See, e.g., Davison, "Date."

29. Mark, "The Gods."

30. Victor Ehrenberg, "The Foundation of Thurii," *AJP* 69 (1948): 156.

31. Richard Garner, *Law and Society in Classical Athens* (New York: St. Martin's Press, 1987), 39.

32. J. S. Morrison, "The Place of Protagoras in Athenian Public Life," *CQ* 35 (1941): 4.

33. Michael Nill, *Morality and Self-Interest in Protagoras, Antiphon, and Democritus* (Leiden: Brill, 1985).

34. A. W. H. Adkins, *Merit and Responsibility: A Study in Greek Values* (Oxford: Clarendon Press, 1960).

35. A. W. H. Adkins, "*Aretê, Technê,* Democracy and Sophists: *Protagoras* 316b-328d," *JHS* 93 (1973): 4.

36. Havelock, *The Greek Concept of Justice* (Cambridge, MA: Harvard U. Press, 1978); Adkins, *Merit,* 195–214.

37. DL 3.37, 57 = DK 80 B5.

38. Guthrie, *HGP IV,* 437.

39. See Havelock, *Justice,* 305. For the argument that Protagoras' social theory is the basis for Plato's *Republic,* see Stanley Moore, "Democracy and Commodity Exchange: Protagoras versus Plato," *HPQ* 5 (1988): 357–68.

40. Havelock, *Justice,* 297.

41. Ibid., 300.

42. Ibid., 305.

43. Trevor J. Saunders, "Protagoras and Plato on Punishment," in Kerferd, *Legacy,* 136–41.

44. Ibid., 134.

45. Havelock, *The Liberal Temper in Greek Politics* (New Haven: Yale U. Press, 1957), 174.

46. Saunders, "Protagoras," 134.

47. Guthrie, *HGP III,* 67.

48. Havelock, *Temper,* 174.

49. Ibid., 155–90; Kerferd, *SM,* 144; Reimer Müller, "Sophistique et démocratie," *Positions de la Sophistique,* ed. Barbara Cassin (Paris: Vrin, 1986), 179–93.

50. Ober, *Mass and Elite,* 6–7.

51. Adolf Menzel, "Protagoras, der älteste Theoretiker der Demokratie," *Zeitschrift für Politik* 3 (1910): 205–38; Havelock, *Temper,* 170. On the biases of this sort of portrayal, see Riane Eisler, *The Chalice and the Blade* (New York: Harper, 1987), esp. ch. 3.

52. See Aeschylus, *Prometheus* 1035–38; Thucydides 1.78.

53. Martin Ostwald, *Plato: Protagoras* (Indianapolis: Bobbs-Merrill, 1956); B. A. F. Hubbard and E. S. Karnofsky, *Plato's* PROTAGORAS: *A Socratic Commentary* (Chicago: U. of Chicago Press, 1982); C. C. W. Taylor, *Plato: Protagoras* (Oxford: Clarendon Press, 1976); W. K. C. Guthrie's translation is in Edith Hamilton and Huntington Cairns, *The Collected Dialogues of Plato* (Princeton: Princeton U. Press, 1961); W. R. M. Lamb, *Plato: Laches, Protagoras, Meno, Euthydemus* (Cambridge, MA: Harvard U. Press, 1924); Havelock, *Temper.*

54. Lines 1050, 1242, trans. in *Greek Tragedies,* Vol. 1, ed. David Greene and Richard Lattimore (Chicago: U. of Chicago Press, 1960).

55. 318e5–7; 322e2–323a2; 323c3–5; 324c5–7.

56. Auguste Bayonas, "L'art politique d'après Protagoras," *Revue Philosophique* 157 (1967): 51; Havelock, *Temper*, 167.

57. On the speech's authenticity and on Thucydides' accuracy see A. W. Gomme, *A Historical Commentary on Thucydides* (Oxford: Clarendon Press, 1956), 2:104, 121–36. On accuracy and objectivity in Thucydides in general see John T. Kirby, "Narrative Structure and Technique in Thucydides VI-VII," *Classical Antiquity* 2 (1983): 183–211; Virginia J. Hunter, *Thucydides: The Artful Reporter* (Toronto: Hakkert, 1973); F. M. Cornford, *Thucydides Mythistoricus* (New York: Greenwood Press, 1969).

58. William M. A. Grimaldi, *Studies in the Philosophy of Aristotle's Rhetoric* (Weisbaden: Franz Steiner, 1972), 25. Cf. Harold Barrett, *The Sophists: Rhetoric, Democracy, and Plato's Idea of Sophistry* (Novata, CA: Chandler and Sharp, 1987), 40.

59. Jaap Mansfeld, "Protagoras on Epistemological Obstacles and Persons," in Kerferd, *Legacy*, 47.

60. LSJ s.vv. *homologeô, homonoia.*

61. Bayonas, "L'art politique," 50–52; T. A. Sinclair, *A History of Greek Political Thought* (London: Routledge and Kegan Paul, 1951), 53–54.

62. Klaus Döring suggests that Protagoras' historical contribution probably was the advancement of the notion of community decision-making through collective agreement (*gemeinsamem Einvernehmen*). See his "Die politische Theorie des Protagoras," in Kerferd, *Legacy*, 109–15. Cf. Dupréel, *Sophistes*, 19.

63. DK 68 B181, translation based on that by Guthrie, *HGP II*, 496. See also KRS, 432–33.

64. Mansfeld, "Protagoras," 44.

65. Kerferd, *SM*, 62.

66. Havelock, *Temper*, 212–13.

67. Ibid., 191–239.

68. See esp. Book 8 of *Topics;* cf. Guthrie, *HGP VI*, 150–55.

69. See Havelock, *Temper*, 191–239.

12

PROTAGORAS "VERSUS"
PLATO AND ARISTOTLE

The long-standing tradition is that the paucity of extant fragments by Protagoras is due in large measure to the treatment his teachings received by Plato and Aristotle. There is both truth and falsity in this tradition. It is true that the neglect of the Sophists' writings by members of Aristotle's Lyceum contributed to the loss of those writings. It is also true that both Plato and Aristotle attacked Protagoras' doctrines in some of their most important works. I believe, however, that the relationship between the thinking of Plato and Aristotle and that of Protagoras is more subtle than is usually imagined. In this chapter I want to reconsider the relationship between Protagoras and the two fourth-century philosophers.

THE REFUTATION OF PROTAGORAS

Plato's and Aristotle's two most significant objections to Protagoras' doctrines were that his human-measure statement refuted itself and that it violated the law of noncontradiction. These objections represent enduring arguments against certain versions of relativism, as is indicated by their reemergence in recent literature concerning rhetoric as a way of knowing.[1] Given the persistence of the arguments, it is important

190

to understand each objection and to consider what Protagoras might have offered as a defense.

Plato's initial interpretation in the *Theaetetus* is generally accepted as a reasonable paraphrase of Protagoras' human-measure statement: "Everything is, for me, the way it appears to me; and is, for you, the way it appears to you."[2] Plato suggested that Protagoras asserted that if a person (or persons) were to judge that A is B, then in fact A *is* B. Likewise if a person (or persons) were to judge that A is not-B, then in fact A is not-B. The objection runs as follows: If a person is a judge of what-is and what-is-not, and if many people believe that Protagoras' human-measure statement is *not* true, then by Protagoras' own logic his statement is proved false. As Barnes puts it, the human-measure statement "suffers an about-turn: it marches to its own ruin."[3] Plato argued in the *Theaetetus:*

> And what about Protagoras himself? Isn't it necessarily the case that, if he didn't himself think a man is the measure, and if the masses don't either, as in fact they don't, then that *Truth* which he wrote wasn't the truth for anyone? Whereas if he did think so himself, but the masses don't share his view, then, in the first place, it's more the case that it isn't the truth than it is: more in the proportion by which those to whom it doesn't seem to be outnumber those to whom it does.[4]

Thus, Plato concluded that "since it's disputed by everyone, it would seem that Protagoras' *Truth* isn't true for anyone."[5] The self-refutation argument was a popular objection to Protagoras' positions, appearing in the works of Democritus and Sextus Empiricus, among others.[6] In Sextus the argument appears as: "If every appearance is true, then the belief that not every appearance is true—once this belief takes the form of an appearance—will also be true, and so the belief that every appearance is true will become false."[7]

In recent times Jack Orr has charged that rhetorical theorist Barry Brummett's intersubjectivist criterion of truth-as-agreement is subject to a similar inconsistency: "The definition of truth as agreement validates views of truth that intersubjectivism itself denies."[8] And a considerable number of modern philosophers are still debating whether or not Protagorean relativism is "really" self-refuting.[9] Though the continued interest in Protagorean relativism is significant, most of the debates are based on contemporary appropriations rather than historical reconstructions, and hence are not examined in depth here.[10]

The second objection to Protagoras' philosophy is that it violates the

191

principle of noncontradiction. The principle can be summarized as "It is a property of being itself that no being can both have and not have a given characteristic at one and the same time."[11] If human(ity) is the measure, then Protagoras must allow that "things" can *be* in two contradictory ways at the same time: good and bad, true and false, etc. Plato and Aristotle added to their attack of the human-measure statement an interpretation of Protagoras' *ouk estin antilegein* doctrine, which understood "impossible to contradict" as denying the "law" of noncontradiction. Plato complained that "the argument always seems extraordinary in the way it overthrows not only other arguments but itself too."[12] Aristotle's objection was more direct: "If this is so, it follows that the same thing both is and is not, and is bad and good, and that the contents of all other opposite statements are true, because often a particular thing appears beautiful to some and ugly to others, and that which appears to each man is the measure."[13]

Though the two objections proved persuasive historically, both are premised on a distortion of Protagoras' relativism. Both ignore Protagoras' assumption that things (or experiences) are not independent or in themselves, but *are* only relative to a frame of reference or "measure." Put another way, Protagoras acknowledged no "being" other than "being-for-the-subject."[14] Plato's portrayal of Protagorean relativism in the *Theaetetus* makes it clear that Plato recognized the significance of the qualification "for X."[15] In contemporary parlance, predications gain ontological status only relative to an experiencing subject who constitutes Protagoras' frame of reference.[16] As I stressed in my earlier examination of Protagoras' fragments, A is B is always true for X.

The concept of a frame of reference frees Protagoras' human-measure statement from the arguments of self-refutation and contradiction. Plato's initial paraphrasing clearly indicated that Protagoras had a notion of frame of reference in mind. While a contradiction may be implied by the competing claims that "A is B" and "A is not-B," there is no contradiction implied by the more Homeric and Protagorean statements "A is B for X" and "A is not-B for Y."

Plato sought to put Protagoras' doctrine into the form "the human-measure statement is true *absolutely*." He dropped the essential qualifying phrase "for X."[17] When this omission was disregarded, it was easy for Plato to make it appear that Protagoras' formulation led to absurdity. The omission introduced a frame of reference to which Protagoras would not have agreed. Aristotle's comments in the *Metaphysics* contain a similar distortion. Aristotle argued that if two parties disagree about what-is and what-is-not, one of the parties must be mistaken (1063a). Both Plato and Aristotle argue from an either/or logic, whereas Protagoras used a both/and logic. To him experience was rich and variable enough to be capable of multiple—and even inconsistent—accounts.

Plato and Aristotle no doubt knew their refutations were not entirely satisfying logically. Plato in the *Euthydemus* and Aristotle in *Sophistical Refutations* specifically discussed and rebuked the strategy of dropping qualifiers from statements in order to create the appearance of inconsistency and contradiction.[18] Modern commentators disagree about the motives of Plato and Aristotle in passages where they use logical procedures or argumentative moves that they acknowledge as invalid in other writings. For my purposes it is sufficient to observe that neither Plato nor Aristotle was likely to have believed that he had logically "refuted" Protagoras. They did, however, render his doctrines less popular. Their efforts may have been aimed chiefly at fourth-century rivals, who may have been the so-called Protagoreans, or the arguments presented may have been intended to lay the basis for Plato's and Aristotle's treatment of being and knowledge, or both agendas may have been at work.[19]

REJECTION OR ASSIMILATION?

Though Plato and Aristotle obviously differed with Protagoras in important ways, certain elements of his thinking appear to have been accepted in their respective philosophies more than either philosopher's writings explicitly acknowledged. I have already discussed Plato's "Protagorean" theory of perception and the resonance between Aristotle's and Protagoras' views on *logos* and *krisis*. Michael Gagarin's reading of the *Protagoras* suggests that Plato and Protagoras were in substantial agreement on the teachability of *aretê*.[20] There was also a parallel between Protagoras' and Aristotle's thinking on the need for civic training. According to Aristotle, humans are "political animals" because they have the power of *logos* (*Politics* 1253a15–18). Just as Protagoras' Great Speech declared that people incapable of developing civic virtues (*aretai*) cannot survive, Aristotle claimed that those incapable of sharing in a political life are "beasts" (*Politics* 1253a27–29). The cornerstone of Aristotle's political and ethical theory was the concept of practical wisdom, or *phronêsis*. For Aristotle, *phronêsis* is "an adult power of insight into practical matters, the outcome of an initial aptitude cultivated and developed by experience."[21] *Phronêsis* is the sort of *sophia* needed to live

193

the good life and to lead the state successfully. A. W. H. Adkins declares that Sophists were among Aristotle's sources for his political theorizing.[22] He suggests that *phronêsis* was similar to the sophistic notion of *orthos logos* (correct reasoning). This is plausible, since the sort of practical training Protagoras advocated in Plato's dialogue to develop civic *aretê* is similar to the sort of teaching Aristotle said was necessary to develop *phronêsis:* "These men must 'know what they are doing': they have no philosopher-kings to do their thinking for them. Aristotle is commending to his audience the same skills, with their implications now more fully understood, as those which the sophists offered to their pupils."[23]

I believe that Protagoras' role in the development of Plato's and Aristotle's metaphysics has been underestimated. Protagoras was a pivotal figure in the transition between two stages of metaphysical explanation. In particular, Protagoras was a key figure between what Julius Moravcsik calls stage 2 explanation, in terms of composition or constituency, and stage 3 explanation in terms of entities and their qualities.[24] Protagoras' treatment of the relationship between *logoi* and "things" provided what Gerald Holton has called "thematic preparation" for Plato's and Aristotle's treatment of things and their qualities.[25] Protagoras' two *logoi* in opposition—one weaker and one stronger—parallels Plato's treatment of physical change as the alternation of stronger elements with weaker ones and Aristotle's description of potential qualities becoming actual. The evidence I offered earlier is sufficient to demonstrate that Protagoras' doctrines extended Heraclitean explanation in such a way that it was a small step from Protagoras' *logoi* to the Platonic and Aristotelian "qualities."[26] Protagoras' theorizing did more than provide a target for Plato and Aristotle; it provided conceptual tools—Holton's "thematas"—that became part of their philosophies. Certain aspects of Protagoras' relativism were not so much rejected by Plato and Aristotle as they were assimilated.

NOTES

1. See Barry Brummett, "Some Implications of 'Process' or 'Intersubjectivity': Postmodern Rhetoric," *PR* 9 (1976): 21–51; C. Jack Orr, "How Shall We Say 'Reality is Socially Constructed through Communication'?" *CSSJ* 29 (1978): 263–74; Earl Croasmun and Richard A. Cherwitz, "Beyond Rhetorical Relativism," *QJS* 68 (1982): 1–16; Barry Brummett, "On to Rhetorical Relativism," *QJS* 70 (1984): 425–37.

2. 152a, trans. John McDowell, *Plato: Theaetetus* (Oxford: Clarendon Press, 1973).

3. Jonathan Barnes, *The Presocratic Philosophers* (London: Routledge and Kegan Paul, 1982), 543.

4. 170e–171a, *Theaetetus,* trans. McDowell.

5. 171c5, ibid.

6. M. F. Burnyeat, "Protagoras and Self-refutation in Later Greek Philosophy," *The Philosophical Review* 85 (1976): 44–69; David K. Glidden, "Protagorean Relativism and the Cyrenaics," *American Philosophical Quarterly,* monograph 9 (1975): 113–40.

7. DK 80 A15.

8. Orr, "How Shall," 267.

9. See, e.g., James E. Jordan, "Protagoras and Relativism: Criticisms Bad and Good," *Southwestern Journal of Philosophy* 2 (1971): 7–29; Edward N. Lee, " 'Hoist with His Own Petard': Ironic and Comic Elements in Plato's Critique of Protagoras," *Exegesis and Argument: Studies in Greek Philosophy Presented to Gregory Vlastos,* ed. E. N. Lee, A. P. D. Mourelatos, R. M. Rorty (Assen: Gorcum, 1973), 225–61; F. C. White, "Protagoras Unbound," *Canadian Journal of Philosophy* supp. 1 (1974): 1–9; M. F. Burnyeat, "Protagoras and Self-refutation in Plato's *Theaetetus,*" *The Philosophical Review* 85 (1976): 172–95; Jack W. Meiland, "Is Protagorean Relativism Self-refuting?" *Grazer Philosophische Studien* 9 (1979): 51–68; E. P. Arthur, "Plato, *Theaetetus* 171A," *Mnemosyne* 35 (1982): 335–36; David K. Glidden, "Protagorean Obliquity," *HPQ* 5 (1988): 321–40.

10. Contemporary appropriations and historical reconstructions are not necessarily in tension, but I think most of the studies cited in the previous note supply concepts or theories to the debate that cannot be grounded in the available evidence concerning the *mid fifth century.* A typical example is James Haden ("Did Plato Refute Protagoras?" *HPQ* 1 [1984]: 223–40), who is interested in the refutation of Protagoras' relativism as developed by Plato (a sort of phenomenalism) and, despite noting the importance of sticking to the text, imports William James' psychology to explain Protagoras' position.

11. Alasdair MacIntyre, "Ontology," *Encyclopedia of Philosophy* (New York: Macmillan, 1967), 5:542.

12. *Euthydemus* 286c = DK 80 A19.

13. *Metaphysics* 1062b15–20 (= DK 80 A19); see also 1007b17–23, 1009a6–7.

14. Gomperz, *SR,* 207–9.

15. See chs. 7 and 8 of this book.

16. W. V. O. Quine, *Ontological Relativity and Other Essays* (New York: Columbia U. Press, 1969), 26–68.

17. Joseph P. Maguire, "Protagoras—or Plato?" *Phronesis* 18 (1973): 135–36; Gregory Vlastos, *Plato's "Protagoras"* (Indianapolis: Bobbs-Merrill, 1956), xivn.

18. Rosamond Kent Sprague, *Plato's Use of Fallacy* (New York: Barnes and Noble, 1962), and "Plato's Sophistry," *The Aristotelian Society,* supp. 51 (1977): 45–61.

19. Cf. G. B. Kerferd, "Le sophiste vu par Platon: un philosophe imparfait," *Positions de la Sophistique,* ed. Barbara Cassin (Paris: Vrin, 1986), 13–25.

20. Michael Gagarin, "The Purpose of Plato's *Protagoras,*" *TAPA* 100 (1969): 133–64.

21. Guthrie, *HGP VI,* 346.

22. A. W. H. Adkins, *Merit and Responsibility: A Study in Greek Values* (Oxford: Clarendon Press, 1960), 334–36.

23. Ibid., 336. Two useful essays on *phronêsis* and Aristotelian rhetoric are: Lois S. Self, "Rhetoric and *Phronêsis:* The Aristotelian Ideal," *PR* 12 (1979): 130–45; Christopher Lyle Johnstone, "An Aristotelian Trilogy: Ethics, Rhetoric, Politics, and the Search for Moral Truth," *PR* 13 (1980): 1–24.

24. Julius M. Moravcsik, "Heraclitean Concepts and Explanations," *Language and Thought in Early Greek Philosophy,* ed. Kevin Robb (La Salle, IL: Hegeler Institute, 1983), 134–52.

25. Gerald Holton, *Thematic Origins of Scientific Thought* (Cambridge, MA: Harvard U. Press, 1973).

26. Cf. Kurt von Fritz, "Protagoras," *RE* 23 (1957): 914. For the link between Protagoras and certain aspects of Aristotelian relativism, see J. D. G. Evans, "Aristotle on Relativism," *Philosophy Quarterly* 24 (1974): 193–203.

13

PROTAGORAS' LEGACY
TO RHETORICAL THEORY

This chapter will pull together some of the arguments offered in previous chapters in order to summarize Protagoras' contributions to rhetorical theory.[1] My objective is to identify those aspects of his theory and practice that functioned paradigmatically, i.e., as exemplars or "shared examples" for imitation and development.[2] To begin with, Protagoras was one of the first thinkers to put into practice a *metalanguage*. Traditionally his contribution has been described as that of "inventing grammar." However, as Foucault argued, such depictions tend to privilege the "object" (in this case grammar) and understate the subjective, historical process of forming discourse such as we now label "the study of grammar."[3] What Protagoras did was to discourse about discourse—to turn *logos* into something to be examined. By introducing conceptual language with which to analyze discourse, Protagoras' lectures constituted a practice that was imitated and extended. Hence what is historically most significant about Protagoras' contribution is not so much that he "invented grammar" as that he introduced a new way of thinking and speaking about the world, the world of discourse in particular.[4]

A second aspect of Protagoras' theory and practice that functioned paradigmatically was his popularization and perhaps standardization of specific forms of discourse as *methods of inquiry*, specifically the professional prose lecture, the informal dialogue, and the debate. The practice of lecturing has, of course, become the standard form used by teachers through the ages to transmit their knowledge, but in the fifth century the idea and form were new. Dialogue became dialectic with Plato and was further formalized as a means of inquiry by Aristotle. Protagoras' contest of *dissoi logoi* was dubbed *antilogikê* by Plato and survives to this day in the form of two-sided debate. I do not mean to imply that Protagoras was single-handedly responsible for the "invention" of lecturing, dialectic, and debate.[5] Again, his contribution is best understood as part of a wider effort to thematize *logos*.[6] The evidence is sufficient, however, to assign Protagoras' methods of teaching the status of exemplars (shared examples) which were imitated and adapted by others, and in that sense functioned paradigmatically. It could be argued that the significance of his innovations owed a great deal to the educational and philosophical revolution in progress in the fifth century due to the rise of analytical thinking and written prose. But it can be said with equal force that the revolution in conceptual thinking and speaking also owes a great deal to Protagorean theory and practice.

The third aspect of Protagoras' theory and practice that functioned paradigmatically was his *literal analogy* between the practice of *logos* and the art of medicine. A variety of fragments by and statements about the Older Sophists make it clear that the analogy (*logos* is to the soul/ psyche as medicine is to the body) became common in the late fifth century, and it appeared in Plato's and Aristotle's works as well. The analogy was an important part of how *technai* of discourse came to be understood, at least by some, in classical Greece, and Protagoras is the earliest thinker with whom the analogy can be identified.

SUMMARY OF CONTRIBUTIONS

To conclude my inquiry of Protagoras' role in the development of what soon would be called the art of rhetoric, I will bring together and recapitulate earlier arguments and observations:

1) Protagoras did not author a *technē* about *rhêtorikê*. Rather, he conceptualized the scope and function of *logos* in a way that, in restrospect, can be identified as an incipient philosophy of rhetoric.

2) Though the Sophists shared a general preference for oral prose over poetry and a humanistic *logos* over *mythos*, their views and practices were sufficiently diverse that a specific sophistic view proper of rhetoric

cannot yet be identified with confidence. An adequate recovery of nascent sophistic rhetorical theories requires a series of individual studies.

3) Protagoras was the first professional Sophist to analyze and critique epic poetry. By providing a metapoetic perspective and terminology he helped to challenge the mythic-poetic tradition in education. Though Protagoras generally favored a humanistic *logos* over *mythos,* his aphoristic and narrative styles of writing are evidence of his responsiveness to the continued demands of an oral culture.

4) Protagoras' teaching methods probably included a formal expository lecture style, verbal exchange in small, informal discussion groups, and antithetical formulations of public positions. These methods cumulatively represent a significant change in fifth-century education.

5) The purpose of Protagoras' theory and practice of *logos* was to change people for the better. The objective was understood as literally analogous to the art of medicine. The thesis that people can be made more excellent marked a departure from the traditional belief that *aretê* was a function of wealth or noble birth.

6) Protagoras' teachings functioned ideologically to advance the precepts of Periclean democracy and to oppose the aristocratic implications of Eleatic monism. For Protagoras, *logos* was the means through which citizens deliberated and came to collective judgments. Protagoras contributed to the theoretical defense of consensual decision-making, and he may have been the first to provide rules to facilitate the orderly conduct of debate and discussion.

The task of describing Protagoras' legacy to rhetorical theory has been complicated by the fact that during his time there was no clearly recognized discipline of *rhêtorikê* per se. Rather, there were competing conceptualizations of *logos* with some application toward success in persuasion and deliberation in public forums. The difference between a theory of *logos* and a theory of rhetoric can be illustrated in a preliminary manner by contrasting Protagoras and Aristotle. Aristotle's *Rhetoric* focuses on three specific settings which correspond to fourth-century expectations about the roles of *rhêtores:* the law courts, the assembly, and certain civic ceremonies. Aristotle's definition of rhetoric as "the faculty of observing in any given case the available means of persuasion" (1355b25–26) can be broadly interpreted, but Aristotle makes a concerted effort to distinguish the scope of rhetoric from the scope of other cognitive and practical activities.[7] Matters capable of certain demonstration are the province of science, and contingent matters may be treated by rhetoric *or* by its parallel art (*antistrophê*), dialectic.[8]

By contrast, Protagoras' conceptualization of *logos* was undifferentiated and precategorical; that is, it was independent of context and did not distinguish between types of discourse on the basis of distinctive principles or degrees of certainty. Plato's description of Protagoras' educational activities did not limit him to the oratorical training of *rhêtores* in the sense the term was used in the fifth and fourth centuries. Protagoras probably would have agreed with Isocrates' description of *logôn paideia* as training for the mind as physical training is for the body (*Antidosis* 181). Similarly, Protagoras' notion of *orthos logos,* understood as correct account or correct understanding, should place him squarely in the "mixed" tradition Kennedy has called "philosophical rhetoric."

CONCLUSION

Throughout this book my focus has been on Protagoras and *logos*. While I do not believe that *logos*-theorizing is precisely the same as theorizing about *rhêtorikê,* the former deserves to be included in any thorough history of the development of rhetorical theory. The study of the manner in which the introduction of the specific term and concept of rhetoric transformed theories of *logos* promises to be interesting and important, but such a study pertains to the analysis of the fourth century BCE, not the fifth, and accordingly has not been pursued here. It must suffice to note that one characteristic of most intellectual disciplines is that they tend toward increasing specialization and reduction of their subject into specific concepts, rules, and practices. It is not surprising, then, that holistic fifth-century concepts such as *kairos* were deemphasized once rhetoric became disciplinized. As Kennedy notes: "*Kairos* as a rhetorical term is largely restricted to the classical period.... The subject is, of course, one that by nature cannot be reduced to rules, which is one of the reasons it did not receive great attention in the handbooks."[9] Furthermore, Platonic and Aristotelian philosophical world views came to replace those of their presocratic predecessors. Theoretical conceptions of *logos* that were closely linked to presocratic world views came to be understood only after being "translated" into (primarily) Aristotelian terminology. This would explain why Protagoras' ontology of twofold *logoi* was appropriated by the history of rhetoric as the commonplace that "there are two sides to every issue."

I hope my observations and arguments have done some justice to the predisciplinary character of fifth-century thinking. Many of the dichotomies traditionally used to distinguish "philosophy" from "rhetoric" simply are not useful for describing Protagoras' account of *logos*. If scholars persist in defining rhetoric as success-seeking and philosophy as truth-seeking, and if they persist in using such a dichotomy as a means of distinguishing the Older Sophists from their contemporaries and successors, then the result will be an incomplete historical account. If, on the other hand, we take our cue from the multivocal meanings of fifth-century *logos*, a more defensible historical account is possible. Both the substance and the method of *logos* in Protagoras' teachings were revolutionary and seminal, earning him an important place in the history of ideas—including the ideas of "philosophy" and "rhetoric."

The account of Protagoras that I have provided in this book portrays a major fifth-century thinker, educator, and speaker who was a significant figure in the transition between *mythos* and *logos*. The "divide" between *mythos* and *logos* has often been described in an exaggerated manner. As a result, the Older Sophists have sometimes been described in an overly aestheticized or "irrational" fashion or in excessively rationalistic terms.[10]

Susan C. Jarratt has attempted to bridge the gap between *mythos* and *logos* with the term *nomos*. In the fifth century BCE *nomos* meant something "believed in, practised or held to be right."[11] For the Sophists "*nomos* signifies the imposition of humanly determined patterns of explanations for natural phenomena in contrast to those assumed to exist 'naturally' or without the conscious intervention of human intellect."[12] The virtue of Jarratt's *mythos-nomos-logos* framework is that it acknowledges the sophistic advances over the mythic-poetic tradition while resisting the habit of equating sophistic *logos* with the sort of formal rationality one finds, for example, in Aristotle's works on logic: "*Nomos* marks, on the one hand, a difference from social order and law under a mythic tradition, and, on the other, looking toward the fourth century, an epistemological alternative to philosophy as the ground of logic and timeless truth."[13]

I am in complete agreement with Jarratt's wish to mark out a conceptual space for the Older Sophists that avoids being collapsed into part of the "grand dichotomy" of *mythos/logos*. A central theme of this book has been that the Older Sophists should be viewed on their own terms, as transitional figures. Protagoras' use of *logos* is not the same as Plato's or Aristotle's. Protagoras' view of discourse, to borrow a phrase Jarratt uses to describe Gorgias' thinking, was that of "a holistic *logos*."[14] At the same time, Protagoras' conceptualization of *logos* was different from that of Gorgias.[15] A similar point can be made with respect to *nomos:* The Older Sophists held divergent, even antithetical, views toward the *nomos/physis* controversy, as did fifth-century thinkers not normally called Sophists.[16] While it is possible to generalize about the common interests of the Older Sophists, such as *nomos* or *logos*, their differences underscore the need to study the Sophists as individuals.

Just what other Sophists contributed to theories of *logos*-cum-rhetoric needs to be determined by further individual studies. I hope to have shown that despite scarcity of extended "doctrinal" statement from such figures, it is still possible to reason out what an individual's chief contributions and limitations as a theorist were. Furthermore, the initial results of taking seriously the relatively late appearance of the term *rhêtorikê* suggest that interpretations of fifth- and fourth-century texts that treat rhetoric as a conceptual given must be reevaluated. Both Plato's and Aristotle's efforts to systematize the verbal arts of rhetoric, dialectic, eristic, and antilogic deserve an examination which gives equal weight to their creative and their delimiting features.

I hope also to have shown both the relevance and the usefulness of paying close attention to intellectual and linguistic developments from the fifth to fourth centuries BCE. These developments have become an increasingly important consideration in literary, philosophical, and rhetorical studies. Since the 1930s such figures as Milman Parry and Albert B. Lord have pressed the importance of recognizing the peculiarities of preliterate substance and forms in literary studies. Eric A. Havelock, Walter Ong, Jack Goody, and others have made similar points concerning study of more pragmatic communication. I have been much indebted to their work and, in important ways, to their critics. Efforts to establish oral theory and to develop reliable tests for distinguishing preliterate from literate discourse have been challenged from a number of directions, but few have challenged the fundamental point that people living in Greek oral culture did not express themselves the same way as people moving toward or living in the more literate fourth century. That has been a central assumption of this book, and I hope to have shown that new and valuable insights come to us when we study a writer or speaker keeping clearly in mind the notion that concepts, forms of expression, patterns of explanation, and vocabularies evolve, especially when social practices and problems are changing. I believe I have shown that attention to such matters yields an account of Protagoras that is more reasonable, more intelligible, and probably more reliable than the account traditional scholarship has given us.

NOTES

1. There is little consensus regarding the defining characteristics of a rhetorical theory. See Richard L. Johannesen, *Contemporary Theories of Rhetoric* (New York: Harper, 1971), 2; Sonja K. Foss, Karen A. Foss, and Robert Trapp, *Contemporary Perspectives on Rhetoric* (Prospect Heights, IL: Waveland Press, 1985), 13–14; Robert L. Scott, "On Not Defining Rhetoric," *PR* 6 (1973): 81–96. It is unavoidable, therefore, that the process of describing Protagoras' legacy to the history of rhetorical theory is somewhat subjective, since "rhetorical theory" was and is a fluid construct. Nonetheless, histories of rhetorical theory require at least a working definition (see Carole Blair and Mary L. Kahl, "Revising the History of Rhetorical Theory," *WJSC* 54 [1990]: 148–59). For my purposes, "rhetorical theory" in general denotes the activity of theorizing or conceptualizing about persuasive discourse. The clearest sign of theorizing, from a historical standpoint, is the development of a specific, usually technical, vocabulary (see Thomas S. Kuhn, *The Essential Tension* [Chicago: U. of Chicago Press, 1977], xx-xxii). A more specific historical subject is the development of rhetoric as a self-conscious discipline. Sophistic theorizing about *logos* obviously set the stage for the emergence of rhetoric as a distinct discipline, yet clearly deserves study on its own merits. See George A. Kennedy's distinction between self-conscious rhetoric and conceptual rhetoric (*Classical Rhetoric and Its Christian and Secular Tradition from Ancient to Modern Times* [Chapel Hill: U. of North Carolina Press, 1980]).

2. Central to the success of theories are exemplars or "shared examples": practical "problem solutions accepted by the group as . . . paradigmatic" and which are widely imitated (Kuhn, *Essential Tension*, 298). Considerable work has been done demonstrating the applicability of Kuhn's treatment of exemplars and paradigms to nonscientific theories (Gary Gutting, *Paradigms and Revolutions: Applications and Appraisals of Thomas Kuhn's Philosophy of Science* [Notre Dame: Notre Dame U. Press, 1980]). Douglas Ehninger ("On Systems of Rhetoric," *PR* 1 [1968]: 131–44) and Henry W. Johnstone, Jr. ("Some Trends in Rhetorical Theory," *The Prospect of Rhetoric*, ed. Lloyd F. Bitzer and Edwin Black [Englewood Cliffs, NJ: Prentice Hall, 1971], 78–90) have pointed out that rhetorical theories arise out of the felt needs of particular cultures (cf. Maurice Bloch, *Political Language and Oratory in Traditional Society* [London: Academic Press,1975]). Their views are similar to Kuhn's analysis of paradigms (theoretical world views) that are employed by scientists in solving particular problems. In communication studies Barry Brummett's definition of a rhetorical theory as a form or pattern of "how a person might experience a rhetorical transaction" accords with an exemplar-centered approach to describing theories ("Rhetorical Theory as Heuristic and Moral: A Pedagogical Justification," *Communication Education* 33 [1984]: 103). While it is true that Kuhn's term "paradigm" was initially criticized for its ambiguity, his subsequent explanation—that widely imitated problem-solving exemplars (shared examples) are the most important aspect of paradigms—provides sufficient clarity, I believe, that his terminology can be used without excessive confusion (see Margaret Masterman, "The Nature of a Paradigm," *Criticism and the Growth of Knowledge,* ed. Imre Lakatos and Alan Musgrave [Cambridge: Cambridge U. Press, 1970], 59–90, and Kuhn's clarifications of "paradigms" in the postscript

of *The Structure of Scientific Revolutions* [Chicago: U. of Chicago Press, 1970], esp. 187–91, and "Second Thoughts on Paradigms," in *Essential Tension,* 293–319).

3. Michael Foucault, *The Archaeology of Knowledge* (New York: Pantheon, 1972).

4. For a very different account of Protagoras' views on language (an account I believe has more in common with fourth-century thinkers than Protagoras), see Michel Narcy, "A qui la parole? Platon et Aristote face à Protagoras," *Positions de la Sophistique,* ed. Barbara Cassin (Paris: Vrin, 1986), 75–90.

5. Protagoras' notion of twofold *logoi* has been described as "the core of the adversary system of justice, legislative deliberations, and academic debate" (Harold Barrett, *The Sophists: Rhetoric, Democracy, and Plato's Idea of Sophistry* [Novata, CA: Chandler and Sharp, 1987], 10–11).

6. For the argument that efforts to formulate self-conscious oratory date to the time of Homer, see Richard L. Enos, "Emerging Notions of Heuristic, Eristic, and Protreptic Rhetoric in Homeric Discourse: Proto-Literate Conniving, Wrangling, and Reasoning," *Selected Papers from the 1981 Texas Writing Research Conference,* ed. Maxine C. Hairston and Cynthia L. Selfe (Austin: U. of Texas Press, 1981), 44–64.

7. William M. A. Grimaldi, *Aristotle, Rhetoric: A Commentary,* Vol. 1 (New York: Fordham U. Press, 1980).

8. For a recent survey of the controversies over the relationship between rhetoric and dialectic in Aristotle, see Lawrence D. Green, "Aristotelian Rhetoric, Dialectic, and the Traditions of 'Αντίστροφος," *Rhetorica* 8 (1990): 5–27.

9. Kennedy, *APG,* 67.

10. Susan C. Jarratt, "The First Sophists and the Uses of History," *Rhetoric Review* 6 (1987): 67–77, and "The Role of the Sophists in Histories of Consciousness," *PR* 23 (1990): 85–95.

11. Jarratt, "Role of the Sophists," 89, citing Guthrie, *HGP III,* 55.

12. Jarratt, "Role of the Sophists," 90.

13. Ibid.

14. Ibid., 91, 93.

15. Contrast my analysis of Protagoras' *logos* with that of Charles P. Segal, "Gorgias and the Psychology of the Logos," *HSCP* 66 (1962): 99–155.

16. Felix Heinimann, *Nomos und Physis* (Basel: F. Reinhardt, 1945); Martin Ostwald, *From Popular Sovereignty to the Sovereignty of Law: Law, Society, and Politics in Fifth-Century Athens* (Berkeley: U. of California Press, 1986), esp. 199–333.

AFTERWORD

It has been over a decade since publications by Thomas Cole (*The Origins of Rhetoric in Ancient Greece*) and myself challenged assumptions that informed traditional and revisionist accounts of "sophistic rhetoric." Traditional accounts, largely based on Plato's unflattering portrayals of fifth and fourth century BCE Sophists, had reduced the historical role of the so-called Older Sophists to the teaching of amoral and atheoretical rhetoric. Revisionist accounts differed by discipline. In philosophy, some sophistic texts were redeemed by the judgment that their content was legitimately philosophical after all. In communication studies and English, sophistic rhetoric has been heralded as a rival philosophy, practice, or pedagogy to that found in the texts of Plato and Aristotle. Though the texts of the Older Sophists may be polyvalent, they generally have not been treated as polysemous; that is, the primary difference between traditionalists and revisionists has not been about what the Older Sophists' texts say, but how their doctrines and practices should be valued. Both traditionalists and revisionists have treated the concept of "sophistic rhetoric" as coherent and useful. It is fair to say that such assumptions are now open to question.

What changed in recent years, I believe, are our assumptions about how we should describe what the Older Sophists were doing. By far, the most animated discussions that the first edition of this book generated stemmed not from substantive claims made about Protagoras but from claims advanced in chapters 3 and 4 concerning the historical assumptions we bring to the study of the Sophists. Accordingly, in this afterword I return to those assumptions. First, I describe the role of theoretical presuppositions in classical historiography and describe what I call "rhetorical salience." In the process, I briefly revisit the distinction

205

made in the first edition of this book between historical reconstruction and contemporary appropriation. Second, I revisit certain persistent questions involving Plato and the term *rhêtorikê*, and the historiographical status of "sophistic rhetoric."

RHETORICAL SALIENCE AND ROLE OF THEORY

What I have in mind by "theory" is simply a web of beliefs that helps us to understand and describe some aspect of the world. Some classicists have resisted the notion that their work is informed by theory because they treat theory as a dogmatic set of beliefs that predetermines the readings of texts with insufficient historical and critical nuance. Indeed, sometimes that happens. But *every* classicist approaches *every* text and fragment with a set of beliefs that inform their interpretations—how could we "read" otherwise? Such beliefs include psychological assumptions about how people think, linguistic assumptions about how people communicate, and technological assumptions about the available media through which people communicate. I can think of no good reason *not* to describe such a set of beliefs a "theory," as long as we use the term loosely to describe any reasonably coherent set of beliefs that seeks to understand and explain some aspect of the world.

Eric Havelock's work on what he described as the "literate revolution" in classical Greece has been alternately praised and maligned. For Cole and myself, Havelock's influence was substantial as it led us to ask questions and read texts in a manner we otherwise would never have pursued. One example must suffice. First and foremost, Havelock encouraged me to look at what writers such as Gorgias or Protagoras were *doing,* not just what they were saying. While there is considerable disagreement about the precise cognitive implications of the growing literacy in classical Greece, there is little question that the fifth century BCE witnessed far-reaching changes in the *uses* of literacy. Compositional practices and modes of description and explanation changed radically between the time when Parmenides composed his account of Being in epic hexameters and when Aristotle wrote his *Metaphysics* in his distinctive prose. What makes a text like Gorgias's *Helen* interesting to me is that Gorgias is practicing a relatively new form of investigation that is performed in a prose style like no other. To appreciate Gorgias's historical significance requires us to appreciate his particularity, which is why

206

I tend to cringe when he is put in anachronistic categories, like "anti-essentialist."

Although I have opinions on the relative merits of different assumptions about reading classical texts, at the moment I do not intend to argue that some theories are right and some are wrong. Rather, my point is that when we engage texts, we are looking for something, and what we are looking for—and what we *notice*—is guided by beliefs that can be called theoretical. These beliefs create what I call *rhetorical salience* for specific features of a text. For nineteenth-century pragmatists, for example, what was rhetorically salient about Protagoras was his explicit humanism, his religious agnosticism, and what I have described previously as his "objective relativism." What was salient for me was how he took Heraclitean insights and advanced new modes of description that Moravcsik calls "second stage compositional explanations" (see chapters 5 and 6 of this book). As few and far between as Protagoras's fragments are, there has never been a shortage of alternative readings, each guided by what the scholar finds salient.

That our readings are informed by our particular values and interests is hardly news, but it is my hope that the notion of rhetorical salience can help us better understand and make sense of competing interpretations. It may help us recognize that some readings rely on the salience of too little of a text (such as when Gorgias's whole career is reduced to his use of the term *paignion*) and it may help distinguish the values and interests informing historical reconstructions and contemporary appropriations. My examples, I confess, are a bit self-serving, but they may prove useful.

For better or for worse, I learned early to expect a certain amount of zeal and vehemence from my critics. For years I thought no one could top the ad hominem assault that met my earliest work, but since that time I have been likened twice to those Holocaust revisionists typically pilloried for their callous anti-Semitism. Aside from the pain such a description evoked, what I find significant about these two readings of my work is that they came from opposite ends of the academic ideological continuum.

On one side comes Victor Vitanza, who defies and personally resists labeling but who, for the purposes of this narrative, can be summed up as a poststructuralist Vitanzian-Deleuzian. In his book *Negation, Subjectivity, and the History of Rhetoric*, Vitanza describes me as a traditional-modernist-philological-"metaphysical" formalist, as well as a part-time

207

Platonist and Aristotelian (32–34). Invoking Lyotard's notion of a *differ-end*, and his critique of the rules of evidence that characterize litigation, Vitanza compares my historical arguments for considering the construct "sophistic rhetoric" suspect to Holocaust revisionists who claim that no reliable evidence exists that the Holocaust happened. Because I question the genus "sophist," I commit a form of genocide ("Genus-cide") that seeks the ex-*termi*nation of "the sophists" ("Sophist-cide"): "Schiappa is engaging in a very violent and potentially dangerous and pernicious *differend*. Schiappa's thinking is much like the contemporary historians' thinking who would deny—given the rules of evidence in the court-room—the less-than-factual testimony of the Holocaust survivors" (45).

Now, not surprising, I disagree with Vitanza's description of me and of my argument concerning sophistic rhetoric. My work, in this book and in *The Beginnings of Rhetorical Theory in Classical Greece*, has ques-tioned the historical utility of the adjective "sophistic," especially when joined with the noun "rhetoric," but I have never said, as Vitanza claims, that the Sophists "never existed." Quite the contrary—my goal was to recover the historical contributions of Older Sophists like Gorgias and Protagoras. Following Kerferd, I have noted that many wise men were called "sophists" and the basic point of the work Vitanza engages can be summarized as the simple caution "do not overgeneralize." But this story does not end with Vitanza.

From a quite different perspective, Rainer Friedrich—classicist, Homer scholar, and critic of postmodernism—reacted passionately to a reviewer's description in the *Bryn Mawr Classical Review* of my account of how facts are socially constructed.[1] In the same article (subsequently included as a chapter in *Beginnings*) that Vitanza critiques, I use the example of the statement that "JFK was killed in 1963" as an example of a reliable fact that was nonetheless socially constructed and could, in theory, be revised someday as our conceptualizations of time, identity, and mortal-ity evolve. I noted that rejecting the statement "JFK died in 1881" does not make me a "traditionalist, positivist, objectivist, foundationalist who labors under the delusion that I have access to objective and unin-terpreted facts" (*Beginnings*, 60). Friedrich *likes* these labels and is appalled that I would distance myself from them: "Let me use an untriv-ial example. If I reject as false, on the strength of cogent evidence, the assertion that the Nazi genocide of the European Jewry in the early for-ties of the twentieth century did not happen, and am therefore branded as a 'traditionalist, positivist, objectivist, foundationalist who labors under the delusion that I have access to objective and uninterpreted facts'—

what would this branding of me amount to? It would amount to a subtle form of Holocaust denial, and it would place my detractors in the most odious company!" In other words, my commitment to social constructionism is sufficient for Friedrich to brand me as a dangerous postmodernist, and he dismisses my book, without having read it, based on a favorable review in *Bryn Mawr Classical Review* wherein my reviewer praised a "levelheaded approach that incorporates healthy portions of poststructuralist theory along with what we call rational interpretation."[2]

I find it fascinating that two scholars from such disparate theoretical starting points would be united in their efforts to portray my argumentative framework as one that facilitates Holocaust deniers, and it is perplexing that they would do so based on the same text. Yet this nicely illustrates rhetorical salience. At the risk of psychologizing, I think one can diagnose their readings as follows: Vitanza reads my concern with categories as symptomatic of an essentializing Aristotelian worldview. Combined with my professed fondness for well-evidenced historical reconstructions, my claim that the construct "sophistic rhetoric" is one that we can do without replicates a metaphysical and epistemological set of commitments that can, and has, been put to evil purposes to marginalize, harm, and kill innocent human beings. For Vitanza and other poststructuralist critics, the *salient* portions of my text are those that reveal, to them, my dark side commitments. My efforts to distance myself from such a stance are ignored or declared "greatly disingenuous."[3] In Friedrich's case, quite different features of my text are salient. Indeed, Friedrich accepts my efforts to carve out a space for a social constructionist historiography as genuine, but for him it is postmodern skepticism that leads to Holocaust denial. While Vitanza wants to protect feelings from the tyranny of facts (48), Friedrich believes that facts are the shield we need against the tyranny of hate.[4]

I can respect where each scholar is coming from, but still I wonder what has this got to do with me? I think it is fair for me to complain that both reacted more to what they believe my work leads to than what it says, and neither engages any of my arguments directly. My lament can be reduced to this hermeneutic: what to me is most salient about my text is not what seems to be salient to these critics. I suspect that when authors complain that they have been misread, typically it amounts to the complaint that what *they* thought was valuable about their work is being undervalued. For over a decade I have argued that it is valuable to create a theoretical space that describes history as a distinct and valuable social practice that need not entail positivism. Those, like Crafton, who share such values and interests, experience a different text than those guided by other agendas.

Now, back to the Sophists. While I have the opportunity to respond to those who write about my work, they do not. But there seems to me to be an ethical obligation (described in *Beginnings*, 167–68) to ponder the question of what Gorgias or Protagoras might have thought was most salient about their texts in their own historical moments. As imperfect as any answer may be, *one* defensible research program (among many) is to ask what they and their contemporaries found valuable and interesting about their work. Historical reconstruction, as I understand it, is at least partially motivated by an effort to understand the historical Other. When that happens, what becomes salient is not so much those features of the text that are similar to our favorite contemporary pieties, but what seems most distant and strange. Thus, when we acknowledge all readings are guided by our values and interests (glossed as our theory), let us not leave out a consideration of ethical relationship to those whom we study (including each other).

Some scholars have argued that the distinction between historical reconstruction and contemporary appropriation cannot be maintained because both scholarly pursuits involve interpretation and translation, and both are activities guided by the values and interests of the scholar. I remain unpersuaded that from such premises it necessarily follows that a distinction cannot be made, and I think the concept of rhetorical salience helps to explain why.

A nonacademic analogy may be useful here. One might take a piece of medieval music and do an historical reconstruction; that is, use instruments either from medieval times or recreations as faithful to what they used then as possible. Is this the same thing as capturing the past as it "really" happened? Of course not. But there is a purpose here—a *social* purpose—that is clearly recognizable and that is quite different than a contemporary appropriation that puts the music to a disco beat and uses electric instruments. The latter might be more fun, but clearly the social purposes to which the music is being put are quite different than the historical reconstruction.

The analogy illustrates how the values and methods of the two activities are distinct. Recreationists (whether from the Civil War or medieval music) often worry about "authenticity" and the avoidance of anachronism. Someone putting medieval music to a modern dance beat is guided by other values. Both activities are human attempts to make music, situated in a given moment in history—both are limited by available socially constructed knowledge of music and instrumentation—but it is not hard to see that they can be discussed intelligently as different activities, and that they are guided by different socially constructed norms.

The piece of medieval music is a "text" that can be put to a variety of purposes (just like the texts of the Sophists). A given performance or use of that text can be judged by whatever norms people decide to use; that is, what is *salient* about the text will vary according to one's tastes, values, and interests. One might prefer a disco version because one can dance to it, or because it is more like one's own favorite music. Or one might prefer the (always incomplete) effort to recreate the sound that people living in medieval times might have heard. The bottom line is that I do not see anything among the tenets of poststructuralism and social constructionism that precludes drawing social and rhetorical distinctions between historical reconstruction and contemporary appropriation. It is only if and when someone tries to explain the difference in grand metaphysical terms (such as those critiqued in Richard Rorty's *Philosophy and the Mirror of Nature*) that charges of "positivism" or other problematic philosophical "isms" become relevant.

One last point on the distinction between historical reconstruction and contemporary appropriation should be made. On several occasions over the past decade, in debates over the Sophists and historiography, the question of whether we can escape our hermeneutic situation and "break the bonds of the present" (as historians imply we can) has arisen.[5] Not surprisingly, my answer to such a question is somewhat different than those of my critics. Obviously what I have in mind is something other than time travel and is better phrased by asking "can we learn something new and different than we already knew?" Scholars who value historical reconstruction suggest that we can. For example: Why might someone prefer a historical reconstruction of medieval music? One motivation might be the pleasure and insight gained by exposing oneself to something different. We *change* from such encounters. Encounters with beliefs, values, or aesthetics that are different from our own offer us an opportunity to become someone other than who we were five minutes ago. We do not go to museums of history only to laugh and jeer at how stupid those past cultures were since they are different from us, but hopefully to try to understand those past cultures and open ourselves to the possibilities they offer.

Difference can be measured in space or time. When we travel and encounter a current culture different than what is already familiar to us, we can resist that difference, or we can embrace it and see where it takes

211

us. This is why in my chapter on Isocrates in *The Beginnings of Rhetorical Theory in Classical Greece* I argue an analogy between different sorts of human relationships and how we approach historical texts. To me, if I am involved in the social practice of writing history, I feel an ethical obligation to treat the Other (text), such as those of Protagoras and Gorgias, as much as I can on its own terms and context. "As much as I can" and "to the extent possible" are important qualifications, since even the act of translating Greek to English imposes an interpretation. Is there a "pure" meaning of Protagoras and Gorgias's texts, some perfect interpretation that is what they "really meant"? Of course not. Can we ever totally know and understand another human being? No. But there is a vast gulf between rejecting or accepting "differences," thus between imposing your own description of an Other versus giving them an opportunity to supply the vocabulary for their description.[6] The fact that such an opportunity can never be perfect (since even the questions we ask limit the answers we seek), does not mean that there is no difference between scholarly projects that try to avoid anachronism and those that do not.

PLATO, *RHÊTORIKÊ*, AND THE SOPHISTS

Cole and I independently surmised that the word *rhêtorikê* may have been coined by Plato. We were both coaxed to this conclusion, already widely noted in various Greek lexicons, partly by the conspicuous absence of the term in any texts of the fifth century BCE (and from most in the fourth century BCE). This includes texts where one could reasonable expect to find the term if it were in common usage, such as Aristophanes's parodies of newfangled terms, or in the discussion of verbal arts in chapter 8 of *Dissoi Logoi,* or in any of the extant texts and fragments of the Older Sophists. We named Plato as our chief suspect also because of his documented penchant for coining terms ending with "*ikê*"—especially for terms denoting verbal arts. Almost no one challenges the idea that Plato coined the term for dialectic, for example, despite the long history of dialectical interaction that predates him. Similarly, despite a long history of suasive speech, we think it likely, or at least plausible, that Plato coined the term *rhêtorikê.*

After an initial flurry of "no, he didn't," "yes, he might have" exchanges,[7] two persistent questions can be identified: First, Is Plato's *Gorgias* the earliest extant use of *rhêtorikê*? Second, does the dating of the term matter for our understanding of the Sophists?

212

With respect to Plato's *Gorgias,* it is possible that Alcidamas's *Against the Sophists* predates *Gorgias.* I personally doubt this, given apparent references to Isocrates' middle work, but it is fair to say there is no scholarly consensus on the issue.[8] Plato's first use of the term in *Gorgias* remains a puzzlement. His use of the phrase *tên kaloumenên rhêtorikên* might signal a self-conscious or novel use of the term, but not necessarily. The weakest argument here, in my estimation, is the claim that Plato is faithfully representing late fifth century BCE terminology; this is a problematic argument to make in light of the anachronisms and linguistic novelties of *Gorgias.* Sir Kenneth Dover notes "Plato writes not as a scholar" but "from first to last as an advocate." "It would be wrong to imagine," Dover suggests, that Plato "necessarily observes the standards of veracity which we demand of a historian."[9] And, of course, many scholars have expressed considerable doubt as to whether Plato represents the historical positions of Socrates—let alone Socrates' vocabulary —with accuracy.

The last point I wish to make about this first question is that it does not much matter who coined the term. While it delights some and outrages others to think of Plato as the creator of a term for an art he apparently reviled, absent time travel we will never know with confidence who first introduced the term or why. The question we *can* productively engage is whether the introduction of the term can or should alter the way we understand the texts of the fifth and fourth centuries BCE. Here we can consider the following equivalent to the social scientist's notion of the null hypothesis: Is it reasonable to believe that the introduction of the term *rhêtorikê* makes *no* difference? Put differently, should we *ignore* the philological data that *rhêtorikê* appears in no fifth century text? The question can be made more concrete with respect to an individual author's *corpus:* Should we ignore the fact that Isocrates, for example, never uses the term but uses others, including *philosophia,* to describe his educational program?

Despite Gerard Pendrick's elaborate plea[10] that we ignore all this and go back to our work as if Cole or I had never published anything, the philologists' love of language precludes a hasty acceptance of the null hypothesis. After all, if there is one belief that all of us in Classics, English, Communication Studies, and Philosophy share, surely it is that language matters. Words matter. Names matter.

In previous work I tried to outline psychological, semiotic, and rhetorical reasons for believing that the introduction of a term that designates a category as culturally significant as "art of the rhetor" alters the linguistic and intellectual landscape in nontrivial ways (i.e., reasons to reject the null hypothesis), but clearly the matter cannot be settled *a priori*. It is only through the tedious work of *revisiting* fifth and fourth century BCE texts without the traditional philosophy versus rhetoric bifocals that we can produce a new historical account of the Sophists and the origins of rhetorical theory.

Such work has been forthcoming, though it is clear that one's disciplinary starting point can play a significant role in what gets talked about—that is, which features of the Sophists' texts are most salient. For those in English, the most salient features of the Sophists' texts often are those that resonate with ongoing pedagogical and theoretical concerns.[11] Steve Mailloux has persuaded me that there is a legitimately felt need in some quarters of the humanities for *some* notion of "sophistic rhetoric" as a counterweight to Platonic and Aristotelian models; so long as that is true, contemporary appropriations of the Sophists should continue. Scholars in Classics, Philosophy, and Communication Studies have generated quite different readings.[12] It is not surprising that accounts of the Sophists turn out so differently when crafted by scholars in different disciplines. Nor, in retrospect, should I be surprised that the needs, interests, and reactions of a multidisciplinary audience can be contradictory (no one from an English department has ever described me as a postmodernist, and no one from Classics has ever called me a traditionalist).

How is current scholarship on the Sophists different than it was in the 1980s? No single generalization will suffice, but there are at least two trends that one can safely identify. First, there is now less generalization about the Sophists as a group and more attention to the contributions of individual Sophists, especially Protagoras, Gorgias, and Isocrates. Second, there is greater reflexivity now concerning the types of claims advanced about the Sophists and rhetorical theory in the fifth century. Victor Vitanza's notion of a Third Sophistic—and my own label, "neosophistic rhetoric"—have, for the most part, supplanted the anachronistic and overbroad label of "sophistic rhetoric."

The most remarkable advancement has been Michael Gagarin's provocatively titled essay, "Did the Sophists Aim to Persuade?" in which he argues that the long-held belief that the primary activity of the Sophists was to teach rhetoric qua persuasion is mistaken.[13] Gagarin's description of the Older Sophists' educational efforts is consistent with the account provided in this book for Protagoras, and he has continued his account in his recent book, *Antiphon the Athenian*.

214

Clearly, we have come a long way from the days when all of the Sophists' teachings and writings were reduced to a mostly platonic notion of "rhetoric." It is my hope that this book has made a modest addition to the continuing effort to understand the Older Sophists' contributions, no matter what labels for those contributions are ultimately deemed most satisfactory.

NOTES

1. See John Michael Crafton's review of *The Beginnings of Rhetorical Theory in Classical Greece* (*Bryn Mawr Classical Review* 2001.03.09), followed by Rainer Friedrich's response (2001.04.16) and my reply (2001.04.26), all of which is accessible online at: http://ccat.sas.upenn.edu/bmcr/.

2. Ibid.

3. Victor Vitanza, *Negation, Subjectivity, and the History of Rhetoric* (Albany: State U. of New York Press, 1997), 46.

4. Facts and feelings need not be thought of as distinct; they can be thought of as inseparable as energy and matter. Deconstruct any "fact" and one finds *nothing but* feelings—impressions, emotions, beliefs, interests, and values. When such feelings coalesce and are shared linguistically, facts may be one socially constructed result.

5. See, for example, Scott Consigny, *Gorgias, Sophist and Artist* (Columbia: U. of South Carolina Press, 2001), 11. I have responded to Consigny's critiques in previous publications: Edward Schiappa, "Some of My Best Friends Are Neosophists: A Reply to Consigny," *Rhetoric Review* 14 (1996): 272–79; Schiappa, "Protagoras and the Language Game of History: A Response to Consigny," *Rhetoric Society Quarterly* 25 (1995): 220–23.

6. The same opportunity to become more than we already are is available when learning a foreign language. Many of us have had that interesting experience of dreaming in a new language. Boom! At that moment, we are no longer merely translating words that are different to those that are familiar. We have changed through our acceptance of the world that a previously "other" language offers.

7. Most of these exchanges are discussed in my *Beginnings of Rhetorical Theory in Classical Greece* (New Haven: Yale U. Press, 1999), chap. 2.

8. See the entry on Alcidamas in Appendix B of this book. For summaries of the relevant literature see Neil O'Sullivan, *Alcidamas, Aristophanes, and the Beginnings of Greek Stylistic Theory* (Stuttgart: Steiner, 1992) and J. V. Muir, *Alcidamas: The Works and Fragments* (London: Bristol Classical Press, 2001).

9. Kenneth Dover, *Plato: Symposium* (Cambridge: Cambridge U. Press, 1980), viii, 9.

10. Gerard J. Pendrick, "Plato and *Rhêtorikê*," *Rheinisches Museum für Philologie*, 141 (1998): 10–23.

11. See, for example, Consigny, *Gorgias;* Susan C. Jarratt, *Rereading the Sophists* (Carbondale: Southern Illinois U. Press, 1991); Bruce McComiskey, *Gorgias and the New Sophistic Rhetoric* (Carbondale: Southern Illinois U. Press, 2002).

12. See, for example, Michael Gagarin, *Antiphon the Athenian* (Austin: U. of Texas Press, 2002); John Poulakos, *Sophistical Rhetoric in Classical Greece* (Columbia: U. of South Carolina Press, 1995); Takis Poulakos, *Speaking for the Polis: Isocrates' Rhetorical Education* (Columbia: South Carolina U. Press, 1997); Yun Lee Too, *The Rhetoric of Identity in Isocrates* (Cambridge: Cambridge U. Press, 1995); Robert Wardy, *The Birth of Rhetoric: Gorgias, Plato and Their Successors* (London: Routledge, 1996). I limit myself

here to books, but obviously the point could be amplified by a systematic review of journal literature.

13. Michael Gagarin, "Did the Sophists Aim to Persuade?" *Rhetorica* 19 (2001): 275–91.

APPENDIX A

CHRONOLOGY OF PROTAGORAS' LIFE

The scant evidence concerning the basic details of Protagoras' life is collected in several widely available sources.[1] My purpose here is not to analyze the evidence, but to provide a brief summary for those not already familiar with the literature.[2] The following outline is based on the chronologies provided by J. S. Morrison and J. A. Davison.[3] All dates are approximations: the years indicated are outside parameters during which the event listed is likely to have occurred. Because Morrison and Davison differ, I have included both scholars' estimated dates. In general, I believe that Morrison's are more reliable.[4]

Event	Morrison	Davison	Age
Birth at Abdera	490/484	492/1	0
Pupil of Persian *magi*	—	480/79	11–13
Settles as Sophist in Athens	460/454	464/3	27–30
Expelled from Athens (?)	—	458/7	33–35
Expulsion decree revoked (?)	—	445/4	39–48
Leaves Athens for Thurii	444	444/3	40–49
Returns to Athens	433	433	51–59
(Dramatic date of *Protagoras*)			
Leaves Athens	430	—	54–63
(Decree of Diopeithes?)			
[Death of Pericles]	[429]	[429]	[55–64]
Returns to Athens	422	422/1	62–71
Asebeia accusal (?)	421/415	421/20	63–72
and death			

Appendix A

There are various accounts of Protagoras' death. Most tend to accept the story that he was prosecuted for *asebeia* and consequently sentenced to death or banished from Athens. Based on Plato's claim that Protagoras was nearly seventy when he died, most commentators assign his death to about 420. Untersteiner conjectured that his death was the result of the temporary overthrow of the democracy in 411, since Diogenes Laertius lists his accuser as "Pythodorus, son of Polyzelus, one of the Four Hundred" (9.54).[5] But Diogenes' account does not say that Protagoras was prosecuted during the reign of the Four Hundred, it merely identifies the accuser with his most prominent historical characteristic. As Morrison points out, Protagoras was closely affiliated with various anti-Spartan figures, including Pericles: "There were at least two occasions, in 418 and again in 415, when the peace-party might have taken advantage of the unpopularity of Alcibiades to rid themselves of Protagoras. Either of these dates agrees with the testimony of Plato: the date of 411 does not."[6]

If, alternatively, the whole story of Protagoras' *asebeia* trial is considered fictional, then we have no clear event by which to fix Protagoras' death except Plato's claim that he died at "nearly seventy."[7] Since the available information suggests that his birth was about 490, this would place his death at about 420.[8]

NOTES

1. The ancient evidence is collected in section 80 of Diels and Kranz (DK), translated into English in Rosamond Kent Sprague, ed. *The Older Sophists* (Columbia: U. of South Carolina Press, 1972). Mario Untersteiner edited a four-volume collection titled *Sofisti: testimonianze e frammenti* (Firenze: La Nuova Italia, 1949–62); Vol. 1 includes Protagoras. See also Antonio Capizzi, *Protagora* (Firenze: G. C. Sansoni, 1955).
2. The evidence is assessed by Kurt von Fritz, "Protagoras," *RE* 23 (1957): 908–11; J. A. Davison, "Protagoras, Democritus, and Anaxagoras," *CQ* 47 (1953): 33–38; J. S. Morrison, "The Place of Protagoras in Athenian Public Life," *CQ* 35 (1941): 1–16; Guthrie, *HGP III*, 262–69; Capizzi, *Protagora*, 219–34.
3. Morrison, "Place of Protagoras," 7; Davison, "Protagoras," 38.
4. In general, Morrison's chronology is followed by Kerferd, *SM*, 42–44, and Guthrie, *HGP III*, 262–69. Both assign 420 as the likely year of Protagoras' death.
5. Untersteiner, *Sophists*, 4.
6. Morrison, "Place of Protagoras," 4.
7. For a discussion of whether the trial was fact or fiction, see ch. 9 above.
8. For the argument that Plato's *Protagoras* deliberately conflated facts from two visits to Athens by Protagoras (433, 420), see John Walsh, "The Dramatic Dates of Plato's *Protagoras* and the Lesson of *Aretê*," *CQ* 34 (1984): 101–6.

218

APPENDIX B

DATA FROM THE TLG SEARCH FOR ῥητορικ-

The *Thesauraus Linguae Graecae* (hereafter TLG) project is in the process of completing a comprehensive computer-based data bank of all available ancient Greek texts.[1] It is, therefore, an invaluable resource for researchers interested in the history of Greek words such as ῥητορική. My hypothesis that Plato's *Gorgias* represents our earliest instance of ῥητορική was formed on the basis of dissertation-related research done exclusively with lexicons and concordances in printed form.[2] After defending my dissertation, I submitted the essay "Did Plato Coin *Rhêtorikê?*" (chapter 3 of this book) to the editor of the *American Journal of Philology*, George A. Kennedy. At his suggestion I requested that Theodore F. Brunner, Director of TLG, run a search of the entire TLG data base, including all corrected and uncorrected texts, for the stem ῥητορικ-. The results of that search, conducted on May 5, 1989, confirmed my original hypothesis. In March of 1990 searches through all corrected and uncorrected texts for ἐριστικ-, ἀντι-λογικ-, and διαλεκτικ- subsequently supported my argument that these terms also first appear in Plato's works.

Data in any field are subject to interpretation. A recent exchange in the journal *Philosophy and Rhetoric* has convinced me that "facts" seldom "speak for themselves": The persuasiveness of TLG data depends, at least in part, on the interpretive framework of the observer.[3] Accordingly, in what follows I have listed all instances of where the TLG search produced apparent matches between ῥητορικ- and texts the TLG identifies as written prior to, or roughly contemporaneous with, Plato's *Gorgias*. For each author I provide the number of matches found, followed by an explanation of why I do not believe the match(es) invalidates my hypothesis. I have also provided original source references in brackets

219

so that readers may investigate each match for themselves. The explanations are coded as follows:

M = Masculine forms, such as ῥητορικός (meaning "of a speaker"). To indicate "art" or "skill" *per se* requires the feminine form, ending in -ική, either modifying *technê* or standing alone as a substantive.

SR = Secondary reference. This means the passage is not claimed to be from before the fourth century BCE, but is simply a discussion *about*, say, the Older Sophists in which ῥητορικ-appeared. For example: Because ῥητορικ- appeared in the same sentence as the name Lysias, the TLG search indicated a match in the collected fragments of Lysias. However, upon closer inspection it turned out that the match is a passing reference to Lysias and rhetoric in the tenth century Suda. Sometimes these are references in which the author is clearly not making a direct link between *rhêtorikê* and a pre–fourth-century figure; the "match" is incidental.

Because Plato closely associates the Sophists with *rhêtorikê*, most later writers do so as well. The fact that later writers employ Platonic terminology does not mean that such terminology was in use in the fifth century. I am well aware that it is possible that ῥητορική was in use prior to Plato's *Gorgias* but that no written examples survived. However, the absence of ῥητορική in a wide variety of fifth- and fourth-century texts that should reasonably be expected to use the term suggests that it had not yet been coined. Accordingly, I consider secondary references to be unreliable guides to the dating of the term ῥητορική.

UN = Uncertain text or questionable dating. This includes fragments of dubious authority or much later claims that cannot be verified (such as references to a *technê rhêtorikê* written by a fifth-century Sophist).

L = A match from the fourth century BCE, but clearly late enough not to challenge the hypothesis that Plato's *Gorgias* is the earliest extant use of *rhêtorikê*.

Acesander 1 M, SR. [Felix Jacoby, *Die Fragmente der griechischen Historiker* (Leiden: Brill, 1964): III B, 425. Hereafter cited as *FGrH*.]

Aeschines (Orator) 2 L. Aeschines was born in 390; matches are from his speeches: *Rhêtorikôs* in *Against Timarchus* 71 (dated 345); *Rhêtorikên* in *Against Ctesiphon* 163 (dated 330). [Charles Darwin Adams, *The Speeches of Aeschines* (Cambridge, MA: Harvard U. Press, 1919), 60, 436.]

Aeschines (Philosopher) 1 UN. Included as an "uncertain" fragment. [H. Dittmar, *Aischines von Sphettos: Philologische Untersuchungen*, Vol. 21 (Berlin: Weidmann, 1912); fragment 51.]

Aeschylus 5 M, UN, SR. All are matches from alleged Aeschylean fragments in texts from much later than the fifth century. Three are attributed to, or about, various lost plays: #73 = M, UN; #231d = UN; #363 = M, UN. Two are from "Fragments of Unknown Origin": #634 = M, SR; #711 = M, UN. [Hans Joachim Mette, *Die Fragmente der Tragödien des Aischylos* (Berlin: Akademie Verlag, 1959), 26, 83, 93, 225, 241.]

Aesop 5 UN. There is a story in the Aesopian corpus that is explicitly about the art of rhetoric. However, only a handful of the fables attributed to Aesop are authentic; the rest were added over the centuries to the Aesopian corpus by later storytellers. These later-written fables are considered Aesopian only by virtue of the moral and stylistic features they share with the Aesopic tradition. The oldest extant collection of Aesopian fables is fully 800 years removed from the historical sixth-century BCE Aesop. The story in question, "Sailor and Son," was not part of that collection; it was written well afterward. Ben Edwin Perry, perhaps the world's foremost authority on Aesop, provided a conclusive case for dating the story sometime in the Middle Ages. He concluded: "It is obvious from the language and style in which these stories are written that the man who composed them lived sometime in the Middle Ages, and they are not, like the *Life* and *Fables* of Aesop in the same manuscripts, descended from an ancient book" ("Two Fables Recovered," 10–11). For the early history of Aesop's Fables, see B. E. Perry, *Aesopica* (Urbana: U. of Illinois Press, 1952), viii-xii. [B. E. Perry, "Two Fables Recovered," *Byzantinische Zeitschrift* 54 (1961): 5–6. Cf. B. E. Perry, "Some Traces of Lost Medieval Storybooks," *Humaniora,* ed. W. D. Hand and G. O. Arlt (Locust Valley, NY: J. J. Augustin, 1960), 151–160. Earlier editions of the story in collections of Aesop are reconstructions based on a mutilated text. Perry's "Two Fables Recovered" presents the recently discovered complete text.]

Alcidamas 2 L. The matches to Alcidamas are authentic; the only question is the date of his pamphlet titled *On the Sophists* or *On the Writers of Written Discourses.* The text is in Radermacher, B XXII 15 (cited below) and twice uses *rhêtorikê* (1.5, 2.5). For an English translation and analysis see LaRue Van Hook, "Alcidamas versus Isocrates," *Classical Weekly* 12 (1919): 89–94.

Though the pamphlet has been dated by Hook as written between 391 and 380 BCE, a closer textual analysis would date it well *after* 380 and hence well after the *Gorgias.* Hook's argument is that Alcidamas' pamphlet was in response to Isocrates' *Against the Sophists* (392 BCE) and that Isocrates' reply appeared in the *Panegyricus* (380 BCE). The basis for Hook's chronology is a passage in the *Panegyricus* (11) which seems to respond to Alcidamas' attacks (*On the Sophists* 6, 12–13), but the link is tenuous at best. Alcidamas' pamphlet attacks those who teach the writing of speeches rather than extemporaneous speaking. In 6 Alcidamas argues that extemporaneous speaking is more difficult than writing speeches, hence by mastering his art a student will be trained to both speak *and* write, but that writing does not train one to speak. The *Panegyricus* (11) *does not* respond to the difference between speaking and writing, but rather to the difference between plain and elegant styles. Isocrates *does* respond more directly to Alcidamas' argument at 6 in the *Antidosis* (49) ca. 354/3 BCE. In 12–13 Alcidamas says extemporaneous speaking is perceived as more spontaneous and hence more sincere by the audience. If Isocrates is responding to this charge in the *Panegyricus* (11) as suggested by Reinhardt (cited by Hook, 92, n46), his defense is not particularly direct, but there does seem to be a direct reference to Alcidamas' description of Isocrates' style as akin to poetry (2, 12) in Isocrates' *Antidosis* (46–7). Hence I believe a chronology that does more justice to Isocrates' argumentative skills would have him answering Alcidamas' charges in the *Antidosis*, not in the *Panegyricus*.

Furthermore, there is good evidence in Alcidamas' text to suggest that it is in response to the *Panegyricus* rather than the other way around (as argued by Hook). The evidence includes: 1) Alcidamas' reference to Isocrates' vanity. Hook's own examples of Isocrates' vanity are from the *Panegyricus* (4–14) or even later works. 2) References that apparently refer to a whole career of writing, not the beginning of a school (*On the Sophists* 1–2). 3) Alcidamas' complaint (4) that written works are the product of long premeditation and revision seems to be a direct reference to the *Panegyricus,* which took Isocrates ten years to complete (Quintilian 10.4.4). 4) Alcidamas' complaint (4) that written works have the luxury of assembling thoughts from many sources seems to be a direct response to Isocrates' *Panegyricus* (see 4, 7–10, 74; and Hook, 91 n41). 5) Alcidamas' complaint (4) that Isocrates revised his texts based on the advice of others *could* be the result of information in Alcidamas' possession early in Isocrates' career, but the practice is not mentioned by Isocrates until *To Philip* (17), ca. 346 BCE (see also *Panathenaicus* 200, 233).

My suggested revised chronology thus has Alcidamas' *On the Sophists* coming sometime after the *Panegyricus* (380 BCE) and before Isocrates' *Antidosis* (354/3 BCE). Such a chronology makes better sense of both authors' arguments. This dating also preserves the possibility that Alcidamas' criticism of written texts in 27–28 is, in fact, based on Plato's *Phaedrus* 275d. This possibility is acknowledged by Hook, but must be rejected if one accepts a pre-380 date for *On the Sophists*. Finally, it should be noted that Alcidamas' passing reference to classifications of public speaking (9) seems more appropriate to mid-fourth-century rhetorical theory than that around 385 BCE (see Kennedy, *APG*, 86). On the dates of Alcidamas see also Guthrie, *HGP III*, 311–13, esp. 311 n5. [Ludwig Rademacher, "Artium scriptores: Reste der voraristotelischen Rhetorik," *Österreichische Akademie der Wissenschaften: Philosophisch-historische Klasse*, Sitzungsberichte, 227. Band 3 (1951) B XXII 15 (135–41).]

Anaxagoras 1 SR. [DK 59 A15 = Plato, *Phaedrus* 269e.]

Anaximenes 2 L; 3 SR. The so-called *Rhetoric to Alexander* has been dated from no earlier than 341 BCE. The TLG matches are either to the title and introduction, which are commonly regarded as an even later addition, or are merely later, secondary discussions of the text. For the date and title see Kennedy, *APG*, 114–24; H. Rackham, introduction, *Rhetorica ad Alexandrum* (Cambridge, MA: Harvard U. Press, 1937), 258–62. [*FGrH*, II A, p. 112–16 (*testimonia* 8, 16).]

Antiphon 1 UN; 2 SR; 1 M, SR. Some of the Older Sophists were said to have authored books on the art of rhetoric. In Antiphon's case, his alleged *technê* was probably another name given to his *Tetralogies*. For arguments that the Older Sophists did not author handbooks called *Technê Rhêtorikê*, see chapter 3 of this book and Thomas Cole, *The Origins of Rhetoric in Ancient Greece* (Baltimore: John Hopkins U. Press), 71–112. For a recent collection of Antiphon's works and fragments in English, see J. S. Morrison's translation in *The Older Sophists*, ed. Rosamond Kent Sprague (Columbia: U. of South Carolina Press, 1972), 106–240. [DK 87 A6, B3, B93; L. Gernet, *Antiphon: Discours* (Paris: Les Belles Lettres, 1923), 167.]

Demades 2 L, M, SR. Demades was born about 380. Additionally, the two TLG matches are masculine. For Demades' life see J. O. Burtt, *Minor Attic Orators* (Cambridge, MA: Harvard U. Press, 1954), 2:329–32. [V. de Falco, *Demade orator: Testimonianze e frammenti* (Naples: Libreria Scientifica Editrice, 1955), fragment 52.4; and *FGrH*, II B, 955.]

Demetrius 9 L. Demetrius of Phaleron lived roughly from 350 to 280 BCE; see Kennedy, *APG*, 284–90. [F. Wehrli, *Demetrios von Phaleron*, in *Die Schule des Aristoteles* (Basel: Schwabe, 1968), 4:21–44.]

Democritus 1 M, SR. The match appears in Diogenes Laertius' concluding paragraph (9.49) about Democritus in which he lists the careers of other people sharing Democritus' name. Since the match refers to a later rhetorician named Democritus, it obviously does not link the fifth-century philosopher to *rhêtorikê*. [DK 68 A1 = DL 9.49.]

Dinarchus 1 L, UN. Dinarchus was born about 361. Also, the match is from an uncertain fragment. On his life see J. O. Burtt, *Minor Attic Orators* 2:161–62. [N. C. Conomis, *Dinarchi orationes cum fragmentis* (Leipzig: Teubner, 1975), 145.]

Empedocles 5 SR. Most references to Empedocles and rhetoric are derived from Aristotle's claim that Empedocles "invented" rhetoric; none purports to be a direct quotation from an Empedoclean text or fragment. For a more thorough discussion of the Empedocles' "invention" myth, see chapter 3 of this book. [DL 8.57, 58; and DK 31 A1, A5, A19.]

Epicurus 10 L. Epicurus was born about 341. [Graziano Arrighetti, *Epicurus, Opere* (Turin: G. Einaudi, 1960), entry 19 of *Deperditorum librorum reliquiae*.]

Gorgias 11 SR, UN. Five matches are from Plato's *Gorgias*; three are later references to an alleged *technê*, probably the *Helen*; two are of the irrelevant masculine form; one is a later reference to Gorgias' oratorical abilities. Refer to the discussion of Antiphon above as well as chapter 3 of this book. [DK 82 A2, A3, A4, A22, A27, A28, B5a, B14.]

Heraclides Ponticus 1 L, UN. A late, reconstructed fragment. [F. Wehrli, *Herakleides Pontikos*, in *Die Schule des Aristoteles*, Vol. 7 (Basel: Schwabe, 1969), fragment 22.]

Hippocrates 1 M, UN. The term is *rhêtorikôtaton*, and it is probably not from the fifth century. [É. Littré, *Oeuvres complètes d'Hippocrate*, Vol. 2 (1840; Paris: Baillière, 1961), "De diaeta acutorum" 23.4.]

Hyperides 1 L, UN. Hyperides was born about 390. Also, the match is from an uncertain fragment. On his life see J. O. Burtt, *Minor Attic Orators* 2:363–66. [C. Jensen, *Hyperidis orationes sex* (Leipzig: Teubner, 1917), fragment 63.]

Idomeneus 1 M, SR. [DL 2.19]

Isocrates 2 M; 3 SR. Only the masculine form is found in the authentic texts of Isocrates. The other three matches are secondary discussions or refer to Isocrates' "lost" *technê*. For the argument that Isocrates would never have written a *technê*, complete with an summary of the relevant literature, see Michael Cahn, "Reading Rhetoric Rhetorically: Isocrates and the Marketing of Insight," *Rhetorica* 2 (1989): 121–44. [Isocrates' *Nicocles* 8, *Antidosis* 256; and Georges Mathieu and Émile Brémond, *Isocrate* (Paris: Les Belles Lettres, 1962), 4:229, 231, 235.]

Lysias 1 SR. [Theodorus Thalheim, *Lysiae Orationes,* editio maior, 2nd ed. (Leipzig: Teubner, 1913), 368.]

Nausiphanes 3 L. The matches may be authentic, but Nausiphanes dates from the late fourth century to the early third century. [DK 75 A1, B1.]

Philistus (Syracusanus) 2 SR, UN. From the Suda. [*FGrH,* III B, 551.]

Philistus (Naucratites) 2 SR, UN. Probably post–fourth century. [*FGrH,* III C, 122.]

Polycritus 1 M, SR. [DL 2.63.]

Protagoras 1 SR. [Aristotles' *Rhetoric* 1402a27 = DK 80 A21.]

Pythagoristae 1 SR. Match is from Iamblichus' (3/4 CE) "Life of Pythagoras." [DK 58 D1: p. 468, line 13.]

Speusippus 2 L. Nephew of Plato. [L. Taran, *Speusippis of Athens: Philosophia Antiqua,* Vol. 39 (Leiden: Brill, 1981), fragments 5a and 68c.]

Theodectes 1 L, SR. A contemporary of Aristotle's, hence not a problematic match. [*FGrH,* II B, 525.]

Theophrastus 1 L. Student of Aristotle. [F. Wimmer, *Theophrasti Eresii opera, quae supersunt, omnia* (1866; Frankfurt am Main: Minerva, 1964), fragment 65.1.]

Theopompus 3 L. The historian from the fourth century, not the earlier comic. Two matches are secondary references; one is masculine. [*FGrH,* II B, testimonia 20a, 45.]

Thrasymachus 6 SR, UN. All matches are either secondary discussions or references to a *technê*. [DK 85 A1, A13, B7a.]

Timaeus 1 M, SR. [*FGrH,* III B, 581.]

Zeno 3 SR. All matches are incidental; they occur in passages referring to Aristotle's claim that Zeno invented dialectic and Empedocles invented rhetoric. [DK 29 A1, A2, A10.]

NOTES

1. For an overview of the TLG project see Luci Berkowitz and Karl A. Squitier, *Thesaurus Linguae Graecae: Canon of Greek Authors and Works,* 3rd ed. (NY: Oxford U. Press, 1990), vii–xxviii.

2. Specifically Henry George Liddell and Robert Scott, *A Greek-English Lexicon,* 9th ed. (Oxford: Clarendon Press, 1940); J. E. Powell, *A Lexicon to Herodotus,* 2nd ed. (Hildesheim: Georg Olms, 1977); Henry Dunbar, *A Complete Concordance to the Comedies and Fragments of Aristophanes* (Oxford: Clarendon Press, 1883); and Leonard Brandwood, *A Word Index to Plato* (Leeds: W. S. Maney and Sons, 1976).

3. See Edward Schiappa, "Neo-Sophistic Rhetorical Criticism or the Historical Reconstruction of Sophistic Doctrines?" *PR* 23 (1990): 196–98; John Poulakos, "Interpreting Sophistical Rhetoric: A Response to Schiappa," *PR* 23 (1990): 221–23; and Edward Schiappa, "History and Neo-Sophistic Criticism: A Reply to Poulakos," *PR* 23 (1990): 307–15.

APPENDIX C

THREE SPURIOUS ATTRIBUTIONS

There are two ancient references to Protagoras and one assignment of author-ship that I have not previously discussed. All three ascriptions deserve mention in any thorough treatment of Protagoras.

THE MILLET SEED PUZZLE

Aristotle's *Physics* (250a19–22) makes reference to what is now commonly referred to as Zeno's millet seed argument, and it is presented in a fuller version in a later commentary by Simplicius:

> In this way [Aristotle] solves the problem which Zeno the Eleatic set for Protagoras the Sophist. "Tell me, Protagoras," he said, "does a single millet seed make a sound when it falls? Or the ten-thousandth part of a seed?" Protagoras said that it didn't. "What about a bushel of millet seed," he said, "does that make a sound when it falls, or not?" He said that the bushel did make a sound. "Well," said Zeno, "isn't there a ratio between the bushel and the single seed, or the ten-thousandth part of a single seed?" He agreed. "Well then," said Zeno, "won't the sounds too stand in the same ratios to one another? For as the sounders are, so are the sounds. And if that's so, then if the bushel makes a sound, the single seed and the ten-thousandth part of a seed will make a sound too."[1]

The original source of the exchange is unknown. No one asserts that the passage records an actual discussion between Zeno and Protagoras, and it is unlikely that Zeno wrote a dialogue in which he himself was a character.[2] The fact that the puzzle is mentioned by Aristotle suggests that it was legitimately linked to Zeno, though Protagoras' role appears to be a later, fictional, addition. The common opinion is that the argument represents part of Zeno's support of Parmenides' exhortation to consider the senses untrustworthy.[3] Since Plato's *Theaetetus* portrays Protagoras as a champion of sense perception, it is perfectly understandable that he would be cast as Zeno's foil in later reproductions of the argument.

THE SUIT AGAINST EUATHLUS

The following anecdote is reported by Diogenes Laertius: "A story is told of the time [Protagoras] demanded his fee from Euathlus, a pupil of his. Euathlus refused to pay, saying, 'But I haven't won a victory [in court] yet.' Protagoras replied, 'But if I win this dispute I must be paid because I've won, and if you win it I must be paid because you've won.'"[4] The story has no authority, and is probably a simple revision of a story told of Corax and Tisias.[5] Both stories are almost certainly fictitious, but the Corax and Tisias story has older roots and hence should be considered the original.[6]

There is an interesting difference in the endings of the respective stories. One is left with the impression from Diogenes Laertius that Protagoras won his suit by putting Euathlus in an insoluble dilemma. Hence the point of the story could have been that Protagoras was very clever or that one ought not try to haggle with Sophists.[7] In the case of Corax's suit, Tisias defends himself by saying if he wins he need not pay, but if he loses he ought not pay since Corax's training will have proven to be useless. Corax counters by saying if Tisias loses, he legally must pay, but if Tisias wins he ought to pay since his training will have proven to be useful. The suit was thrown out with the punning epigram "a bad egg from a bad crow (*korax*)."[8] In this version of the story the objective would appear to be to lampoon the art of rhetoric in general and rhetoric's "inventors" in particular.[9]

ON THE ART

Theodor Gomperz argued that the Hippocratic work *On the Art* was authored by Protagoras.[10] W. H. S. Jones, in his edition of the Hippocratic corpus, tentatively agreed with Gomperz.[11] If Protagoras was in fact the author, then the text would be an extremely valuable guide to Protagoras' views and style of argument. Unfortunately, as tempting as the attribution to Protagoras is, there are good reasons to reject Gomperz's suggestion.

Gomperz cites a passage from Plato's *Sophist* which claims "Protagoras wrote on wrestling and the other arts" (232d9-e1) as evidence that Protagoras wrote on a variety of "special arts." *On the Art* contains a promise that "the scope of the other arts shall be discussed at another time and in another discourse" (9.1–2), which Gomperz sees as corroborating the reference in Plato. There are two problems with these complementing bits of evidence. First, there is no evidence that Protagoras wrote on any subject as a *technê*. Indeed, the use of *technê* to designate a discrete art, craft, or system became common only in the fourth century (see LSJ). Diogenes Laertius' reference (9.55) to a book by Protagoras omits reference to an art and is simply titled *On Wrestling* (*Peri Palês*). Second, it is doubtful that Protagoras ever wrote on the physical sport of wrestling specifically. Physical combat in general and wrestling in particular were often used to describe the process of arguing.[12]

There are two passages in *On the Art* that suggest Protagorean influence. One is a discussion of how "correctness" and "incorrectness" (*orthon* and *ouk orthon*) are provided by art, and the other is a discussion of cures by the use of opposites (5.32–34). The latter theme is common in the Hippocratic works, and hence is no assurance of Protagoras' authorship. "Correctness," too, is a common sophistic theme in the late fifth and early fourth centuries, so it suffices only to show Protagoras' influence, not authorship.

There are three passages which suggest that the author was *not* Protagoras. The first suggests that names (*onomata*) come into being by convention and not by nature (2.16–18; cf. 6.17–18). Such a claim is at odds with Protagoras' identification of *logos* and *onoma* with reality (*pragma*), which is echoed in the *Dissoi Logoi* (1.11) as late as 400 BCE. The second is the author's claim, "First I will define what I conceive medicine to be" (3.5–6). The sort of logic and syntax this sentence represents originates with Plato in the fourth century, and provides justification for dating *On the Art* after the death of Protagoras.[13] The third passage refers to men who see "only with [their] eyes" as "obscure" and their refusal to see with the "eye of the mind" as evidence of their "obscurity" (11.1–13). The use of *adêla* as "obscurity" in this passage is grossly inconsistent with its usage in Protagoras' "concerning the gods" fragment and the alleged "new" fragment (see chapter 9 in this book). If Protagoras made a distinction between perception and cognition, which is unlikely, he would have drawn a conclusion opposite to that of the author of *On the Art*.

On the whole, the evidence leans toward a fourth-century rather than a fifth-century date for *On the Art*. Since Plato displayed ambivalence toward the *technê* of medicine, *On the Art* seems as much at home with the philosophical controversies of the early fourth century as it does with those of the fifth.[14] Even by Jones' analysis the style of the text could date it well into the fourth century.[15] Accordingly, the most that can be taken from *On the Art* is its evidence for the affinity of sophistic and medical thinking. Fifth-century Sophists obviously influenced the text, but did not author it.

228

NOTES

1. Simplicius, *Commentary on the Physics* 1108.14–28, trans. by Jonathan Barnes in *The Presocratic Philosophers* (London: Routledge and Kegan Paul, 1982), 258 = Jonathan Barnes, *Early Greek Philosophy* (London: Penguin, 1987), 158. The Greek text is available in DK 29 A29 or Mario Untersteiner, *Sofisti: testimonianze e frammenti* (Firenze: La Nuova Italia, 1961), 1:84.

2. Guthrie, *HGP II*, 81.

3. Ibid., 97. See also Barnes, *Presocratic*, xix-xx, 258–60. J. Moline has argued that Zeno's millet seed argument gave Eubulides the idea of the "soritical" arguments ("Aristotle, Eubulides, and the Sorites," *Mind* 78 [1969]: 393–407). Though Barnes once thought the millet seed argument soritical, he now claims that Zeno "derived his conclusion by the aid of a principle of proportionality that has nothing to do with the sorites," even if it was later associated with them ("Medicine, Experience and Logic," *Science and Speculation*, ed. Jonathan Barnes, Jacques Brunschwig, Myles Burnyeat, Malcolm Schofield [Cambridge: Cambridge U. Press, 1982], 36–39).

4. DL 9.56 = DK 80 A1 ¶56, trans. by Michael J. O'Brien in Rosamond Kent Sprague, ed. *The Older Sophists* (Columbia: U. of South Carolina Press, 1972), 6. See also DL 9.54 = DK 80 A1 ¶54; DK 80 A4, B6.

5. The oldest version of the story can be found in Chistianus Walz, *Rhetores Graeci* (Stuttgart: J. G. Cottae, 1836), 6:4–30, or Hugo Rabe, *Prolegomenon Sylloge* (Leipzig: Teubner, 1931), 18–43.

6. The Corax and Tisias trial story *might* date back to the fourth century BCE, according to Georgius (Jerzy) Kowalski, *De Arte Rhetorica* (Leopoli: Polonorum, 1937), 84. Stanley Wilcox concluded that it is impossible "to determine when all the details of this story originated" ("Corax and the 'Prolegomena,'" *AJP* 64 [1943]: 20). See also A. W. Verrall, "Korax and Tisias," *JP* 9 (1880): 208–9.

7. Friedrich Blass, *Die Attische Beredsamkeit von Gorgias bis zu Lysias* (Leipzig: Teubner, 1868), 20, 27.

8. As retold by Kennedy, *APG*, 59.

9. Georgius (Jerzy) Kowalski, *De Artis Rhetoricae Originibus* (Leopoli: Sumptibus Societatis Litterarum, 1933), 43.

10. Theodor Gomperz, *Greek Thinkers* (London: John Murray, 1901), 1:466–70.

11. W. H. S. Jones, *Hippocrates* (Cambridge, MA: Harvard U. Press, 1923), 2:187.

12. Ernst Heitsch, "Ein Buchtitel des Protagoras," *Hermes* 97 (1969): 292–96 (= Classen, *Sophistik*, 298–305).

13. Cf. Havelock, *The Greek Concept of Justice* (Cambridge, MA: Harvard U. Press, 1978), 312–19.

14. Jones, *Hippocrates*, 2: xxxvii-xl; cf. Ludwig Edelstein, *Ancient Medicine: Selected Papers of Ludwig Edelstein*, ed. Owsei Temkin and C. Lilian Temkin (Baltimore: Johns Hopkins U. Press, 1967), 3–64.

15. Jones, *Hippocrates*, 1: xxxii.

BIBLIOGRAPHY

Ancient Greek texts concerning Protagoras are collected in section 80 of Diels and Kranz (DK), translated into English in Rosamond Kent Sprague, ed., *The Older Sophists*. More complete collections appear in Greek and Italian in volume 1 of Mario Untersteiner's *Sofisti: Testimonianze e frammenti* and Antonio Capizzi's *Protagora*.

The following is a list of sources cited more than once in the text or works that may be of particular interest to those studying Protagoras and early rhetorical theory.

Adkins, A. W. H. *Aretê, Technê*, Democracy, and Sophists: *Protagoras* 316b–328d." *Journal of Hellenic Studies* 93 (1973): 3–12.

———. *Merit and Responsibility: A Study in Greek Values*. Oxford: Clarendon Press, 1960.

Allen, R. E. *The Dialogues of Plato*. Vol. 1. New Haven: Yale U. Press, 1984.

Arrowsmith, William. *Aristophanes: The Clouds*. Ann Arbor: U. of Michigan Press, 1962.

Arthur, E. P. "Plato, *Theaetetus* 171A." *Mnemosyne* 35 (1982): 335–36.

Aulitzky, [ ]. "Korax 3." *Paulys Real-Encyclopädie der classischen Altertumswissenschaft* 11 (1922): 1379–81.

Austin, Scott. *Parmenides: Being, Bounds, and Logic*. New Haven: Yale U. Press, 1986.

Barilli, Renato. *Rhetoric*. Minneapolis: U. of Minnesota Press, 1989. Originally published as *La Retorica*. Milan: Arnoldo Mondadori, 1983.

Barnes, Jonathan. "Aphorism and Argument." *Language and Thought in Early Greek Philosophy*, ed. Kevin Robb. La Salle, IL: Hegeler Institute, 1983. 91–109.

———. *The Complete Works of Aristotle*. 2 vols. Princeton: Princeton U. Press, 1984.

———. *Early Greek Philosophy*. London: Penguin, 1987.

230

———. "The Presocratics in Context." *Phronesis* 33 (1988): 327–44.

———. *The Presocratic Philosophers*, rev. ed. London: Routledge and Kegan Paul, 1982.

Barrett, Harold. *The Sophists: Rhetoric, Democracy, and Plato's Idea of Sophistry*. Novata, CA: Chandler and Sharp, 1987.

Bayonas, Auguste. "L'art politique d'après Protagoras." *Revue Philosophique* 157 (1967): 43–58.

Beattie, Paul. "Protagoras: The Maligned Philosopher." *Religious Humanism* 14 (1980): 108–15.

Beck, Frederick A. G. *Greek Education: 450–350 B.C.* New York: Barnes and Noble, 1964.

Bernal, Martin. *Black Athena: The Afroasiatic Roots of Classical Civilization* Vol. 1. New Brunswick: Rutgers U. Press, 1987.

Bernsen, N. O. "Protagoras' Homo-Mensura Thesis." *Classica et Mediaevalia* 30 (1974): 109–44.

Bett, Richard. "The Sophists and Relativism." *Phronesis* 34 (1989): 139–69.

Binder, Gerhard, and Leo Liesenborghs. "Eine Zuweisung der Sentenz οὐκ ἔστιν ἀντιλέγειν an Prodikos von Keos." *Museum Helveticum* 23 (1966): 37–43. Rpt. in Classen, *Sophistik,* 452–62.

Blank, David L. "Socratics versus Sophists on Payment for Teaching." *Classical Antiquity* 4 (1985): 1–49.

Blass, Friedrich. *Die Attische Beredsamkeit von Gorgias bis zu Lysias*. Leipzig: Teubner, 1868.

Bloch, Maurice. *Political Language and Oratory in Traditional Society*. London: Academic Press, 1975.

Bloom, Allan David. "The Political Philosophy of Isocrates." Ph.D. diss., University of Chicago, 1955.

Bodrero, Emilio. "Le opere di Protagora." *Rivista di Filologia* 31 (1903): 558–95.

Brumbaugh, Robert S. *The Philosophers of Greece*. New York: Crowell, 1964.

Bryant, Donald C. *Ancient Greek and Roman Rhetoricians*. Columbia, MO: Artcraft Press, 1968.

Burnet, John. *Early Greek Philosophy*. 4th ed. London: Adam and Charles Black, 1930.

———. *Greek Philosophy: Thales to Plato*. London: Macmillan, 1964. Originally published in 1914.

Burns, Alfred. "Athenian Literacy in the Fifth Century B.C." *Journal of the History of Ideas* 42 (1981): 371–87.

Burnyeat, M. F. "Protagoras and Self-refutation in Later Greek Philosophy." *The Philosophical Review* 85 (1976): 44–69.

———. "Protagoras and Self-refutation in Plato's *Theaetetus*." *The Philosophical Review* 85 (1976): 172–95.

Burrell, P. S. "Man the Measure of All Things: Socrates versus Protagoras." *Philosophy* 7 (1932): 27–41, 168–84.

Bury, R. G. *Sextus Empiricus.* 4 vols. Cambridge, MA: Harvard U. Press, 1933.

Buxton, R. G. A. *Persuasion in Greek Tragedy: A Study of "Peithô."* Cambridge: Cambridge U. Press, 1982.

Caizzi, Fernanda Decleva. "La tradizione Protagorea ed un Frammento di Diogene di Enoanda." *Rivista di Filologia* 104 (1976): 435–42.

Calogera, Guido. "Protagora." *Enciclopedia Italiana.* Roma: Fondata da Giovanni Treccani, 1949. 28: 368–70.

Capizzi, Antonio. *Protagora: le testimonianze e i frammenti, edizione riveduta e ampliata con uno studio su la vita, le opere, il pensiero e la fortuna.* Firenze: G. C. Sansoni, 1955.

Cappeletti, Angel J. "El Agnosticismo de Protagoras." *Dianoia* 28 (1982): 51–55.

Carpenter, Rhys. "The Antiquity of the Greek Alphabet." *American Journal of Archaeology* 37 (1933): 8–29.

――――. "The Greek Alphabet Again." *American Journal of Archaeology* 42 (1938): 58–69.

Cassin, Barbara, ed. *Positions de la Sophistique.* Paris: Vrin, 1986.

Caujolle-Zaslawsky, Françoise. "Sophistique et scepticisme. L'image de Protagoras dans l'uvre de Sextus Empiricus." *Positions de la Sophistique,* ed. Barbara Cassin. Paris: Vrin, 1986. 149–65.

Cherniss, Harold. *Aristotle's Criticism of Presocratic Philosophy.* New York: Octagon Books, 1935.

Chilton, C. W. "An Epicurean View of Protagoras." *Phronesis* 7 (1962): 105–9.

Clark, Donald Lemen. *Rhetoric in Greco-Roman Education.* New York: Columbia U. Press, 1957.

Classen, Carl Joachim. "Aristotle's Picture of the Sophists." *The Sophists and Their Legacy,* ed. G. B. Kerferd. Wiesbaden: Franz Steiner, 1981. 7–24.

――――. "The Study of Language Amongst Socrates' Contemporaries." *The Proceedings of the African Classical Association* 2 (1959): 33–49. Rpt. in *Sophistik,* 215–47.

Classen, Carl Joachim, ed. *Sophistik* (Wege der Forschung 187). Darmstadt: Wissenschaftliche Buchgesellschaft, 1976.

Cole, Thomas. "The Apology of Protagoras." *Yale Classical Studies* 19 (1966): 101–18.

――――. *The Origins of Rhetoric in Ancient Greece.* Baltimore: Johns Hopkins U. Press, 1991.

――――. "The Relativism of Protagoras." *Yale Classical Studies* 22 (1972): 19–45.

Conley, Thomas M. "Dating the So-called *Dissoi Logoi:* A Cautionary Note." *Ancient Philosophy* 5 (1985): 59–65.

Connors, Robert J. "Greek Rhetoric and the Transition from Orality." *Philosophy and Rhetoric* 19 (1986): 38–65.

Consigny, Scott. *Gorgias, Sophist and Artist.* Columbia: U. of South Carolina Press, 2001.

Cooper, Lane. *The Rhetoric of Aristotle.* Englewood Cliffs, NJ: Prentice-Hall, 1932.

Cope, Edward Meredith. "The Sophists." *Journal of Classical and Sacred Philology* 1 (1854): 145–88.

———. "On the Sophistical Rhetoric." *Journal of Classical and Sacred Philology* 2 (1855): 129–69; 3 (1856): 34–80, 252–88.

———. *The Rhetoric of Aristotle with a Commentary.* 3 vols. Cambridge: Cambridge U. Press, 1877.

Cornford, Francis Macdonald. *Plato's Theaetetus.* Indianapolis: Bobbs-Merrill, 1957.

———. *Plato's Theory of Knowledge.* London: Routledge and Kegan Paul, 1935.

———. *Thucydides Mythistoricus.* New York: Greenwood Press, 1969. Originally published London: Edward Arnold, 1907.

Davison, J. A. "The Date of the *Prometheia.*" *Transactions and Proceedings of the American Philological Association* 80 (1949): 66–93.

———. "Protagoras, Democritus and Anaxagoras." *Classical Quarterly* 47 (1953): 33–45.

Decharme, Paul. *Euripides and the Spirit of His Dramas.* Trans. J. Loeb. New York: Macmillan, 1906.

Denniston, J. D. "Technical Terms in Aristophanes." *Classical Quarterly* 21 (1927): 113–21.

Diels, Hermann, and Walther Kranz. *Die Fragmente der Vorsokratiker,* 3 vols. 6th ed. Berlin: Weidmann, 1951–52.

Dodds, E. R. *The Greeks and the Irrational.* Berkeley: U. of California Press, 1951.

———. *Plato: Gorgias.* Oxford: Clarendon Press, 1959.

Döring, Klaus. "Die politische Theorie des Protagoras." *The Sophists and Their Legacy,* ed. G. B. Kerferd. Wiesbaden: Franz Steiner, 1981. 109–15.

Dover, Kenneth J. *Aristophanes: Clouds.* Oxford: Clarendon Press, 1968.

———. "The Freedom of the Intellectual in Greek Society." *Talanta* 7 (1976): 24–54.

Dupréel, Eugène. *Les Sophistes: Protagoras, Gorgias, Hippias, Prodicus.* Neuchâtel: Éditions du Griffon, 1948.

Eden, Kathy. "Hermeneutics and the Ancient Rhetorical Tradition." *Rhetorica* 5 (1988): 59–86.

Ehninger, Douglas. "On Systems of Rhetoric." *Philosophy and Rhetoric* 1 (1968): 131–44.

Ehrenberg, Victor. "The Foundation of Thurii." *American Journal of Philology* 69 (1948): 149–70.

Eisler, Riane. *The Chalice and the Blade.* New York: Harper, 1987.

Eldredge, Laurence. "Sophocles, Protagoras, and the Nature of Greek Culture." *Antioch Review* 25 (1969): 8–12.

Engnell, Richard A. "Implications for Communication of the Rhetorical Episte-mology of Gorgias of Leontini." *Western Journal of Speech Communication* 37 (1973): 175–84.

Enos, Richard Leo. "Aristotle, Empedocles, and the Notion of Rhetoric." *In Search of Justice: The Indiana Tradition in Speech Communication,* ed. R. Jensen and J. Hammerback. Amsterdam: Rodopi, 1987. 5–21.

———. "The Epistemology of Gorgias' Rhetoric: A Re-examination." *Southern Speech Communication Journal* 42 (1976): 35–51.

———. "Emerging Notions of Argument and Advocacy in Hellenic Litigation: Antiphon's 'On the Murder of Herodes.'" *Journal of the American Forensic Association* 16 (1980): 182–91.

———. "Emerging Notions of Heuristic, Eristic, and Protreptic Rhetoric in Homeric Discourse: Proto-Literate Conniving, Wrangling, and Reasoning." *Selected Papers from the 1981 Texas Writing Research Conference,* ed. Maxine C. Hairston and Cynthia L. Selfe. Austin: University of Texas, 1981. 44–64.

Epps, P. H. "Protagoras' Famous Statement." *Classical Journal* 59 (1964): 223–26.

Erickson, Keith V. *Aristotle: The Classical Heritage of Rhetoric.* Metuchen, NJ: Scarecrow Press, 1974.

———. *Aristotle's Rhetoric: Five Centuries of Philological Research.* Metuchen, NJ: Scarecrow Press, 1975.

———. *Plato: True and Sophistic Rhetoric.* Amsterdam: Rodopi, 1979.

Evans, J. D. G. "Aristotle on Relativism." *Philosophical Quarterly* 24 (1974): 193–203.

Farenga, Vincent. "Periphrasis on the Origin of Rhetoric." *Modern Language Notes* 94 (1979): 1033–55.

Fehling, Detlev. "Protagoras und die ὀρθοέπεια." In Classen, *Sophistik,* 341–47.

Finnegan, Ruth. *Orality and Literacy: Studies in the Technology of Communication.* Oxford: Basil Blackwell, 1988.

Foucault, Michel. *The Archaeology of Knowledge.* Trans. A. M. Sheridan Smith. New York: Pantheon, 1972.

Frede, Michael. "Philosophy and Medicine in Antiquity." *Human Nature and Natural Knowledge,* ed. A. Donagan, A. N. Perovich, Jr., and M. V. Wedin. Dordrecht: D. Reidel, 1986. 211–32.

Freeman, Kathleen. *Ancilla to the Presocratic Philosophers.* Cambridge, MA: Harvard U. Press, 1978.

———. *Companion to the Presocratic Philosophers.* 2nd ed. Oxford: Basil Blackwell, 1949.

Freese, J. H. *Aristotle, "Art" of Rhetoric.* Cambridge, MA: Harvard U. Press, 1926.

Frings, Manfred S. "Protagoras Rediscovered: Heidegger's Explication of Protagoras' Fragment." *Journal of Value Inquiry* 8 (1974): 112–23.

234

Fritz, Kurt von. "*Nous, Noein,* and their Derivatives in Pre-Socratic Philosophy." *The Presocratics,* ed. A. P. D. Mourelatos. New York: Anchor Books, 1974. 23–85. First published *Classical Philology* 40 (1945): 223–42; 41 (1946): 12–34.

———. "Protagoras." *Paulys Real-Encyclopädie der classischen Altertumswissenschaft* 23 (1957): 908–21.

Fuller, Benjamin Apthorp Gould. *History of Greek Philosophy.* Vol. 2: *The Sophists, Socrates, Plato.* New York: Henry Holt, 1931.

———. *A History of Philosophy.* Rev. ed. New York: Henry Holt, 1945.

Gagarin, Michael. *Antiphon the Athenian.* Austin: U. of Texas Press, 2002.

———. "Did the Sophists Aim to Persuade?" *Rhetorica* 19 (2001): 275–91.

———. *Early Greek Law.* Berkeley: U. of California Press, 1986.

———. "The Nature of Proofs in Antiphon." *Classical Philology* 85 (1990): 22–32.

———. "Plato and Protagoras." Ph.D. diss., Yale University, 1968.

———. "The Purpose of Plato's *Protagoras.*" *Transactions of the American Philological Association* 100 (1969): 133–64.

Gaonkar, Dilip. "Plato's Critique of Protagoras' Man-Measure Doctrine." *Pre/ Text* 10 (1989): 71–80.

Garner, Richard. *Law and Society in Classical Athens.* New York: St. Martin's Press, 1987.

Gercke, A. "Die älte τέχνη ῥητορική und ihre Gegner." *Hermes* 32 (1897): 348–58.

Giannantoni, Gabriele. "Il frammento 1 di Protagora in una nuova testimonianza platonica." *Rivista critica di storia della filosofia* 65 (1960): 227–37.

Gillespie, C. M. "The *Truth* of Protagoras." *Mind* 19 (1910): 470–92.

Glidden, David K. "Protagorean Obliquity." *History of Philosophy Quarterly* 5 (1988): 321–40.

———. "Protagorean Relativism and the Cyrenaics." *American Philosophical Quarterly,* monograph 9 (1975): 113–40.

———. "Protagorean Relativism and *Physis.*" *Phronesis* 20 (1975): 209–27.

Gomme, A. W. *A Historical Commentary on Thucydides.* Vol. 2. Oxford: Clarendon Press, 1956.

Gomperz, Heinrich. *Sophistik und Rhetorik.* Aalen: Scientia Verlag, 1985. First published Leipzig: Teubner, 1912.

Gomperz, Theodor. *Greek Thinkers: A History of Ancient Philosophy,* Trans. Laurie Magnus. 4 vols. London: John Murray, 1901.

Gonda, Joseph P. "*Politikê Technê* in *Protagoras* 309–338." Ph.D. diss., Pennsylvania State University, 1975.

Goody, Jack, and Ian Watt. "The Consequences of Literacy." *Literacy in Traditional Societies,* ed. Jack Goody. Cambridge: Cambridge U. Press, 1968. 27–68.

Graeser, Andreas. "On Language, Thought, and Reality in Ancient Greek Philosophy." *Dialectica* 31 (1977): 360–88.

Green, Lawrence D. "Aristotelian Rhetoric, Dialectic, and the Traditions of 'Αντίστροφος." *Rhetorica* 8 (1990): 5–27.

Grimaldi, William M. A. *Aristotle, Rhetoric: A Commentary.* 2 vols. New York: Fordham U. Press, 1980, 1988.

———. "A Note on the ΠΙΣΤΕΙΣ in Aristotle's *Rhetoric,* 1354–1356." *American Journal of Philology* 78 (1957): 188–92.

———. *Studies in the Philosophy of Aristotle's Rhetoric.* Wiesbaden: Franz Steiner, 1972.

Gronbeck, Bruce E. "Gorgias on Rhetoric and Poetic: A Rehabilitation." *Southern Speech Communication Journal* 38 (1972): 27–38.

Gronewald, M. "Ein neues Protagoras-Fragment." *Zeitschrift für Papyrologie und Epigraphik* 2 (1968): 1–2.

Grote, George. *A History of Greece.* 2nd ed. 10 vols. London: John Murray, 1851.

Guthrie, W. K. C. "Aristotle as Historian." *Journal of Hellenic Studies* 77 (1957): 35–41.

———. *A History of Greek Philosophy.* 6 vols. Cambridge: Cambridge U. Press, 1962–81.

Haden, James. "Did Plato Refute Protagoras?" *History of Philosophy Quarterly* 1 (1984): 223–40.

Hamilton, Edith, and Huntington Cairns. *The Collected Dialogues of Plato.* Princeton: Princeton U. Press, 1961.

Hansen, Mogens Herman. "The Athenian 'Politicians,' 403–322 B.C." *Greek, Roman, and Byzantine Studies* 24 (1983): 33–55.

———. "Initiative and Decision: The Separation of Powers in Fourth-Century Athens." *Greek, Roman, and Byzantine Studies* 22 (1981): 345–70.

———. "*Rhêtores* and *Stratêgoi* in Fourth-Century Athens." *Greek, Roman, and Byzantine Studies* 24 (1983): 151–80.

Harris, William V. *Ancient Literacy.* Cambridge, MA: Harvard U. Press, 1989.

Havelock, Eric A. *The Greek Concept of Justice.* Cambridge, MA: Harvard U. Press, 1978.

———. *The Liberal Temper in Greek Politics.* New Haven: Yale U. Press, 1957.

———. "The Linguistic Task of the Presocratics." *Language and Thought in Early Greek Philosophy,* ed. Kevin Robb. La Salle, IL: Hegeler Institute, 1983. 7–82.

———. *The Literate Revolution in Greece and Its Cultural Consequences.* Princeton: Princeton U. Press, 1982.

———. *The Muse Learns to Write.* New Haven: Yale U. Press, 1986.

———. *Origins of Western Literacy.* Toronto: Ontario Institute for Studies in Education, 1976.

———. *Preface to Plato.* Cambridge, MA: Harvard U. Press, 1963.

Hegel, G. W. F. *Lectures on the Philosophy of History.* Trans. J. Sibree. London: G. Bell and Sons, 1914.

Heinimann, Felix. "Eine vorplatonische Theorie der τέχνη." *Museum Helveticum* 18 (1961): 105–30. Rpt. in Classen, *Sophistik*. 127–69.
———. *Nomos und Physis*. Basel: F. Reinhardt, 1945.
Heitsch, Ernst. "Ein Buchtitel des Protagoras." *Hermes* 97 (1969): 292–96. Rpt. in Classen, *Sophistik*. 298–305.
Hicks, R. D. *Diogenes Laertius*. 2 vols. Cambridge, MA: Harvard U. Press, 1925.
Hinks, D. A. G. "Tisias and Corax and the Invention of Rhetoric." *Classical Quarterly* 34 (1940): 61–69.
Holland, R. F. "On Making Sense of a Philosophical Fragment." *Classical Quarterly,* new series, 6 (1956): 215–20.
Hook, LaRue Van. "Alcidamas versus Isocrates." *Classical Weekly* 12 (1919): 89–94.
Hubbard, B. A. F., and E. S. Karnofsky. *Plato's* PROTAGORAS: *A Socratic Commentary*. Chicago: U. of Chicago Press, 1982.
Hunter, Virginia J. *Thucydides: The Artful Reporter*. Toronto: Hakkert, 1973.
Jacoby, F. "The First Athenian Prose Writer." *Mnemosyne: Bibliotheca classica Batava* 13 (1947): 13–64.
Jaeger, Werner. *Paideia: The Ideals of Greek Culture*. Vol. 1. Rev. ed. Trans. Gilbert Highet. New York: Oxford U. Press, 1945.
———. *Theology of the Early Greek Philosophers*. Oxford: Clarendon Press, 1947.
Jarratt, Susan C. "The First Sophists and the Uses of History." *Rhetoric Review* 6 (1987): 66–77.
———. *The Return of the Sophists: Classical Rhetoric Refigured*. Carbondale: Southern Illinois U. Press, 1991.
———. "The Role of the Sophists in Histories of Consciousness." *Philosophy and Rhetoric* 23 (1990): 85–95.
———. "Toward a Sophistic Historiography." *Pre/Text* 8 (1987): 9–26.
Jarrett, James L. *The Educational Theory of the Sophists*. New York: Teachers College Press, 1969.
Jebb, Richard C. *The Attic Orators from Antiphon to Isaeos*. 2 vols. New York: Russell and Russell, 1962.
Johnstone, Christopher Lyle. "An Aristotelian Trilogy: Ethics, Rhetoric, Politics, and the Search for Moral Truth." *Philosophy and Rhetoric* 13 (1980): 1–24.
Jones, W. H. S. *Hippocrates*. 4 vols. Cambridge, MA: Harvard U. Press, 1923–31.
Jordan, James E. "Protagoras and Relativism: Criticisms Bad and Good." *Southwestern Journal of Philosophy* 2 (1971): 7–29.
Jowett, Benjamin. *The Dialogues of Plato*. London: Macmillan, 1892.
Kahn, Charles H. *Anaximander and the Origins of Greek Cosmology*. New York: Columbia U. Press, 1960.
———. *The Art and Thought of Heraclitus*. Cambridge: Cambridge U. Press, 1979.

———. "The Greek Verb 'to be' and the Concept of Being." *Foundations of Language* 2 (1966): 245–65.

———. *The Verb "Be" in Ancient Greek.* Dordrecht: D. Riedel, 1973.

Kaster, Robert A. *Guardians of Language: The Grammarian and Society in Late Antiquity.* Berkeley: U. of California Press, 1988.

Kauffman, Charles. "The Axiological Foundations of Plato's Theory of Rhetoric." *Central States Speech Journal* 33 (1982): 353–66.

Kennedy, George A. *The Art of Persuasion in Greece.* Princeton: Princeton U. Press, 1963.

———. *Classical Rhetoric and Its Christian and Secular Tradition from Ancient to Modern Times.* Chapel Hill: U. of North Carolina Press, 1980.

———. "The Earliest Rhetorical Handbooks." *American Journal of Philology* 80 (1959): 169–78.

Kerferd, G. B. "The First Greek Sophists." *Classical Review* 64 (1950): 8–10.

———. "The Future Direction of Sophistic Studies." *The Sophists and Their Legacy,* ed. Kerferd. 1–6.

———. "Plato's Account of the Relativism of Protagoras." *Durham University Journal* 42 (1949): 20–26.

———. "Protagoras." *The Encyclopedia of Philosophy.* Vol. 6. New York: Macmillan, 1967.

———. "Protagoras' Doctrine of Justice and Virtue in the *Protagoras* of Plato." *Journal of Hellenic Studies* 73 (1953): 42–45.

———. "Le sophiste vu par Platon: un philosophe imparfait." *Positions de la Sophistique,* ed. Barbara Cassin. Paris: Vrin, 1986.

———, ed. *The Sophists and Their Legacy.* Wiesbaden: Franz Steiner, 1981.

———. *The Sophistic Movement.* Cambridge: Cambridge U. Press, 1981.

———. "Sophists." *The Encyclopedia of Philosophy.* Vol. 7. New York: Macmillan, 1967.

Keuls, Eva C. *The Reign of the Phallus: Sexual Politics in Ancient Athens.* New York: Harper, 1985.

Kimball, Bruce A. *Orators and Philosophers: A History of the Ideal Liberal Education.* New York: Teachers College Press, 1986.

Kirby, John T. "Narrative Structure and Technique in Thucydides VI-VII." *Classical Antiquity* 2 (1983): 183–211.

Kirk, G. S. , J. E. Raven, and Malcolm Schofield. *The Presocratic Philosophers: A Critical History with a Selection of Texts,* 2nd ed. Cambridge: Cambridge U. Press, 1983.

Kitto, H. D. F. *The Greeks.* Harmondsworth: Penguin, 1957.

Kowalski, Georgius (Jerzy). *De Artis Rhetoricae Originibus.* Leopoli: Sumptibus Societatis Litterarum, 1933.

———. *De Arte Rhetorica.* Leopoli: Polonorum, 1937.

Kraus, Manfred. *Name und Sache: ein Problem im frühgriechischen Denken.* Amsterdam: Grüner, 1987.

Kretzmann, Norman. "History of Semantics." *The Encyclopedia of Philosophy.* Vol. 7. New York: Macmillan, 1967.

Kroll, Wilhelm. "Rhetorik." *Paulys Real-Encyclopädie der classischen Altertumswissenschaft* supp. 7 (1940): 1039–1138.

Kuhn. Thomas S. *The Structure of Scientific Revolutions.* Rev. ed. Chicago: U. of Chicago Press, 1970.

Lambridis, Helle. *Empedocles.* University, AL: U. of Alabama Press, 1976.

Lana, Italo. *Protagora.* Torino: Università di Torino Pubblicazione, 1950.

Ledger, Gerard R. *Re-counting Plato: A Computer Analysis of Plato's Style.* Oxford: Clarendon Press, 1989.

Lee, Edward N. " 'Hoist with His Own Petard': Ironic and Comic Elements in Plato's Critique of Protagoras." *Exegesis and Argument: Studies in Greek Philosophy Presented to Gregory Vlastos,* ed. E. N. Lee, A. P. D. Mourelatos, and R. M. Rorty. Assen: Van Gorcum, 1973. 225–61.

Lentz, Tony M. *Orality and Literacy in Hellenic Greece.* Carbondale: Southern Illinois U. Press, 1989.

Levi, Adolfo. "The Ethical and Social Thought of Protagoras." *Mind* 49 (1940): 284–302.

———. "Studies on Protagoras. The Man-Measure Principle: Its Meaning and Applications." *Philosophy* 40 (1940): 147–67.

Levin, Saul. "The Origin of Grammar in Sophistry." *General Linguistics* 23 (1983): 41–47.

Liddell, Henry George, and Robert Scott. *A Greek-English Lexicon.* 9th ed. Rev. and augmented by Henry Stuart Jones. Oxford: Clarendon Press, 1940.

Lloyd, G. E. R. "Hot and Cold, Dry and Wet in Early Greek Thought." *Studies in Presocratic Philosophy.* Vol. 1. Ed. David J. Furley and R. E. Allen. New York: Humanities Press, 1970. 255–80. Originally published in *Journal of Hellenic Studies* 84 (1964): 92–106.

———. *Magic, Reason and Experience.* Cambridge: Cambridge U. Press, 1979.

———. *Polarity and Analogy.* Cambridge: Cambridge U. Press, 1966.

Loenen, Dirk. *Protagoras and the Greek Community.* Amsterdam: Noord-Hollandsche Uitgevers Maatschappij, 1940.

Loraux, Nicole. *The Invention of Athens: The Funeral Oration in the Classical City.* Trans. Alan Sheridan. Cambridge, MA: Harvard U. Press, 1986.

Lukasiewicz, J. "Aristotle on the Law of Contradiction." *Articles on Aristotle.* Vol. 3: *Metaphysics.* Ed. Jonathan Barnes, Malcolm Schofield, and Richard Sorabji. New York: St. Martin's Press, 1979. 50–62.

McDiarmid, J. B. "Theophrastus on the Presocratic Causes." *Harvard Studies in Classical Philology* 61 (1953): 85–156.

McDowell, John. *Plato: Theaetetus.* Oxford: Clarendon Press, 1973.

MacIntyre, Alasdair. *After Virtue: A Study in Moral Theory.* Notre Dame: Notre Dame U. Press, 1981.

———. *Whose Justice? Which Rationality?* Notre Dame: Notre Dame U. Press, 1988.

McNeal, Richard A. "Protagoras the Historian." *History and Theory* 25 (1986): 299–318.

Maguire, Joseph P. "Protagoras—or Plato?" *Phronesis* 18 (1973): 115–38.

———. "Protagoras ... or Plato? II. The *Protagoras.*" *Phronesis* 22 (1977): 103–22.

Mailloux, Steven, ed. *Rhetoric, Sophistry, Pragmatism.* Cambridge: Cambridge U. Press, 1995.

Makin, Stephen. "How Can We Find Out What Ancient Philosophers Said?" *Phronesis* 33 (1988): 121–32.

Mansfeld, Jaap. "Protagoras on Epistemological Obstacles and Persons." *The Sophists and Their Legacy*, ed. G. B. Kerferd. Wiesbaden: Franz Steiner, 1981. 38–53.

Mark, Ira S. "The Gods on the East Frieze of the Parthenon." *Hesperia: Journal of the American School of Classical Studies at Athens* 53 (1984): 289–342.

Martin, Josef. *Antike Rhetorik: Technik und Methode.* München: Beck, 1974.

Mason, Richard. "Parmenides and Language." *Ancient Philosophy* 8 (1988): 149–66.

McComiskey, Bruce. *Gorgias and the New Sophistic Rhetoric.* Carbondale: Southern Illinois U. Press, 2002.

Meiland, Jack W. "Is Protagorean Relativism Self-refuting?" *Grazer Philosophische Studien* 9 (1979): 51–68.

Mejer, Jørgen. "The Alleged New Fragment of Protagoras." *Hermes* 100 (1972): 175–78. Rpt. in Classen, *Sophistik.* 306–11.

———. "Protagoras and the Heracliteans: Some Suggestions Concerning *Theaetetus* 151d–186e." *Classica et Mediaevalia* 29 (1972): 40–60.

Menzel, Adolf. "Protagoras, der älteste Theoretiker der Demokratie." *Zeitschrift für Politik* 3 (1910): 205–38.

———. "Protagoras als Gesetzgeber von Thurioi" and "Die Sozialphilosophischen Lehren des Protagoras." *Hellenika: Gesammelte kleine Schriften.* Baden bei Wien: R. M. Rohrer, 1938. 66–82, 83–107.

Michalaros, Demetrios A. *Protagoras: A Poem of Man.* Chicago: Syndicate Press, 1937.

Michelini, Ann Norris. *Euripides and the Tragic Tradition.* Madison: U. of Wisconsin Press, 1987.

Minar, E. L. "Parmenides and the World of Seeming." *American Journal of Philology* 70 (1949): 41–53.

Moore, Stanley. "Democracy and Commodity Exchange: Protagoras versus Plato." *History of Philosophy Quarterly* 5 (1988): 357–68.

Moravcsik, Julius M. "Heraclitean Concepts and Explanations." *Language and Thought in Early Greek Philosophy*, ed. Kevin Robb, La Salle, IL: Hegeler Institute, 1983. 134–152.

Morrison, J. S. "The Place of Protagoras in Athenian Public Life." *Classical Quarterly* 35 (1941): 1–16.

Mortley, R. J. "Plato and the Sophistic Heritage of Protagoras." *Eranos: Acta Philologica Suecana* 67 (1969): 24–32.

Moser, S., and G. L. Kustas. "A Comment on the 'Relativism' of Protagoras." *Phoenix* 20 (1966): 111–15.

Mourelatos, A. P. D. *The Route of Parmenides.* New Haven: Yale U. Press, 1970.

Muir, J. V. "Protagoras and Education at Thourioi." *Greece and Rome* 29 (1982): 17–24.

Müller, Carl Werner. "Protagoras über die Götter." *Hermes* 95 (1965): 140–59. Rpt. in Classen, *Sophistik.* 312–40.

Müller, Reimar. "Sophistique et démocratie." *Positions de la Sophistique,* ed. Barbara Cassin. Paris: Vrin, 1986. 179–93.

Murphy, C. T. "Aristophanes and the Art of Rhetoric." *Harvard Studies in Classical Philology* 49 (1938): 69–113.

Murphy, James J. *A Synoptic History of Classical Rhetoric.* New York: Random House, 1972.

Mutschmann, Hermann. "Die Älteste Definition der Rhetoric." *Hermes* 53 (1918): 440–43.

Nahm, Milton C. *Selections from Early Greek Philosophy.* 4th ed. Englewood Cliffs, NJ: Prentice-Hall, 1964.

Narcy, Michel. "A qui la parole? Platon et Aristote face à Protagoras." *Positions de la Sophistique,* ed. Barbara Cassin. Paris: Vrin, 1986. 75–90.

Naveh, Joseph. *Early History of the Alphabet.* Jerusalem: Magnes Press, 1982.

Nehamas, Alexander. "Eristic, Antilogic, Sophistic, Dialectic: Plato's Demarcation of Philosophy from Sophistry." *History of Philosophy Quarterly* 7 (1990): 3–16.

Neumann, Alfred. "Die Problematik des Homo-mensura Satzes." *Classical Philology* 33 (1938): 368–79. Rpt. in Classen, *Sophistik.* 257–70.

Nill, Michael. *Morality and Self-interest in Protagoras, Antiphon and Democritus.* Leiden: Brill, 1985

Norlin, George. *Isocrates.* 2 vols. Cambridge, MA: Harvard U. Press, 1928–29.

Ober, Josiah. *Mass and Elite in Democratic Athens: Rhetoric, Ideology, and the Power of the People.* Princeton: Princeton U. Press, 1989.

O'Brien, D. *Empedocles' Cosmic Cycle: A Reconstruction from the Fragments and Secondary Sources.* Cambridge: Cambridge U. Press, 1969.

Ong, Walter S. J. *Orality and Literacy: The Technologizing of the Word.* London: Methuen, 1982.

Osborne, Catherine. *Rethinking Early Greek Philosophy.* London: Duckworth, 1987.

Ostwald, Martin. *From Popular Sovereignty to the Sovereignty of Law: Law,*

Society, and Politics in Fifth-Century Athens. Berkeley: U. of California Press, 1986.

———. *Plato: Protagoras.* Indianapolis: Bobbs-Merrill, 1956.

Parry, Milman. "Studies in the Epic Technique of Oral Verse-Making. I: Homer and Homeric Style." *Harvard Studies in Classical Philology* 41 (1930): 73–147.

———. "Studies in the Epic Technique of Oral Verse-Making II: The Homeric Language as the Language of an Oral Poetry." *Harvard Studies in Classical Philology* 43 (1932): 1–50.

Pattison, Robert. *On Literacy: The Politics of the Word from Homer to the Age of Rock.* New York: Oxford U. Press, 1982.

Payne, David. "Rhetoric, Reality, and Knowledge: A Re-examination of Protagoras' Concept of Rhetoric." *Rhetoric Society Quarterly* 16 (1986): 187–97.

Peppler, Charles W. "The Termination –*kos,* as Used by Aristophanes for Comic Effect." *AJP* 31 (1910): 428–32.

Perelman, Chaim, and L. Olbrechts-Tyteca. *The New Rhetoric: A Treatise on Argumentation.* Trans. John Wilkinson and Purcell Weaver. Notre Dame: U. of Notre Dame Press, 1969. Originally published as *La Nouvelle Rhétorique: Traité de l'Argumentation.* Presses Universitaires de France, 1958.

Perlman, S. "The Politicians in the Athenian Democracy of the Fourth Century B.C." *Atheneum* 41 (1963): 327–55.

Pfeiffer, Rudolf. *History of Classical Scholarship from the Beginnings to the End of the Hellenistic Age.* Oxford: Clarendon Press, 1968.

Pilz, Werner. *Der Rhetor im attischen Staat.* Weida: Thomas and Hubert, 1934.

Placido, D. "El pensamiento de Protágoras y las Atenas de Pericles." *Hispania Antiqua* 3 (1973): 29–68.

———. "Protágoras y Pericles." *Hispania Antiqua* 2 (1972): 7–19.

Popper, Karl R. *The Open Society and Its Enemies.* 5th ed. London: Routledge and Kegan Paul, 1966.

Poulakos, John. "Aristotle's Indebtedness to the Sophists." *Argument in Transition: Proceedings of the Third Summer Conference on Argumentation,* ed. David Zarefsky, Malcolm O. Sillars, and Jack Rhodes. Annandale, VA: Speech Communication Association, 1983. 27–42.

———. "Gorgias' *Encomium to Helen* and the Defense of Rhetoric." *Rhetorica* 1 (1983): 1–16.

———. "Hegel's Reception of the Sophists." *Western Journal of Speech Communication* 54 (1990): 160–71.

———. "Interpreting Sophistical Rhetoric: A Response to Schiappa." *Philosophy and Rhetoric* 23 (1990): 218–28.

———. "Rhetoric, the Sophists, and the Possible." *Communication Monographs* 51 (1984): 215–26.

———. "Sophistical Rhetoric as a Critique of Culture." *Argument and Critical Practices: Proceedings of the Fifth SCA/AFA Conference on Argumentation,* ed. Joseph W. Wenzel. Annandale, VA: Speech Communication Association, 1987. 97–101.

———. *Sophistical Rhetoric in Classical Greece.* Columbia: U. of South Carolina Press, 1995.

———. "Toward a Sophistic Definition of Rhetoric." *Philosophy and Rhetoric* 16 (1983): 35–48.

Poulakos, Takis. "Intellectuals and the Public Sphere: The Case of the Older Sophists." *Spheres of Argument: Proceedings of the Sixth SCA/AFA Conference on Argumentation,* ed. Bruce E. Gronbeck. Annandale, VA: Speech Communication Association, 1989. 9–15.

Rabe, Hugo. *Prolegomenon Sylloge.* Leipzig: Teubner, 1931.

Race, William H. "The Word Καιρός in Greek Drama." *Transactions of the American Philological Association* 111 (1981): 197–213.

Rackham, H. *Rhetorica ad Alexandrum.* Cambridge, MA: Harvard U. Press, 1937.

Radermacher, Ludwig. "Artium scriptores: Reste der voraristotelischen Rhetorik." *Oesterreiches Akademie der Wissenschaften, Philosophisch-historische Klasse,* Sitzungsberichte 227, Band 3, 1951.

Rankin, H. D. "*Ouk estin antilegein.*" *The Sophists and Their Legacy,* ed. G. B. Kerferd. Wiesbaden: Franz Steiner, 1981. 25–37.

Reale, Giovanni. *A History of Ancient Philosophy: From the Origins to Socrates.* Ed. and trans. John R. Catan. Albany: SUNY Press, 1987.

Reimer, Milton K. "The Subjectivism of the Sophists: A Problem of Identity." *Journal of Thought* 13 (1978): 50–54.

Rensi, Giuseppe. *Introduzione alla scepsi etica.* Firenze: F. Perrella, 1921.

Ritter, Michelle R. "In Search of the Real Protagoras." *Dialogue* 23 (1981): 58–65.

Roberts, W. Rhys. "The New Rhetorical Fragment (OXYRHYNCHUS PAPYRI, Part III., Pp. 27–30) in Relation to the Sicilian Rhetoric of Corax and Tisias." *The Classical Review* 18 (1904): 18–21.

Robinson, John Mansley. *An Introduction to Early Greek Philosophy.* Boston: Houghton Mifflin, 1968.

Robinson, Richard. *Plato's Earlier Dialectic.* 2nd ed. Oxford: Clarendon Press, 1953.

Robinson, Thomas M. *Contrasting Arguments: An Edition of the Dissoi Logoi.* Salem, NH: Ayer, 1979.

Rogers, Benjamin Bickley. *Aristophanes.* 3 vols. Cambridge, MA: Harvard U. Press, 1924.

Romilly, Jacqueline de. *Les Grands Sophistes dans L'Athènes de Périclès.* Paris: Éditions de Fallois, 1988.

Rorty, Richard. "The Historiography of Philosophy: Four Genres." *Philosophy in History: Essays on the Historiography of Philosophy,* ed. Richard Rorty, J. B. Schneewind, and Quentin Skinner. Cambridge: Cambridge U. Press, 1984. 49–75.

Roseman, N. "Protagoras and the Foundations of His Educational Thought." *Paedagogica Historica* 11 (1971): 75–89.

Saunders, Trevor J. "Protagoras and Plato on Punishment." *The Sophists and Their Legacy,* ed. G. B. Kerferd. Wiesbaden: Franz Steiner, 1981. 129–41.

Schiappa, Edward. *The Beginnings of Rhetorical Theory in Classical Greece.* New Haven: Yale U. Press, 1999.

———. "Did Plato Coin Rhêtorikê?" *American Journal of Philology* 111 (1990): 460–73.

———. "History and Neo-Sophistic Criticism: A Reply to Poulakos." *Philosophy and Rhetoric* 23 (1990): 307–15.

———. "Neo-Sophistic Rhetorical Criticism or the Historical Reconstruction of Sophistic Doctrines?" *Philosophy and Rhetoric* 23 (1990): 192–217.

Schiller, F. C. S. *Plato or Protagoras?* Oxford: Basil Blackwell, 1908.

Scinto, Leonard F. M. *Written Language and Psychological Development.* Orlando, FL: Academic Press, 1986.

Scodel, Ruth. "Literary Interpretation in Plato's *Protagoras.*" *Ancient Philosophy* 6 (1986): 25–37.

Segal, Charles P. "Gorgias and the Psychology of the Logos." *Harvard Studies in Classical Philology* 66 (1962): 99–155.

———. "Literature and Interpretation: Conventions, History, and Universals." *Classical and Modern Literature* 5 (1984/5): 71–85.

———. "Protagoras' *Orthoepeia* in Aristophanes' 'Battle of the Prologues' (*Frogs* 1119–97)." *Rheinisches Museum für Philologie* 113 (1970): 158–62.

Self, Lois S. "Rhetoric and *Phronêsis:* The Aristotelian Ideal." *Philosophy and Rhetoric* 12 (1979): 130–45.

Sesonske, Alexander. "To Make the Weaker Argument Defeat the Stronger." *Journal of the History of Philosophy* 6 (1968): 217–31.

Sidgwick, Henry. "The Sophists." *Journal of Philology* 4 (1872): 288–307; 5 (1873): 66–80.

Simmons, George C. "The Humanism of the Sophists with Emphasis on Protagoras of Abdera." *Educational Theory* 19 (1969): 29–39.

———. "Protagoras on Education and Society." *Paedagogica Historica* 12 (1972): 518–37.

Sinclair, R. K. *Democracy and Participation in Athens.* Cambridge: Cambridge U. Press, 1988.

Sinclair, Thomas Alan. *A History of Greek Political Thought.* London: Routledge and Kegan Paul, 1951.

Smith, Bromley. "Corax and Probability." *Quarterly Journal of Speech* 7 (1921): 13–42.

——. "The Father of Debate: Protagoras of Abdera." *Quarterly Journal of Speech* 4 (1918): 196–215.

Snell, Bruno. *The Discovery of the Mind.* Trans. T. G. Rosenmeyer. Oxford: Basil Blackwell, 1953.

——. "Die Nachrichten über die Lehren des Thales." *Philologus* 96 (1944): 119–28. Rpt. Classen, *Sophistik.* 465–77.

Solmsen, Friedrich. *Intellectual Experiments of the Greek Enlightenment.* Princeton: Princeton U. Press, 1975.

——. Review of *Preface to Plato* by Eric A. Havelock. *American Journal of Philology* 87 (1966): 99–105.

Sommerstein, Alan H. *Aristophanes: Clouds.* Warminster: Aris and Phillips, 1982.

Sprague, Rosamond Kent. "Plato's Sophistry." *The Aristotelian Society* supp. 51 (1977): 45–61.

——. *Plato's Use of Fallacy.* New York: Barnes and Noble, 1962.

Sprague, Rosamond Kent, ed. *The Older Sophists.* Columbia: U. of South Carolina Press, 1972. Reissued 1990.

Stallknecht, Newton P. "Protagoras and the Critics." *Journal of Philosophy* 35 (1938): 39–45.

Starkie, W. J. M. *The Clouds of Aristophanes.* London: Macmillan, 1911.

Stegemann, Willy. "Teisias 6." *Paulys Real-Encyclopädie der classischen Altertumswissenschaft* 5A (1934): 139–50.

Stevenson, Charles L. *Ethics and Language.* New Haven: Yale U. Press, 1944.

Stone, I. F. *The Trial of Socrates.* New York: Anchor Books, 1989.

Street, Brian V. *Literacy in Theory and Practice.* Cambridge: Cambridge U. Press, 1984.

Taylor, A. E. *Plato: The Man and His Work.* 6th ed. London: Methuen, 1949.

Taylor, C. C. W. *Plato: Protagoras.* Oxford: Clarendon Press, 1976.

Thomas, Rosalind. *Oral Tradition and Written Record in Classical Athens.* Cambridge: Cambridge U. Press, 1989.

Turner, E. G. *Athenian Books in the Fifth and Fourth Centuries B.C.* 2nd ed. London: H. K. Lewis, 1977.

Untersteiner, Mario. *Sofisti: testimonianze e frammenti.* 4 vols. Firenze: La Nuova Italia, 1949–62.

——. *The Sophists.* Trans. Kathleen Freeman. Oxford: Basil Blackwell, 1954. Originally published as *I sophisti.* Torino: Einaudi, 1949. A second Italian edition was published in 2 volumes in Milan: Lampugnani Nigri, 1967.

Verrall, A. W. "Korax and Tisias." *The Journal of Philology* 9 (1880): 197–210.

Versényi, Lazlo. "Protagoras' Man-Measure Fragment." *American Journal of Philology* 83 (1962): 178–84. Rpt. in Classen, *Sophistik.* 290–97.

——. *Socratic Humanism.* New Haven: Yale U. Press, 1963.

Vlastos, Gregory. *Plato's "Protagoras."* Indianapolis: Bobbs-Merrill, 1956.

Wallace, Robert W. *The Areopagus Council, to 307 B.C.* Baltimore: Johns Hopkins U. Press, 1989.

245

Bibliography

Walsh, John. "The Dramatic Dates of Plato's *Protagoras* and the Lesson of *Aretê.*" *Classical Quarterly* 34 (1984): 101–6.

Walz, Christianus. *Rhetores Graeci.* 9 vols. Stuttgart: J. G. Cottae, 1832–36.

Webster, T. B. L. *The Tragedies of Euripides.* London: Methuen, 1967.

West, Elinor Jane Maddock. "The Promethean Ethic in the *Protagoras.*" Ph.D. diss., Columbia University, 1967.

Wheelwright, Philip. *Heraclitus.* New York: Atheneum, 1974.

———. *The Presocratics.* New York: Odyssey Press, 1966.

White, F. C. "Protagoras Unbound." *Canadian Journal of Philosophy* supp. 1 (1974): 1–9.

———. "The Theory of Flux in the *Theaetetus.*" *Apeiron* 10 (1976): 1–10

Wilcox, Stanley. "Corax and the *Prolegomena.*" *American Journal of Philology* 64 (1943): 1–23.

———. "The Scope of Early Rhetorical Instruction." *Harvard Studies in Classical Philology* 46 (1942): 121–55.

Windelband, Wilhelm. *History of Ancient Philosophy.* 3rd ed. Trans. Herbert Ernest Cushman. New York: Scribner's, 1924.

Withington, E. T. *Hippocrates.* Vol. 3. Cambridge, MA: Harvard U. Press, 1928.

Woodbury, Leonard. "Aristophanes' *Frogs* and Athenian Literacy: *Ran.* 52–53, 1114." *Transactions of the American Philological Association* 106 (1976): 349–57.

Woodruff, Paul. "Didymus on Protagoras and the Protagoreans." *Journal of the History of Philosophy* 23 (1985): 483–97.

Wright, M. R. *Empedocles: The Extant Fragments.* New Haven: Yale U. Press, 1981.

Zaslavsky, Robert. "The Platonic Godfather: A Note on the 'Protagoras' Myth." *Journal of Value Inquiry* 16 (1982): 79–82.

Zeller, Eduard. *A History of Greek Philosophy.* 2 vols. Trans. S. F. Alleyne. London: Longmans, Green, 1881.

Zeppi, Stelio. *Protagora e la filosofia del suo tempo.* Firenze: La Nuova Italia, 1961.

INDEX

Index

Index